Sweet Tea with Cardamom

SWEET TEA WITH CARDAMOM

A Journey through Iraqi Kurdistan

Teresa Thornhill

An Imprint of HarperCollinsPublishers

Pandora

An Imprint of HarperCollins*Publishers*

77–85 Fulham Palace Road

Hammersmith, London W6 8JB

1160 Battery Street

San Francisco, California 94111–1213

Published by Pandora 1997

10 9 8 7 6 5 4 3 2 1

A catalogue record for this book
is available from the British Library

ISBN 0 04 440984 2 (Paperback)

Printed and bound in Great Britain by
Caledonian International Book Manufacturing Ltd, Glasgow

To Mohammed

CONTENTS

AUTHOR'S NOTE

This book records my two journeys through Iraqi Kurdistan in 1993, during the hopeful days of the Kurdish experiment in democratic self-government which followed the withdrawal of Iraqi government personnel from the region in late 1991. From late 1993 until summer 1996 the experiment foundered, as strife between the two main Kurdish parties developed into near civil war; nevertheless, the Western-protected Safe Haven survived and the Iraqi government was kept at bay. Tragically for the Kurds, those days are now at an end.

On 31 August 1996, Iraqi tanks and Republican Guards rolled into the Kurdish city of Arbil in support of the Kurdistan Democratic Party's attempt to seize control of the city from the Patriotic Union of Kurdistan. The city fell to the KDP within hours and, although Iraqi troops soon withdrew to positions outside Arbil, they left behind large numbers of *mukhaberaat*, Iraqi secret police.

On 9 September KDP forces took control of the city of Sulaymaniyah.

Whether the Iraqi government will now resume domination of the Kurdish 'enclave' remains to be seen, but its penetration by government security personnel appears to be a *fait accompli*. For this reason the names of the majority of Kurds referred to in the book have been changed. The names of well known public figures remain unchanged.

TT
25 September 1996

ACKNOWLEDGEMENTS

I would like to thank the following people for their invaluable assistance, support and encouragement in the writing of this book:

Mubejel Arif Baban, Mawlan Brahim, Geraldine Brooks, Rebwar Fatah, Kemal Farraj, Mohammed Ali, Claudia Lank, Margaret Macadam, Kanan Makiya, Bayan Shali, Afsaneh Najmabadi, Ayad Rahim, Karen Raney, Nazaneen Rashid, Anne Rodford, the late Marion Farouk-Sluglett, Sheila Thornhill, Alan Thornhill, Medea Mahdavi-Walker.

PROLOGUE

My interest in Iraq began with a personal connection: my former partner, Ayad, was an Iraqi Arab. We had been living in Palestine–Israel
when the Gulf crisis began in August 1990. My own background is
partly Jewish and, combining my interest in the Arab–Israeli conflict
with my legal training, I was doing research with Palestinian women
who had been in prison. Ayad was working as a journalist on a Palestinian newspaper. We left Jerusalem shortly before the war, and
together watched the bombing of Baghdad and the suppression of the
Iraqi uprising, first with his family in the US, then back in London.

When it was all over we decided to stay in London, where I went
back to my work as a family law barrister and Ayad became deeply
involved in the renascent Iraqi opposition. This was an extraordinary period for Iraqis living in exile, both Arabs and Kurds. The barrier of fear which had kept so many of them silent for the last 20
years had at last been broken, and people were beginning to emerge
from reclusion and talk to each other. Terrible stories were being
told by newly-arrived refugees, stories of imprisonment, torture and
repression. Some of these were published in the national press and
Ayad came home daily with other stories which had not made the
papers but were equally horrifying.

In 1992 we separated and I moved to the West country, but I
remained nevertheless deeply concerned with and involved in the
fate of Iraq and Iraqis, and I simply could not forget what was happening in their world.

I was trying to settle into my new life, but part of me longed to
return to the Middle East. I had left very reluctantly when the war

broke out and now I began to look out for opportunities to go back, whether to Palestine or Iraq or anywhere else.

Early in 1993 I heard about a two-week tour that was being organised to the Kurdish enclave in northern Iraq. At first I felt uncertain, not liking the idea of being a tourist in war-damaged Kurdistan, but when a friend suggested I should do some interviews with Kurdish women and write them up, I felt able to go. Memories of the rich days I had spent sitting in the homes of Palestinian women listening to their stories were still strong in my mind, and in the two years since the war I had often found myself wondering what it would be like to sit and talk with Iraqi women. I felt sure that they would have some extraordinary stories to tell about their lives under Saddam Hussein. Whether they would want to tell them to me, a Westerner, remained to be seen, but Iraqis I spoke to in Britain thought that my foreign-ness might be an asset. 'Some things it is easier to tell to a complete outsider,' one man said. 'And you are a woman: that is good.'

The Kurdish people, who are thought to be descended from the Medes of central Asia, have for several thousand years inhabited the region of the Zagros mountains which lies to the north of Mesopotamia and to the east of the Euphrates river. Originally Zoroastrians, the Kurds converted to Islam and are mainly Sunni. Kurdish society is tribally based and the culture has some characteristics in common with that of other Middle Eastern peoples, although ethnically the Kurds have no relationship with the Arabs or Turks. Kurdish women traditionally do not veil and they dress in bright colours, but they are subjected to many of the same social constraints as their Arab and Persian counterparts.

The Kurdish language is Indo-European in origin; different dialects are spoken in different parts of Kurdistan. Modern 'Kurdistan', meaning the geographical region predominantly inhabited by Kurds, is divided by the national boundaries of Turkey, Iraq, Iran, Syria and the former USSR. In southern Kurdistan, which includes north western Iran and northeastern Iraq, Sorani is spoken; in central and northern Kurdistan, which includes the northernmost part of Iraqi Kurdistan and most of southeastern Turkey, Kurmanji is the predominant dialect. Speakers of one dialect have considerable difficulty understanding speakers of the other; and the problem is made worse by the fact that, in Turkey, Kurdish is written in the Latin alphabet, whereas in Iran and Iraq it is written in the Arabic alphabet.

When the region was divided into nation states at the end of the First World War, the idea of a Kurdish state was mooted by the Western powers but subsequently rejected. The Kurdish nationalist movements which had begun to develop in the nineteenth century were weak and divided along tribal lines. Since the 1920s the Kurds, who as a people now number between 20 and 25 million, have lived as ethnic minorities in the five states that divide them. They constitute the fourth largest ethnic group in the Middle East after the Arabs, Turks and Persians, and are said to be the largest people in the world who lack a state of their own.

In southeastern Turkey, since 1984, Kurdish guerillas led by the Kurdish Workers' Party (PKK) have been fighting a war with the Turkish army with the aim of creating a Kurdish state. The death-toll exceeded 20,000 by 1996.

Since the creation of the state of Iraq in the 1920s, the Iraqi Kurds, who constitute nearly a quarter of the Iraqi population and number about 4 million, have continually struggled for autonomy. From the days of the British mandate to the present, relations between the Kurds in the northeast of the country and central government in Baghdad have oscillated between low level fighting, uprising and outright war. The Kurds have been treated with great brutality by successive Iraqi regimes, most notably by the present Ba'athist one of Saddam Hussein, which, among other things, has subjected them to torture, chemical attacks and a campaign of genocide.

The Iraqi Kurds have not always been well served by their leaders, however, and conflict between the main political groupings has sometimes led one grouping to form an alliance with Baghdad against the other. Both the Kurdistan Democratic Party (KDP) and the Patriotic Union of Kurdistan (PUK) have done this at different times.

With the Iraqi invasion of Kuwait in August 1990 and the international military response, the Kurds saw an opportunity to rid themselves of Saddam Hussein. The Kurdistan Front had been formed in June 1988, uniting the main Kurdish parties. In March 1991, within days of the Gulf War ceasefire, spontaneous anti-government uprisings occurred in both the south of Iraq and in Kurdistan. The uprisings were put down savagely within two to three weeks by the Republican Guard, whereupon half of the population of Kurdistan fled to the mountainous Iranian and Turkish borders.

When John Major's 'Safe Haven' was set up in April 1991 and many refugees began to come down from the mountains and return to the Kurdish cities, the security personnel of Saddam Hussein's Ba'athist regime were still present. By the late summer, however, following failed negotiations between the Kurds and the regime, the latter withdrew from about 50 per cent of Kurdistan, leaving the Kurdistan Front more or less in control of the area. The Kurdish cities of Mosul and Kirkuk remained under government control; Sulaymaniyah, Arbil and D'hok were in the 'liberated' area. The Kurdistan Front did not, however, have a mandate to govern the area, and after some months a decision was made to hold elections. These took place amid great excitement in May 1992 and a Kurdish administration was formed.

The Iraqi Kurds claimed that they did not wish to establish an independent state: rather they wished to be part of a post-Saddam Iraq under a federal arrangement. The enclave soon became host to the Iraqi National Congress (INC), a coalition of the Iraqi opposition.

The odds stacked against success for the Kurdish administration were tremendous: UN sanctions were still in force against Iraq, hampering the economy of the liberated area as much as that of the south. In addition, Saddam had instituted his own blockade against the Kurds, preventing fuel, food and international aid from reaching them. And Iraqi troops were massed along the lines to which they had withdrawn in late 1991, waiting for an opportune moment to march back in. This was, nevertheless, a rare moment in Kurdish history. The Kurds were governing themselves and Iraqi Kurdistan was now one of the few places in the Middle East where an attempt was being made at democracy.

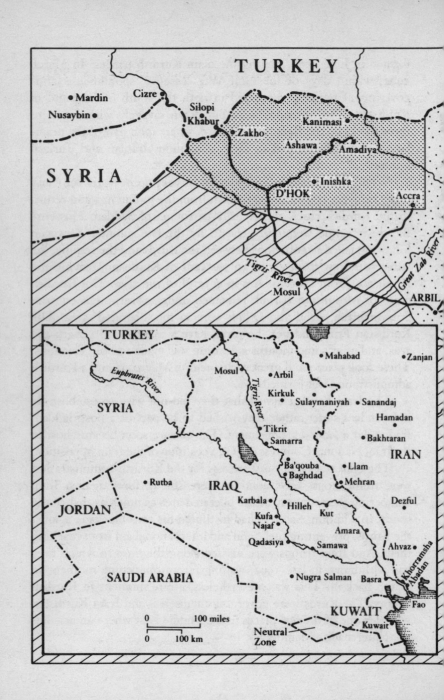

The Kurdish enclave in Northern Iraq in 1993

The Northern No-fly Zone

The Safe Haven

Iraqi controlled territory

Mahabad

Hajj Omran
Diyana

Rawanduz

Sheikh Wisan

Shaqlawa   Ranya

IRAN

Qala Diza

Koysanjaq

36°N

Dokhan

Lesser Zab River

Penjwin

SULAYMANIYAH

Chemchemal

rkuk

Qara Dagh   Said Sadeq

Sanandaj

Sergalou-Bergalou   Halabja   Biyaara

IRAQ

Tawella

Kifri

Sumud   Dobendikhan

z Khurmatu

GERMIYAN

Kalar

0   50 miles

0   50 km

CHRONOLOGY

1200 BC The Medes, who are thought to be ancestors of the Kurds, migrate from central Asia and settle in the Zagros mountains.

AD 1514 Kurdistan is divided between the Ottoman and Persian empires following the Battle of Chaldiran. This boundary endures until the First World War.

1914 The Ottomans side with Germany in the First World War, while Britain persuades the Arabs to fight on their side along with France and Russia, on the basis that it will subsequently support Arab independence from the Ottomans.

1918 At the end of the war Britain occupies the area which later becomes Iraq.

1920 Britain is awarded a mandate over Iraq, and establishes a monarchy and a parliament. However, for the next 12 years real power is wielded by a bevy of British advisers and the RAF.

The Treaty of Sèvres is signed, Article 62 of which provides for the possible creation of a Kurdish state in the future.

1919–22 The Turkish War of Independence, fought by Turkish nationalists against the moribund Sultanate, results in the birth of the modern state of Turkey. The Turkish nationalists refuse to adhere to the Treaty of Sèvres.

1920s Uprisings in Iraqi Kurdistan against outside authority are put down by British troops and the RAF.

1923　The Treaty of Lausanne replaces the Treaty of Sèvres. The new treaty makes no mention of a possible Kurdish state, or indeed of Kurdish rights.

1925　Mosul province becomes part of Iraq.

1932　The British mandate over Iraq is formally ended by a Treaty which fails to contain guarantees as to Kurdish rights. Britain retains many military facilities in Iraq and a major interest in the Iraqi Petroleum Company (IPC).

1934　Iraqi Communist Party (ICP) founded.

1945　Kurdistan Democratic Party (KDP) founded in Iran by Qadhi Mohammed.

1946　January: Kurdish Republic of Mahabad proclaimed in Iran, with military support from Mullah Mustafa Barzani. Kurdistan Democratic Party (KDP) of Iraq founded by Barzani and Hamza Abdullah.
December: Republic of Mahabad is crushed.

1947　Barzani flees to the USSR.

1958　Free Officers' Coup led by Qasim overthrows the monarchy. Barzani returns to Iraq from the USSR.

1961　Relations between Qasim and the Kurds deteriorate and fighting breaks out. The 'Kurdish Revolution' begins.

1963　A Ba'athist–Nationalist coalition overthrows Qasim, but the Ba'athists are subsequently ousted by the Nationalists.

1968　The Ba'athists come to power in a further coup, beginning a period of rule that continues today.

1970　Saddam Hussein travels to Kurdistan and offers an 'Autonomy' plan to the Kurds, to be implemented in 1974, which Barzani accepts.

1974　The 'Autonomy' law is published but the Kurds reject it. Fighting breaks out with the central government.

1975　By now the Iraqi Kurds are receiving military support from the American CIA and Israel, and Iran is allowing them to maintain bases in Iranian Kurdistan. At an OPEC meeting in Algiers, Saddam does a deal with the Shah whereby Iran will close its borders to the Iraqi Kurds in exchange for Iraq ceding rights in the Shatt al-Arab waterway. Iran complies immediately and thousands of Iraqi Kurds are massacred. The military struggle against Baghdad collapses; Barzani flees to the US, where he dies in 1979.

1976 The Patriotic Union of Kurdistan (PUK) founded by Jalal Talabani.

1978 Major purge of Communists by the Ba'athists.

1979 Saddam Hussein becomes president of Iraq.
The Iranian Revolution takes place.

1980–88 The Iraq–Iran war. The Iraqi Kurds assist the Iranians at various junctures during the war.

1987 Ali Hassan al-Majid is appointed to lead the northern command of the Ba'ath party, with the task of finding a 'final solution' to the Kurdish question. He launches chemical attacks against a series of Kurdish villages, including Sheikh Wisan.

1988 February to September: The *Anfal* campaign is waged against rural Kurds. Up to 180,000 perish.
March: Halabja is bombed with chemicals, killing 5,000 people.
The Kurdistan Front is formed.

1990 Saddam Hussein invades Kuwait on 2 August. UN sanctions are imposed against Iraq.

1991 17 January to 28 February: The Gulf War.
March: After the ceasefire, uprisings begin in the south and north of Iraq. As the regime retaliates, Kurds flee to the Iranian and Turkish borders.
April: The Safe Haven is set up and UN personnel begin to operate in Iraq. A 'no-fly' zone is established north of the 36th parallel.
October: All Iraqi government personnel withdraw from an area covering about 50 per cent of Iraqi Kurdistan.

1992 May: Elections are held and the Kurdish administration is established.

1993 November: Fighting breaks out between rival Kurdish groups.

1994 May–June: Serious fighting breaks out between the PUK and KDP. The parliament ceases to function. Economic crisis. The enclave is divided into two zones, with the northwest controlled by the KDP, and Arbil and the southeast controlled by the PUK.

1995 Kurdistan descends into a state of near civil war. Severe economic crisis. Attempts to negotiate a settlement between the PUK and the KDP fail.

1996 Political and military stalemate.

31 August: The KDP takes control of Arbil with the support of Iraqi government tanks and Republican Guard troops. Iraqi security police conduct house-to-house searches, arresting members of the Iraqi opposition and the PUK. The US launches cruise missile attacks on Iraqi air defences in the south but does not defend the Safe Haven.

9 September: KDP forces oust the PUK from Sulaymaniyah and take control of the city. Tens of thousands of PUK supporters flee to the Iranian border.

Organisations

KDP	Kurdistan Democratic Party
PUK	Patriotic Union of Kurdistan
PKK	Kurdish Workers' Party (Turkey)
INC	Iraqi National Congress (umbrella grouping of the Iraqi opposition)
ICP	Iraqi Communist Party
IMIK	Islamic Movement in Kurdistan
KHRO	Kurdish Human Rights Organisation
ADM	Assyrian Democratic Movement

PART ONE

chapter one

SOUTHEASTERN TURKEY, MAY 1993

The road surface was good and we sped along. I was sitting behind
the driver, a thin man with ginger hair who sat up straight and kept
his eyes on the road. I thought he was probably a Kurd, but I wasn't
sure. We had been warned not to use the word 'Kurd' in the airports
at Istanbul and Dyarbakir.

We were crossing a vast plain of green cornfields speckled with
poppies stretching as far as the eye could see. The fields were lush
and beautiful under a low-hanging cloudy sky which gave a hazy,
white light. From time to time it spattered with rain and the driver
pulled his window shut.

Southeastern Turkey was said to be as dangerous now for travellers as Iraqi Kurdistan, with a massive presence of heavily armed,
very jumpy Turkish troops confronting the PKK. If we got
stopped, we were to stress that we were 'tourists' on our way to
Iraq, not fact-finders – and certainly not journalists. If they wanted
to know more, we would say we were going to look at archaeologi-
cal sites.

Relishing the silence and the sense of motion, I let my eyes drift
to the horizon. I had been excited about the trip for weeks, con-
vinced that it was a good idea to come, but right now the main thing
on my mind was danger. Two foreign aid workers had been killed in
Kurdistan since January, by Iraqi government agents. The second, a
young Belgian, had been shot only a month earlier, ambushed on a
lonely road north of Sulaymaniyah. I had heard that individual
Kurds were being offered large sums of money by Saddam Hussein
to kill Europeans.

I had travelled in many Middle Eastern countries, but the Iraqis inspired a special kind of fear. Saddam was trying to inhibit the activities of non-governmental organisations by making Kurdistan a 'no-go' area for Westerners. In the last few days I had begun to feel afraid and, when I thought of the tales of repression and suffering which I knew we were going to hear, to wonder whether I had the necessary strength. I had found myself half-wishing I had chosen to stay at home in the West country, in the green spring which was so lovely and felt so safe...

It was hot in the bus and nearly everyone in our party of seven was dozing except Shireen, who sat next to the driver with a shortwave radio on her lap. She was looking out of the window and smiling quietly to herself. Her Kurdish friends were travelling behind us in a taxi.

Shireen was originally from Sulaymaniyah in Iraqi Kurdistan, but had been living in exile in London for the last 15 years. She was a long-standing member of the Iraqi Communist Party and had had to leave Iraq during the purge of Communists in 1978. She was in her late fifties, a tall, attractive woman with short chestnut hair and a warm, intelligent face. She wore a loose-fitting, grey cotton suit with a pleated skirt well below the knee, the sort of suit that middle-class Iraqi women who live in the West often wear. That sort of suit carries a message of secular respectability, of having grown-up children, a woman who knows where she comes from but has a modern, Westernised outlook.

We had talked on the flight to Istanbul the day before and I had taken a liking to Shireen. It is unusual for Iraqi women to travel alone and I wondered about her situation. 'My sons have all flown the nest,' she told me in her husky-voiced, impeccable English, 'and I've just divorced my husband!' She had asked me where I had learned Arabic and I had told her about my year in Palestine–Israel. Like most of the Iraqis I knew, Shireen still felt angry with the Palestinians for their insistence on seeing Saddam Hussein as a hero and their refusal to acknowledge the terrible suffering he had inflicted on his own people.

'They should have known better. They never had to live under Saddam! The Palestinians have suffered, of course, but not like we suffered.' Her voice was deep with disapproval.

Shireen spoke of the 'liberation' of Kurdistan with great excitement. This was to be her first visit to Sulaymaniyah in 20 years. I wondered how it must feel to have been exiled for so long, and to be returning to her native city under Kurdish control.

I hadn't expected this part of Turkey to be green, or flat. I had seen it in the films of Yilmaz Gunay and what I remembered was sand-coloured mud-brick villages, soldiers and brown rocky hills. By contrast the rippling cornfields looked fertile and serene. To the right a high wire fence stretched parallel to the road for as far as the eye could see: the Syrian border. On the far side, the vast green plain extended to the horizon. The road was empty except for the occasional truck coming the other way; and several times we passed a jeep full of soldiers.

It was getting on for noon. The city of Mardin was far behind us now and the road signs as we flashed past showed that we were eating up the remaining miles to Nusaybin. Nusaybin was the first town on my map; from there it was about 40 miles to Cizre, another 12 to Silopi, the last town in Turkey, and then about eight to Khabur, just inside the Iraqi border.

Somewhere between Nusaybin and Cizre the landscape began to change in an unforgettably dramatic way. We were coasting along at speed on the straight, empty road and suddenly, in the far distance, the silhouette of a mountain range began to loom through the haze. To begin with I thought the blurred bluish shapes were rain clouds, but within a minute they became stronger and I knew that they were mountains. I felt a childlike delight. My map didn't give contours so I could only guess, but I felt sure that this must be the beginning of Iraqi Kurdistan.

By the time we reached Cizre, the others were waking up. It was a sand-coloured, poor-looking town with concrete-block houses built across the side of a hill; then, as we rounded a bend in the road, a big expanse of brownish-green water came into view.

'That's the Tigris,' Jill announced from the back of the bus.

As we left the town, the road curved through an area of mud-flats, spilling over from a big bend in the river. They were cultivated in little plots and people were standing at the water's edge. The water was thick and pale brown, rippling in the white light; as we flashed past I thought that this must be just the way it looked 5,000 years ago; this is the rich muddy water of Mesopotamia from which civilisation sprang.

A mile before Silopi we were stopped by soldiers and asked for our papers. It fell to me to hand the passports out of the window. I beamed and said, '*Tourists.*' Two deeply-tanned soldiers with machine guns and walkie-talkies looked at me doubtfully. They flicked through the passports. They peered through the window at our faces. Then they returned the passports, tried to smile and waved us on.

On the outskirts of Silopi young men stood about on the edge of the road, staring at us vacantly from cafés with Pepsi-cola signs. We were about to stop for a snack when another group of soldiers waved to the driver to pull over. The taxi carrying Shireen's friends was immediately in front of us and they were made to stop too. This time there were more soldiers, five or six. We went through the same performance with the passports, again I smiled and said, '*Tourists*,' and again it went down all right. But Shireen's Kurdish friends were made to get out and the soldiers started to go through their suitcases.

After 10 minutes the soldiers testily returned the men's documents and we set off again. By now the idea of having lunch in Silopi had lost its appeal and we decided to keep going until we reached the border.

chapter two

TEA WITH THE BRITISH ARMY

It was the most spectacular land border I had ever crossed.

On the far side of a rusty metal suspension bridge spanning a narrow river, the mountain range we had seen from the distance rose against the sky in a long, craggy ridge. It was as stunningly beautiful as it was abrupt, like something in a dream. Not until the following day, when we were looking back at the ridge from the far side, did I reflect how inhospitable these mountains had been for the Kurds in 1991 and how many children had died trying to cross them.

On the Turkish side of the bridge, single-storey concrete huts stood on either side of the tarmac. We overtook a long queue of brightly-painted Turkish lorries, evidence that the UN sanctions were still in force. Behind the lorries, over a high fence, I glimpsed a field full of tents, the remains of one of the many refugee camps which were set up on this border following the exodus of Kurds from Iraq in 1988 after the chemical bombing of Halabja.

We were met by Dara Qazzaz, a representative of the year-old Kurdish Ministry of Municipalities and Tourism. Dara was a pale young man of about 30, with plump cheeks which bulged when he smiled and a handlebar moustache. He was wearing a black Western suit in honour of our arrival and had brought a large dark blue coach to pick us up. We were the first group of British 'tourists' to visit Iraqi Kurdistan and it was clear that we were to be treated as VIPs.

After the grim-faced Turkish officials had stamped our passports in three or four places and we had said goodbye to Shireen and her friends, Dara ushered us onto the coach and, with a deafening rattle, we were driven across the metal bridge. On the far side we were greeted cordially by a group of absurdly good-looking, weather-beaten men who rose from the stools on which they'd been sitting in the sun smoking. They were dressed in the traditional Kurdish out-fit of ginger-brown wool *sharwal* – vastly baggy trousers and match-ing tops with colourful cotton cummerbunds wound around their waists – and turbans on their heads; Kalashnikovs dangled from straps across their backs. They gave a cursory glance at our docu-ments and led us into a large dilapidated office for our first glass of Kurdish tea.

Big shabby armchairs were arranged around the walls, leaving the floor space clear. Lilian, John and Steve sat down side by side, and I noticed that they all looked as tired and disorientated as I felt. Lilian was wearing a pudding basin straw hat, with a short brim and a black ribbon, pulled down over her eyebrows. John looked uncom-fortably hot in a tweed jacket. Steve, who was wearing jeans, had his long legs entwined like spaghetti and his arms folded. His expression was very serious.

We were an odd bunch and had met each other for the first time only the week before. Jill, the organiser of the trip, was a human rights activist turned tour operator in her mid-forties with streaky blonde hair that fell in her eyes. She had visited Iraqi Kurdistan three times since the 1991 uprising and had had the idea of bringing parties of British tourists. The Kurds, she said, had been delighted: building links with Westerners was high on their list of political priorities. We were the first group, although none of us were exactly tourists.

Lilian was writing a travel piece for a national newspaper. Steve and John, computer programmer and community health worker respectively, had both come out of general interest in the Kurds. David was an ex-youth worker newly qualified as a barrister. He was a committed Christian and had been involved in Kurdish human rights work for many years. Lastly there was Christine, a photogra-pher who had heard about the trip through her local Labour party and had wanted to take pictures of Kurdish women.

The tea was served in tiny, pear-shaped glasses – *piyala* in Kur-dish – which sat delicately on painted saucers. It was sweet, pale and flavoured with cardamom. Our hosts sat down and drank with us, providing my first sight of what was to become a familiar image: a line of rugged, masculine Kurdish men in *sharwal*, cummerbunds and turbans, sipping tea with incongruous delicacy. I had never seen a Kalashnikov before, except in films, and was fascinated by the way the man sitting nearest me let the long slender black barrel rest against the back of his armchair with the muzzle nestling cosily into the cushion. When he stood up and turned his back I noticed that the magazine was made of wood. Its crescent-shaped curve was surprisingly graceful.

One of the many men who were milling around the office stepped forward, bowed and made a brief welcoming speech in Kurdish, which was translated for us by Dara. We nodded and smiled, but between the seven of us failed to manage more than a few mumbled words in reply. I felt ashamed of our British reserve but was dazed to the point of silence. We had been on the road, without food, since six that morning, and it was now after three in the afternoon. But, perhaps more importantly, I couldn't quite take in that we had actually arrived in Iraqi Kurdistan.

After the tea we boarded the bus again. Dara informed us that our next call would be at the Zakho office of the PUK. Zakho was the first town in Kurdistan, 10 minutes' drive from the border.

'We've been hijacked by the PUK!' Jill whispered to me. 'But it doesn't matter, we'll get to meet the other side too.'

I raised my eyebrows. The PUK, led by Jalal Talabani, shared power in the new government with the KDP, led by Masoud Barzani. We had been warned, come what may, to avoid appearing to favour one party over the other.

The bus stopped on the outskirts of Zakho and we were led through a small rose garden into a one-storey concrete office. The green emblem of the PUK was painted on the outside wall, with 'Patriotic Union of Kurdistan' written in large green letters in English and Kurdish. Inside we were greeted by a tall man in a military-style *sharwal*, in khaki. He had a handlebar moustache like Dara's, but unlike Dara his face was lean and dark. Jill took his hand.

'The last time I saw you was in Islington Town Hall!' she exclaimed, giving him an awkward hug. The idea seemed ridiculous and we all began to laugh.

The Safe Havens policy had been co-ordinated from Zakho. The coalition of French, British, Turkish and American troops was still patrolling above the 36th parallel, flying over the area twice a day and enforcing a 'no-fly' zone in what they termed 'Operation Provide Comfort'. Token though it was, their continued presence was thought to be the main reason why Saddam Hussein had not yet tried to reoccupy Kurdistan. The office of the Safe Havens' Military Command Council was around the corner from where we were. After another glass of tea and another speech, Jill suggested we should drop in on the British commander.

We joked about what sort of reception we could expect to get from the British army, but none of us realised that Jill had not informed them in advance about our visit. The coach pulled up outside a suburban bungalow with a mosquito screen over the door and a patch of lawn in front. A small British flag was flying from a post and an army Landrover was parked outside.

We clambered out of the bus, feeling slightly awkward, as Jill marched bravely up to the Kurd who was guarding the door. I looked round at the group, wondering what sort of sight we were going to present. John had taken off his jacket and was dangling it over his shoulder with one finger through the loop. He looked tired and a bit cross. David was smiling calmly but his eyes were red and he kept rubbing them. Christine was worried about leaving her cameras on the bus. She went back and returned with a heavy black bag dangling from each shoulder. I was hot and tired and wishing I could take my tights off.

After a few seconds a sun-tanned British officer in skin-tight camouflage fatigues came out of the door. He was mopping his forehead with a handkerchief and when he caught sight of us his mouth dropped open. However, when Jill explained who we were and that we would like to come in for a 'chat', he swiftly regained his composure, as if visits by parties of tourists were a daily occurrence.

'OK, fine, give me two minutes, we've just returned from an eight-hour road trip and the boss isn't feeling too well...'

I noticed that his boots were covered in dust and there were beads of sweat on his neck. He disappeared through the mosquito screen door, leaving the Kurdish guard to smile at us in bemusement.

As we stood waiting in the dirt road outside the house it struck me that the atmosphere was remarkably peaceful. A group of children were playing 20 yards away and a handful of men were standing around near us. I felt quite safe, quite relaxed. The afternoon sun was warm, casting a glowing light over the sandy road, it was very quiet and I had the sense of a peaceful, one-horse town whose inhabitants were sleeping the siesta.

After a couple of minutes, the door was opened again, this time by a tall bony soldier with a Glaswegian accent.

'Would ye like to step this way, please?'

We trooped past the mosquito screen into a small reception room with a tiled floor, armchairs and a coffee table. The officer who had come to the door before was sprawled comfortably in the largest chair, in front of a map of Kurdistan which filled the whole of the back wall. The Glaswegian perched silently beside him on a stool. There was no sign of 'the boss', and I vaguely wondered if he was laid out somewhere else in the house suffering from sun-stroke or diarrhoea...

Once we were all seated, our host gazed round at us with a faintly amused expression, and announced: 'Bill Bennett, Commanding Officer of the — Regiment. What can I do for you?'

As Jill explained who we were and what we were doing in Kurdistan, I studied Bill Bennett. He was a fit-looking, sun-tanned man of about 40 who obviously considered himself attractive. His hair was streaked with grey and longer than my stereotype of an army officer said it should have been. He had fleshy cheeks and the sort of body which, had he not been a soldier, would have tended to fat. His fatigues were a pretty, pale moss green with mushroom-coloured blotches and fitted him as snugly as a pair of lycra leggings. His boots – which were the subject of endless discussion between us afterwards – would not have been out of place in a fashionable shoe shop. They were made of very soft sand-coloured canvas with suede trimmings and came half way up his calf.

When Jill had finished speaking, Bill nodded politely and said, 'Well, I expect you could all do with a cup of tea!' He glanced over at the Glaswegian, who scrambled to his feet and opened a door into what was apparently the kitchen.

'Is it tea for ye all, or would any of youse rather cawffee?' he grinned shyly round the room. He was much taller than Bill, and thinner, and his plain green fatigues hung on him loosely. He had a nice face, with piercing, hungry blue eyes. Later in the conversation, when Bill was talking about Kurdish women, I noticed his gaze wandering from one to the other of us four women.

'You've certainly come at an interesting time,' Bill told us. 'No doubt you've heard about the withdrawal of the 25 dinar note?'

I had seen a brief mention of this in the *Guardian* a few days before we left, but I hadn't realised how serious the implications were. Saddam had taken the note out of circulation on very short notice and was refusing to allow any except his closest allies to exchange the money they held in 25-dinar notes for ones which were still legal tender. This was having the intended disastrous effect on the already very fragile Kurdish economy. The dinar had been devalued by nearly 50 per cent. Prior to the Gulf crisis, one Iraqi dinar had been worth three US dollars. By early 1993 it took 250 dinars to buy one dollar; and now the rate was about 35 to the dollar. The big fear was that Saddam might be planning to withdraw the five- or the ten-dinar notes as well, which would effectively leave the Kurds bankrupt.

Bill Bennett told us that the Kurdish authorities were asking the Turkish government to allow the Turkish lira to be used as legal tender in northern Iraq. It seemed that the Military Command Council were often consulted by the Kurdish authorities in times of crisis. The following night on Kurdish television we would see footage of Bill and 'the boss' sitting in the same room, with a delegation of Kurdish MPs, discussing the devaluation.

'The other big problem at the moment is the harvest. It's a fine crop this year, there's even been talk of it being a bumper crop – I expect you'll have heard that last year's harvest was poor – but now we've got a plague of beetles. The whole crop is threatened.

'It's taken a few weeks to organise a delivery of pesticide. It just arrived, last week, so now this week they're starting to spray. The crop won't be as good as it should have been, but, *insha'allah*,' he smiled, raising his eyebrows, 'some of it should be saved.'

I began to get the feeling that Bill was genuinely concerned about the Kurds' predicament, which confounded another of my stereotypes of army officers. I half-liked him, but he was slightly over-confident, and instinct told me that he was a sexual predator.

'What about the Iraqis?' David asked. 'I heard that they were trying to damage the harvest by shelling in some places.'

'The GOI,' Bill frowned, 'will do anything they can to make life difficult for the Kurds, short of coming back in. At the moment, that is.'

' "GOI"?' We looked at him blankly.

'Government of Iraq.' He smiled. 'Army speak.'

He gestured to the map which filled the wall behind him. A series of pins were spaced out across the northeastern corner of Iraq. 'The pins show the approximate position of the GOI troops as of two weeks ago.'

'What happens to Kurds with families on the "GOI" side of the line?' Jill asked. The area to the northeast of the line represented only about half of Kurdistan.

'Kurds who aren't *peshmerga* can come and go.' *Peshmerga* was the Kurdish term for guerilla fighter, which literally translates as 'those who face death'. 'Old people go through all the time to collect their pensions. They have to – can't get 'em here!'

'Why not?'

'Because there's almost no infrastructure here and no money. The GOI ran a highly centralised operation and now they're using that to make life harder for people on this side of the line. There's no postal service, a very restricted telephone system and electricity comes from a central grid in Mosul, so we get constant power cuts.' He smiled. 'No, the Kurdish government can't pay out pensions. It can hardly pay its own employees,' he glanced at Dara, 'so people go through, every month, and collect their pensions in Kirkuk and Mosul. And younger people go through to visit their families.'

'Do they get harassed?'

'Sure they do. Only last week at Chemchemal, so the story goes, women coming through the checkpoint from the GOI-controlled area were forced to take pills, and after they'd taken them they were told that the pills would make them infertile; and men were made to give blood, and then afterwards told that they had contracted AIDS.'

'Is it true?'

Bill raised his eyebrows. 'I dare say they were given pills and had blood taken. Whether the effects will be infertility and AIDS … who knows? More likely they were given vitamin pills, and told they would be infertile to frighten them…'

Suddenly the door swung open and the Glaswegian came in with a tray laden with huge pint mugs of dark, strong army tea. It smelled bitter after the delicate little glasses of golden liquid we had drunk at the border. There was UHT milk in a carton.

Bill was speaking enthusiastically now about the work of the various non-governmental organisations. One of the medical NGOs was working on improving the water supply, another on health education. We should try to visit the Caritas village reconstruction project on the road to Arbil and the artificial limb hospital in Sulaymaniyah.

'You'll get a fantastic welcome from the Kurds everywhere you go,' he assured us, beginning to sound like a tour guide. 'They're the warmest, most hospitable people you could hope to meet. And the children will steal your hearts!'

'My children back in Britain,' Bill went on, 'have collected up their old toys and sent them out here, with strict instructions for me to hand them out in the villages we patrol.' He grinned, revealing buck teeth. 'So what are your special interests? What in particular do you want to see while you're here?' He looked at each of us in turn.

'Well,' I ventured, curious to see what his reaction would be, 'I'm hoping to do some interviews with Kurdish women.'

'Oh, the women!' He looked me hard in the eye. 'You'll see some very beautiful women here, some real stunners. And they're very strong … I think you'll be surprised at the weight they carry on their heads. You'll see them carrying great stacks of firewood.' His eyes lit up as he spoke, and I had a momentary vision of him driving into a Kurdish village in his British army Landrover to eye up women as they gathered firewood. There was something sexually insistent about his gaze; it was not hard to imagine that if you met him in different circumstances, those eyes would undress you in a matter of seconds.

'Oh yes, it's a hard life for the women,' he went on. 'The average stay in the hospital in D'hok after giving birth is half an hour.'

He tossed out this piece of information in a tone which was half-admiring, half-pitying, all the while maintaining eye contact with me, as if trying to gauge my reaction.

'But,' he added, 'they age very young. Too much hard work. You'd be surprised,' and his glance took in all four of us women, as if giving a warning, 'the women here are past it by their late twenties!'

There was something in the way he spoke that clearly demanded a response (of pity, or disgust, or even anxiety that the same terrible fate might await us?), but Christine caught my eye and we both looked away.

There was a pause. A large fly buzzed around the room.

'What about the security situation?' Jill changed the subject. 'D'you have any advice for us?'

Bill Bennett frowned. 'Whereabouts are you thinking of going?'

'Er...' Jill cleared her throat uncomfortably, 'well, actually we've been told not to tell anyone exactly where we're going ... but, strictly for your ears only' (she smiled nervously at Bill, not wanting to offend him) 'as you'd expect, we're going to all the main cities...'

'One after the other, progressing gradually southeast?'

'Er, yes, that's about it.'

'Right.' His tone was efficient now, professional. 'Basically, security gets worse as you get further south and east. As you know, once you're south of the 36th parallel you're outside the 'no-fly' zone and there's no Allied protection at all. But, having said that, Saddam hasn't tried to come back in yet. I'm sure you'll be very well looked after. You're being hosted by the Ministry of Tourism,' he nodded his head at Dara, who was sitting next to me on the sofa, and who looked, I thought, slightly irritated, 'and no doubt you'll have *peshmerga* travelling with you?'

Jill nodded.

'What you must remember,' and at this point Bill pulled himself up in his armchair and looked at us rather sternly 'is that this is, technically speaking, a war zone, and there are undoubtedly risks. Don't wander far off the road: you may encounter land mines. Keep abreast of the news. Always ask your local guides about security conditions and follow their advice. And remember, south of the 36th parallel, there's absolutely nothing we can do for you!'

He didn't seem to regret this.

'Will we see you flying overhead, when we're north of the 36th parallel?'

'You won't see us, we fly too high for that. But you may hear us, from time to time. There *is* a terrorism problem, mainly in the cities. A smaller problem than one might perhaps expect, given the situation. Chiefly car bombs.

'*We* always travel in a convoy of three vehicles,' he went on. 'We spread ourselves out between the vehicles, to minimise the risk of a successful ambush. And of course we always travel with *pesh*.' He smiled indulgently. 'Pesh' seemed to be an affectionate, if patronising, shortening of *peshmerga*.

'Och aye, the *pesh* are brilliant!' the Glaswegian suddenly chimed in. He had been following the conversation intently, so far without contributing a word. Now he smiled round at us shyly with his pale blue eyes and for some reason I felt rather sorry for him. I wasn't sure what his rank was, but he certainly lacked Bill's self-confidence.

'Right, folks,' Jill put her half-drunk mug of tea on the coffee table and began to get up from her chair. 'Time to hit the road. We've another hour's drive to D'hok.' She smiled bravely at Bill Bennett and stretched out her hand.

'Thank you very much for talking to us, and for the tea. That was a wonderful introduction to Kurdistan.'

I glanced again at Dara, wondering how he felt about his first-ever group of tourists being given their introduction to Kurdistan by the British army, rather than by himself as the personal representative of the Minister of Tourism. Not a lot, judging by the look on his face.

'Now, before we get back on the bus,' Jill began, 'would you gentlemen be so kind as to let us use your toilets…?'

'Yes of course!' Bill grinned. 'I was about to suggest it. Would the ladies like to step this way?'

He opened a door and led us through a corridor to the back of the building, past a stack of cardboard boxes marked 'Heinz' to a corridor which housed a washing machine and tumble dryer. At the back a door opened onto a lawn, where a couple of soldiers were relaxing bare-chested in shorts. They did a double take as we walked past.

'Here you are, you have a choice of three toilets,' said Bill magnanimously. 'One here, one in the bathroom,' he pointed, 'and another one up the stairs.'

We had been well warned what to expect of Kurdish toilets, and our last opportunity to relieve ourselves had been a very smelly squat toilet on the Turkish side of the border, so it was a delight to have a last chance to sit on a clean, European-style lavatory seat. I chose to use the one 'up the stairs' in the hope that I might gain some further, fascinating glimpses of Safe Haven-barracks life. How on earth had they got the washing machines here, I wondered. Surely they wouldn't have gone to all the trouble of bringing them in through Turkey? And come to that, what about the lavatories themselves? Could this building have been purpose-built for Allied soldiers, in the short time the Safe Havens had been established? I wondered what the Kurds thought of Western soldiers who couldn't cope with squatting down to do their business...

Back on the bus we drove through the outskirts of Zakho and took a road which wound through a pass in the ridge of mountains. We seemed to be driving in convoy with a white Toyota pick-up truck. I found that reassuring, although I wished we could be in a convoy of three, like the army. Our driver was taking the road extremely slowly. I wondered why: was it safer to go slowly (logic told me it would be safer to go quickly), was it because of the petrol shortage, or was it to enable us 'tourists' to admire the view? The mountains were beautiful – wild, rugged and as green as Wales – but I felt uneasy.

After more than an hour, we rounded a bend to find a large city spread out before us. We had come down from the mountains onto a plain, and grey concrete buildings fanned out in a grid on either side of the main road. It wasn't beautiful, but it was D'hok, and we had arrived.

chapter three

SADDAM'S PALACES

Saddam's palace at Ashawa had been designed around a beautiful natural waterfall, a spot where previously Kurds had come for family picnics. He had appropriated the site in 1988 and built a 15 ft high, 2 mile long stone wall around it.

I had had a good night's sleep and woken up feeling relaxed and enthusiastic. We had breakfasted on flat bread and delicious, lumpy yogourt before setting off at a leisurely pace with Dara and Salim, a second man from the Ministry of Tourism. It was a warm, balmy day with clear blue skies, perfect for the start of a holiday, but the sight of the wall as the bus drew closer reminded me where we were, and I felt fear creeping back into my body. Built of blocks of stone sandwiched together with a thick layer of cement, the wall snaked arbitrarily over the contours of the rough hillside, gleaming a creamy white in the sun.

As we came round a bend I noticed a group of four weatherbeaten women standing by the side of the road. They were dressed in men's *sharwal* with colourful blouses and scarves tied roughly over their hair. One of the women had a bundle of firewood twice her own size balanced on her head, the other three were resting against equally large bundles which lay on the ground.

'These women are *Anfal* widows,' Dara announced. The *Anfal* was the genocidal campaign waged by the Iraqi government in 1988 against rural Kurds, in which up to 180,000 are believed to have perished. I hoped we would offer the women a lift, but, although one of them waved and the others stared at us fixedly, the driver did not slow down. We passed many more such groups in the course of the next few days and I gradually realised that, given our vulnerability as foreigners, our hosts felt it was not safe to offer lifts to anybody.

Ashawa was one of a series of palaces Saddam had built for himself and his retinue in the hills of the D'hok Governorate. In the late 1980s he had talked of bringing his Revolutionary Command Council to spend the hot summers here to escape the intolerable Baghdad heat. But the plan was never put into action and the palace had fallen into rebel Kurdish hands during the uprising.

We drove through a gateway past a cluster of red-roofed villas, built to house guards, which rose angrily from the scrubby moorland, utterly out of place. From here the driveway swept downhill in a great curve and the palace came into view: a large, squat, hard-edged lego-mansion with white walls and a green roof, fronting onto an artificial lake. The water was an unnatural shade between turquoise and petrol blue. I looked up at the sky, trying to work out where the colour came from. But it was pale azure, and the hills which rose behind the palace were a sappy green. I wondered if the water had been tinted with a chemical.

As we walked towards the palace, Salim pointed to a ridge of mountains over to the northwest. 'Those are the mountains we had to cross when we walked to Turkey after the uprising.'

Salim was skinny and small, with a pleasant, rather squashed face and large ears, and he looked older than Dara. Lilian was walking beside him.

'So those are the mountains at the border, that we came through yesterday?'

'Yes.'

'You walked all the way?'

'Yes, with my wife and children. It was very hard.' He spoke quietly. 'Our baby daughter died on the way, she was five months old.'

A long reception hall looked onto the lake, with gaping holes in the walls where doors and windows should have been. The building had been incomplete in March 1991 when it was sacked by the Kurds and the builders and guards were driven out.

Inside, the ceiling was sculpted in the voluptuous shape of a massive sea shell. The walls were pockmarked with bullet-holes and heavily graffitied. I wanted to stop and try to decipher some of it, but was afraid of embarrassing our hosts. Some was obvious – 'Long live the PUK' written in English – but there were also sexually explicit drawings and writing in Kurdish and Arabic.

Six or seven young men were wandering around the palace with us – the *peshmerga* we had been promised. I had discovered this morning that some of them were travelling in the Toyota pick-up which accompanied us; others rode in the back of our bus. They were in their early twenties, with sun-drenched, handsome faces, dressed not in the traditional *peshmerga* outfit of *sharwal* and cummerbunds, but in jeans and T shirts. Kalashnikovs were slung across their shoulders and a camera was being passed around between them.

At one end of the room a mosaic panel was set into the pock-marked wall. It was decorated in pale pinks and green, and some Arabic words were inscribed on it in gold: '*Al-hamdu-lillahi, alathi akramana wa anama aleyna.*'

I was struggling to decipher these when Dara came up and read over my shoulder, 'Thanks be to God, who was generous to us and provided for our needs.'

The choice of words seemed to me highly ironic, but he read in a matter-of-fact tone of voice, without disgust or anger. The construction of Ashawa had begun in 1988, the year of the *Anfal* and of the chemical bombing by the government of the Kurdish town of Halabja, towards the close of the Iraq–Iran war. Five thousand people were killed outright; many thousands more were injured.

Dara had abandoned his black suit today and was dressed more casually in a dark green shirt and trousers. His manner had changed too since the previous day. The formality had melted away, replaced by a friendly hospitality bordering on flirtatiousness. At supper the previous evening he had been delighted to discover that I spoke Arabic, and we had agreed to do a swap in which I would help him with his English and he would help me with my Arabic.

Dara had told us that he was a trained physicist but could find no work in his field in Kurdistan. His job with the Ministry of Tourism and Municipalities was prestigious, but, because the Kurdish government was bankrupt, he was paid a mere 150 dinars a month – about US$ 6.

I had asked Dara whether it was acceptable for me to talk to Kurds in Arabic, as I didn't know Kurdish and few of them spoke English. Since the Iraqi Kurds had suffered so much at the hands of the Arab-dominated central government, I imagined they might see Arabic as the language of their oppression. I liked the idea of learning Kurdish, but knew that it would be unrealistic to try to do so within the time I had available.

'Don't be worried,' Dara had reassured me in his Kurdified English. 'You are a foreigner, so I think people will forgive you for talking Arabic. You will find all our men know Arabic, because until the uprising it was the language used in the schools, but in the villages most of the women speak only Kurdish. They may not understand you, though,' he added with a flicker of friendly mockery, 'you have a Palestinian accent and lots of the expressions you use are different from what we say in Iraqi Arabic...'

Later that afternoon we tried to visit another of Saddam's palaces, at Inishka. Our guides thought it was empty, but when we got to the entrance we found a barrier and uniformed soldiers on guard. The palace had been taken over by the newly-formed Kurdish army. After a few moments' negotiation they agreed to let us in and we went down a driveway to a mansion which was smaller than the one at Ashawa. It stood on a hill, looking out over another artificial lake.

We were invited into the palace and ushered into a large square reception room. As usual the seating was arranged around the walls, only this time the sofas were massive modern ones. We sat along one wall and 20 or 30 soldiers in their bottle-green uniforms arrayed themselves along the other three. The tallest and thinnest of the soldiers, who turned out to be the Colonel, sat facing us from behind a massive mahogany desk. Sunlight streamed into the room from a window set high in the wall.

The Colonel had a beautiful, delicate, bony face. He nodded to us gravely but with warmth and told us, through Dara as interpreter, that we were 'extremely welcome'. He would try to assist us in any way he could and if we wanted anything, we only had to ask. The only thing he asked of *us* was that, since this was a military base, we should refrain from taking photographs. We nodded and the room fell silent.

I was confused as to what was meant by the 'Kurdish army'. I knew that there had been Kurdish conscripts in the Iraqi army – a lot of the men who were sent to Kuwait were Kurds – but I thought that in the liberated part of Kurdistan the only fighters would be *peshmerga*. And yet here were Kurds dressed not in *sharwal* and cummerbunds but in conventional army uniforms.

'Why are they wearing uniforms?' I whispered to Dara.

'Why? Because they are army, Kurdish army,' he whispered back.

'But ... why don't they wear *peshmerga* gear? Whose uniform is it?'

'Iraqi army uniform. Kurdistan is part of Iraq.'

I caught the eyes of Lilian and Steve, who had overheard. We were amazed. How could people who had suffered so much at the hands of the Iraqi army choose to wear its uniform? The Colonel was looking curious, so I asked Dara to put the question to him in Kurdish. As Dara spoke, I looked round at the array of gentle, bronzed faces in their deep maroon berets and told myself that if I had been facing a room full of 'real' Iraqi soldiers, this is what they would have looked like. It was a strange feeling.

While the Colonel was replying to my question, a hunch-backed old man dressed in a black *sharwal* came in with a tray of wet tea glasses and tiny saucers. He wheezed as he toured the room, handing them out with shaking hands.

'We are part of Iraq, this is why we wear the Iraqi army uniform.' The Colonel smiled delicately, almost shyly.

Dara could see that we were still very surprised, so he added: 'Look, we want to remain part of Iraq and we want to make this very clear to the world; it is very important for us that foreign countries understand this. Syria, Iran, Turkey for example: we do not want them to think that we intend to set up a separate state. And we do not intend that.'

We tried to ask how the men felt about wearing Iraqi army uniform. Didn't they find it distasteful? But the response was blank, either because they didn't understand the question or because it was not a question that they could afford to think about. The Colonel politely suggested that if we had any more questions, we might like to ask someone higher up, when we got back to D'hok.

The old man was going round now with a large copper kettle, filling the tiny glasses.

I couldn't take my eyes off the Colonel. He had a dignified, gentle air and his movements were extremely graceful. Ironically, his dark maroon beret suited him perfectly. It was perched diagonally on his narrow head and the angle somehow accentuated the length of his elegant neck.

When we had drunk our tea, one of the Colonel's aides suggested we might like to take a stroll down to the lake. We said we would, whereupon the Colonel pushed back his chair, unfolded his long body and led us out of the building. He was 6 foot 6 inches tall and moved like a gazelle.

We sauntered down the hill towards the lake in a posse of green-uniformed men. I had the feeling that they didn't have anything urgent to be getting on with and were quite happy to idle away the hot afternoon talking to us. The sun was high in the sky and the air was perfectly still. The palace and lake were surrounded by bare, green, scrub-covered mountains, with not a village or a road to be seen. It was peaceful and beautiful and, like the day before in Zakho, I found it strange to think that this was a place that had recently been the scene of terrible suffering.

'Look, up there,' one of the *peshmerga* was at my elbow, pointing to the top of the highest mountain and addressing me in Arabic. I had noticed him earlier. He was the only one with a baggy denim jacket to match his baggy denim jeans, and he had a lithe, agile body and beautiful eyes. 'See?'

I could just make out a white shape against the sky.

'Saddam's palace.'

'Another one? How many did he have?'

'He had lots of palaces, all round here. Maybe ten.'

'Ten! How did he get up there? Is there a road?'

'There is, a very difficult road. But Saddam,' he flapped his arms in the baggy jacket, imitating a bird, 'came by helicopter.'

I remembered the helicopter gunships which the Kurds had pleaded with the Allies to prevent Saddam from using during the uprising. Of course: Saddam could get to anywhere he wanted.

'Who lives up there now?' I asked.

'Now? I don't know,' he shrugged his shoulders and smiled at me.

He was slight and the jacket hung on him loosely, but with style. He had a head of bushy, wiry, thick black hair which curled down almost to his eyebrows, under which his eyes were warm and sad at the same time. A Kalashnikov dangled idly from his right shoulder and as he turned away I noticed a pistol stuck into the waistband of his jeans.

chapter four

A CAMPAIGN OF GENOCIDE

In 1988 the Kurds were subjected to a campaign of genocide in which up to 180,000 rural people were killed. The *Anfal* took place in the same year as the chemical bombing of Halabja; but, unlike Halabja, the facts of the *Anfal* remained concealed from the Western press until 1991.

The Kurds had been intermittently at war with central government from the early 1960s until 1975, when a government plan to grant them autonomy was imposed by force. The Kurdish leadership had rejected the autonomy plan because it offered little of real advantage and excluded the oil-rich parts of Kurdistan. The Iraqi government response was to crush the Kurdish fighters through a deal with Iran whereby the Shah (and the CIA) withdrew their hitherto considerable support for the Kurdish *peshmerga* overnight. Thousands of Kurds were subsequently massacred by the Iraqi government.

While the Iraqi government was boasting of the new Kurdish autonomy deal and celebrating its defeat of the *peshmerga*, it embarked on a campaign of 'Arabising' the oil-producing regions of Kirkuk and Khanaquin by forcibly transferring their Kurdish inhabitants to the south and replacing them with Arabs. Then, in the late 1970s, the Iraqi army began evacuating and destroying Kurdish villages in the mountainous border regions. This was part of a scorched-earth policy aimed at clearing a tract of land 12 miles wide by 500 miles long along the borders with Turkey and Iran. Again the evacuated villagers were forcibly transferred, some to the south of Iraq and others to specially built 'collective towns' on the plains.

Subsequently the border areas were heavily land-mined and designated 'prohibited areas'. The Kurds say that 4,500 of their villages were destroyed by the Iraqi government in the combined ravages of the *Anfal*, the scorched-earth policy and resettlement programmes.

It was the commencement of the eight-year Iraq–Iran war in 1980 which allowed the Kurdish *peshmerga* to reassert themselves in northern Iraq. Many army garrisons in the area were either closed or reduced in size due to the need to send more and more troops to the front, thereby reducing the level of surveillance and control which the Iraqi government could exert over the Kurds. Between 1980 and 1987 many parts of Kurdistan became 'no-go' areas for the army and were effectively controlled by the *peshmerga* of the KDP and the PUK. At different points in the war, both Kurdish parties built alliances with Teheran and assisted Iranian troops in achieving military victories against Baghdad.

Middle East Watch, the US-based human rights organisation, describe this period in their report *Genocide in Iraq: The Anfal Campaign against the Kurds* as follows:

> By [1986] the Iraqi regime's authority over the North had dwindled to control of the cities, towns, complexes and main highways. Elsewhere, the *peshmerga* forces could rely on a deep-rooted base of local support. Seeking refuge from the army, thousands of Kurdish draft-dodgers and deserters found new homes in the countryside. Villagers learned to live with a harsh economic blockade and stringent food rationing, punctuated by artillery shelling, aerial bombardment and punitive forays by the army and the paramilitary *jash*. In response, the rural Kurds built air-raid shelters in front of their homes and spent much of their time in hiding in the caves and ravines that honeycomb the northern Iraqi countryside. For all the grimness of this existence, by *1987* the mountainous interior of Iraqi Kurdistan was effectively liberated territory. This the Ba'ath Party regarded as an intolerable situation.

In the spring of 1987 Saddam Hussein appointed his cousin, Ali Hassan al-Majid, as Secretary General of the Northern Bureau of the Ba'ath Party. Al-Majid was granted sweeping, quasi-presidential powers over northern Iraq and given the remit to 'solve' the Kurdish question once and for all. From March 1987 until April 1989, al-Majid master-minded both the chemical attacks on Halabja and dozens of Kurdish villages, and the *Anfal* campaign. One of the most hated men in Iraq, al-Majid came to be known by the Kurds as 'Ali Anfal' or 'Ali Chemical'.

The term *Anfal* comes from the Qu'ran, where it has the meaning of 'the spoils of war', in the context of *jihad* or holy war. Saddam chose it in order to give a spurious veneer of religious legitimacy to the campaign – spurious since the Kurds are Muslims.

The campaign was carried out in eight phases, each one directed at a different area of rural Kurdistan. The operation began in the southeast and gradually moved to the northwest; seven of the eight areas were once under PUK control. The campaign began with a massive military assault by the Iraqi army on the PUK headquarters at Sergalou-Bergalou in the Qara Dagh on the night of 23 February, 1988.

Each separate *Anfal*, or phase, lasted about two weeks, the last one being concluded in early September 1988. On 6 September the regime declared victory by announcing a general 'amnesty' for all Kurds. Kurdish human rights organisations say that by then 182,000 people were dead.

Each phase of the *Anfal* generally began with a chemical attack aimed at both villagers and *peshmerga* bases, followed by a military blitz against the latter. Shortly after this, ground troops and *jash* (the Kurdish collaborator militias paid by the Iraqi government) would surround the area and round up the terrified inhabitants. The countryside was then combed for fugitives by the *jash* (although in a few cases conscience-stricken *jash* saved lives by spiriting people away to safety across the mountains). In the towns, secret police went house to house hunting for hiding villagers.

Once rounded up, the men and boys above a certain age were separated from the women, children and elderly before all were herded into covered army trucks and driven away. Most were taken to Topzawa military camp near Kirkuk, where they were counted and their names recorded. In most cases the women and children were then trucked on to other camps; thousands of elderly were held in Nugra Salman, a former prison in the desert of southern Iraq. Both groups were held in appalling conditions and many died of starvation, abuse and disease. Those who survived were eventually released in the 'amnesty'.

A different fate awaited the men and boys, few of whom were ever seen again. From the available evidence it appears that they were sent before firing squads in large groups and buried in mass graves outside the Kurdish areas. Middle East Watch interviewed a small number of survivors who would have died in this way but who escaped by extraordinary chance. One 12-year-old boy, named Taymour, described being driven with his relatives and fellow villagers to a remote area of desert in southern Iraq where large pits had been dug in the sand. The exhausted captives were made to stand along the edge of the pits, whereupon firing squads shot them. Taymour fell into the pit with his family but was only lightly wounded and managed to crawl out later under cover of darkness before the bodies were covered with sand. He was taken in by a Bedouin Arab family and eventually returned to Kurdistan to tell his story.

Although mostly women and girls were sent to camps, in a few cases they went before firing squads in the same way as the men. In Taymour's case his mother and sisters were with him: they did not survive.

The locations of three mass graves have been established through the testimony of survivors, but all are within the Iraqi government-controlled parts of the country and thus cannot be investigated. This leaves the widows and families of the men who disappeared in the extraordinarily difficult position of not having any conclusive proof that their men are dead, although there can be no real doubt about it.

When the surviving *Anfal* prisoners were released in September 1988, they were barred from returning to their villages, which were now declared to be in 'prohibited' areas. In fact, little remained of the villages since the army had been given the task of razing them to the ground, destroying homes, schools and clinics, concreting wells, looting possessions and slaughtering all domestic animals. The effect of the *Anfal* upon rural Kurdish life was, as intended, utterly devastating.

chapter five

GALAWESH, A WOMAN MP

We reached the city of Arbil in the late afternoon. Stiff after the long drive through the mountains, Christine and I went out to explore the quarter around the hotel, taking a couple of *peshmerga* with us for protection.

We were close to the area of the *bazaar*, which spilled through several streets at the foot of the *qala'a*, Arbil's prehistoric citadel. It was an ancient stone fortress atop a strangely-shaped sandy rock which rose abruptly in the midst of the flat streets with their single-storey shops and houses. A stone wall climbed gradually upwards along the side of the rock, like a belt holding it in place, masking an unsurfaced road. At the top, the *peshmerga* said, a handful of families were still living in some very old houses behind the fort which the Iraqis had not had time to demolish. Jews had once lived there; one wall remained of a ruined synagogue.

Market stalls lined the pavements offering over-ripe tomatoes, aubergines and piles of small apricots, the skins of which were marked with brown patches. Thin young traders stood about idly, calling to each other and staring hard at Christine and me as we passed. There were no other women to be seen.

The *peshmerga* ushered us onto the pavement as an emaciated donkey ambled past, pulling a wooden cart. A boy of about ten stood on the cart, urging the donkey forward with a strange cry. In the street at the foot of the *qala'a*, piles of men's shirts were displayed on the pavement in neat rows, next to stacks of writing pads. The paper looked as thin as newsprint.

Next to the paper-seller a photographer had set up business with a camera perched on an old-fashioned tripod. On the wall behind the pavement he had pinned up a vast colour photograph showing an Alpine scene complete with azure sky, snow-capped mountains and a Swiss chalet, for his customers to pose against. Christine darted into the road and took a photo without the man noticing.

'Look,' said one of our *peshmerga*, 'a car bomb went off last year right in front of that shop.' He pointed to a tea shop opposite, in front of which several small boys sat at shoe-shiners' stools waiting for business. 'Ten people were killed in one go. They think it was government agents.' The walls were blackened as if from fire.

When we turned back towards the hotel the rays of the sun were still hitting the walls of the citadel, turning them gold, although the streets below had fallen into shadow.

I met Galawesh the following day, during an official visit to the Kurdish parliament. After the timeless poverty of the *souq* and the ancient quality of the *qala'a*, the harsh modernity of the parliament building came as a shock. It was an ugly concrete box which stood on stilts in its own compound, 15 minutes' drive from the hotel. Dara told us it had been built by the Ba'athists, to house the 'Kurdish National Assembly' set up under the Autonomy Law of 1974. The Assembly, he said, had existed as a 'face' only. 'The Iraqi government used it for propaganda, to show off to foreign visitors who were brought here by Mercedes ... it had no powers.'

The stilts were 20 feet high and on top of them the box rose another 40 feet. The front was fluted with thin concrete panels. Somewhere between the panels was glass, but from the boulevard as we walked towards the entrance the impression was of an eyeless container, rearing up like a watertower.

The new parliament was the result of the election of May 1992. It had been an election by party list, in which only parties with more than 7 per cent of the vote were allowed to put up MPs. One hundred and five MPs had gained seats, of whom 50 were PUK, 50 were KDP, four were Assyrian Democratic Movement and one was an independent Assyrian.

Once inside the building, the impression changed completely. There were polished marble floors, a graceful staircase with wooden bannisters that spiralled up through the centre of the building and smiling, gentle people who welcomed us as if we were visiting dignitaries. Our bags were given a cursory check and we were asked to sign the visitors' book, below the names of some people making a film for the BBC who had been here two days before us. Then we were ushered from one large reception room to another, where we were received in turn by the Chief of International Relations and Mass Media, the Deputy Head of the PUK, a representative of the Juridical Committee, the parliamentary head of the KDP and the Speaker of Parliament.

The Speaker was a large, handsome man dressed in a khaki-coloured *sharwal* with flowery chiffon cummerbund and a red and white turban, but most of the MPs we met that day were in Western dress.

Said Hassan, the Deputy Head of the PUK, was a small intelligent-looking man of about 50 with white hair; he wore a grey suit with trousers that were slightly too short. He came to meet us with two women MPs, greeting us with vigorous handshakes. We were taken into a large room with dark timber-panelled walls and comfortable black-cushioned chairs, where some male MPs from the Juridical Committee joined us. They too were wearing lounge suits and looked very Western.

The women, Nahla Mohammed and Galawesh Abdul Jabbar, were introduced to us as 'Mrs Nahla' and 'Mrs Galawesh'. Mrs Nahla was an engineer and head of the Committee for Reconstruction; Mrs Galawesh was a primary school teacher. Mrs Nahla smiled warmly and seemed to be used to receiving foreign visitors, but Mrs Galawesh nodded shyly, sat down at the back of the group of MPs and said not a word. She was wearing a dull brown suit and had her hair scraped back off her face. Mrs Nahla was slightly more stylish in a pale green satin blouse with a bow tied loosely round her neck. Neither of them was older than her mid-thirties, but they didn't conform at all to the glamorous image of my imaginings, and I felt vaguely disappointed.

Said Hassan sank into a large armchair and welcomed us in English. 'This is our first experience of parliament and democracy in

Kurdistan,' he told us. 'It is quite different from the experiences of Turkey or Syria, as you will see for yourselves. We are setting a precedent in the Middle East... We support human rights... You are most welcome to come and inspect democracy in Kurdistan!

'We have many problems, many many. Our economy is in grave difficulty. The UN sanctions prevent us from trading with the outside world and I am sure you have heard about the withdrawal of the 25-dinar note. Inflation is running very, very high. We lacked revenue before, and now the situation is really very serious.'

He drew breath and went on. 'The sanctions are a very great problem for us. We understand why they were imposed against Saddam, but since we are trying to create a democracy here in Kurdistan we feel it is not right that they are enforced against us too.' He sighed. 'We have many resources here in Kurdistan. We have fruit, we have grain, we have tourism ... and we have oil.' He paused and looked around at us slowly, to be sure we had taken this in. 'Yes, we have many good resources, if only we can exploit them. But we need help from the international community. We need the sanctions to be lifted from Kurdistan; and we need help to build an oil refinery...'

I had learned that morning at breakfast that there was an oilfield near Arbil, the three existing wells of which had been sealed up by the Iraqi government. Kirkuk had the biggest oil field in Kurdistan and a functional refinery, but the Iraqi government had made sure that they regained control of the city following the uprising.

'If we are helped by other countries, eventually we will be able to help them, because we are very rich!' Said Hassan added as an afterthought, and smiled a sad, rueful smile, as if he knew that there was precious little hope of getting assistance on that scale from the international community.

'Now,' he nodded, 'I know you will want to know what our government is doing. Of course, all our friends who come from abroad ask us this. Well, we have 14 committees. We have a Committee for Economic Affairs; we have a Juridical Committee' – he gestured towards the men sitting beside him – 'we have a Committee for Health and,' he fumbled for the word, '...Society. Mrs Galawesh is the Head of this Committee.' He turned and jerked his head in her direction.

'Can Mrs Galawesh tell us what her Committee does?' Jill interrupted.

'Yes, yes, of course Mrs Galawesh can tell you,' Mr Hassan replied, and addressed her in Kurdish. From where I was sitting he seemed to speak very fast and in an intimate manner, as if he were addressing his sister.

She began to reply in a soft voice, until one of the men sitting in front of her butted in in English: 'The work of this Committee is principally with the widows from the *Anfal* in 1988. Most of the members of the Committee are doctors. They are trying to do something about the health care in the villages and they are trying to help the *Anfal* Widows' Association. At the moment, the NGOs are feeding the women. The plan is for the government to provide a pension for each woman, some land and assistance with food. Many of these women have large families, five or six children are common. And they have lost all their land.'

One of the men leaned forward in his chair and added: 'You see, the problem for these women is a social one as well as an economic one.' He lowered his voice. 'These are women who lost their husbands in the *Anfal*. They are peasant women, who are not used to working outside of their home village. They would never have worked other than on the land or in the home. Many of them are young women, who might want to remarry. They are used to having a man to support them. But they can't remarry until a court declares that the husband is dead. And that's not possible, at the moment. Nobody knows for certain what happened to the men...'

There was a pause. Then Said Hassan went on, 'Now, since some of you are lawyers, perhaps you would like to hear something about the work of the Juridical Committee.' He turned to the two men seated in front of Mrs Galawesh. 'This is Mr – and this is Mr Ayad Hadinamak. They are both lawyers. Ayad is our youngest member of parliament! He is only 32.' Mr Hassan beamed.

Mr Hadinamak looked very much the lawyer, in a smart black suit and tie. It was funny how newly qualified lawyers had the same shiny, keen look in Iraq as they do in England. He had thick curly black hair and heavy-rimmed glasses, and the expression on his face was both serious and sweet. Next to the other MPs he did look very young.

'In fact, I too am a lawyer and I also sit on this Committee,' Said Hassan went on. 'We are very busy at the moment. We are perhaps the busiest of all the committees! You see, we are in the process of redrafting a great many of our laws.'

David had got out his notebook and was listening intently. 'Can I ask a question?' he ventured.

'Please.'

'Now that you are independent from Baghdad, what law do you apply? I mean, have you repealed all the old Ba'athist laws, in which case you will have to start again from scratch, or are you still applying them?'

'That is a very good question,' Said Hassan nodded at David. 'Actually, the answer is that we are doing both. You see, at the time of our election last year, no laws were being applied, because no one was really governing Kurdistan. We had had the uprising and then a year in which really no one body was in control. You see? And then we had the election and the parliament was established as the governing body for all the liberated areas. At that point we really had no choice but to go on applying the Ba'athist laws. Not in every aspect, for example the law concerning membership of the Ba'ath party, which says that if you are a member and you want to leave the party, you will be killed, this law we do not apply! But in general, the criminal law, the commercial law, we continue to apply them.

'Shortly after the election the Juridical Committee was set up, and now it is their job to propose which of the Ba'athist laws should be abolished and to redraft new laws to take their place. We use the same lower courts as before, but we have had to establish our own Appeal Court because formerly all our appeals went to Baghdad. But even in the lower courts, we are appointing new judges. You see, when the regime was driven out, in 1991, they took many of their people with them. Not just judges: they took experts in every field.'

He sighed and cleared his throat.

'For us, this has been both a good thing and a bad thing. Good, because we now run our own affairs in every respect. But bad, because we lack a lot of the expertise which these people had. And we have to learn to do so many new things at once! Not only in the field of law, but in education, engineering, medicine, in all these fields we are short of highly qualified people.'

Suddenly Mrs Nahla threw her hands in the air and said something in Kurdish.

Said Hassan laughed, 'Yes, it's true. She is saying that the Iraqi government didn't just take away people, they also removed all our equipment. When the government forces left Arbil, they ransacked this building. They took all the machines, they only left the furniture. Photocopiers, fax machines, computers ... this is a new building and it had wonderful facilities. All they left behind was one photocopier which does not work and two manual typewriters!'

Mrs Nahla spoke again, smiling, but not hiding her frustration and anger.

'She is saying that the government soldiers even damaged the microphones in the parliament chamber. You will see the chamber later on, you can come again when we are in session. And now, when we are debating for example a new law, we do not have the facilities to make enough copies of the documents for each MP to have one.'

'What about the family law?' I asked, hoping that the two women MPs would deal with this question. 'The personal status law, has that been redrafted?'

All the MPs began to talk at once, in Kurdish. Then Said Hassan said, 'The *Sharia*, the Islamic code of family law, still applies, so our personal status code is the same as in Baghdad. But it only applies to Muslims, as you know. The Assyrian Christians, for example, have their own personal status laws.'

'The Social Commission,' Mrs Nahla added, 'is trying to reform the Ba'athist interpretation of the *Sharia* law. We have a draft law signed by 30,327 women, which proposes a series of changes to the Islamic personal status code. This is going to be debated in parliament.' She addressed me directly, with a note of pride in her voice.

I had heard about this before leaving London. I watched carefully to see if I could detect the male MPs' reaction, but they seemed to be at least as interested in the subject as the women.

'For example,' Said Hassan began, 'under the *Sharia* law, as it is at present, a man is allowed to have four wives.' They all looked amused. 'We want to abolish this. We want to change the law to say that a man can have only one wife, although there will be an exception.' He consulted with Mrs Nahla, who turned to Mrs Galawesh, then he added, 'If the wife gets ill, mentally ill, that is, or if she fails to produce children, then the man can take a second wife. But the husband is obliged to support the first wife as well as the second one.'

The others nodded and I got the impression that all five thought that the proposed amendment was fair.

'Can you tell us about some of the other proposed amendments?' David had been scribbling fast in his notebook. His forehead was puckered up in a frown and it struck me that he, too, was exhibiting the keenness of a newly-qualified lawyer.

Ayad Hadinamak answered: 'Another point is the right of a man to kill his wife if she goes with another man. We want to change this.'

The other MPs laughed. I couldn't tell whether this was due to embarrassment at the mention of sex or because they found the prospect of a man killing his adulterous wife funny.

'And then,' Said Hassan went on, 'there is a proposal that if a woman sees her husband with another woman, she should be able to go to court and get compensation.'

More laughter.

'And there is a proposed change to the law of inheritance. Under *Sharia* law, the man inherits twice what the woman inherits, except in the case of land, which should be divided equally. But we are not hopeful of getting this change through. We think it is too early...'

As we were getting up to leave, Christine whispered to me, 'This is hopeless! We must try to talk to the women on their own.' Jill overheard and suggested that we invite them to come to the hotel for dinner. It would have been impossible to invite the women without the men, but fortunately David said he would like another opportunity to talk law with them.

The invitation went down very well. The men accepted instantly and said they would be in the hotel foyer at 8 o'clock; the women both said they couldn't promise due to husband- and child-care commitments, but they would do their best. When I explained to Mrs Nahla in Arabic that Christine and I particularly wanted to talk to her and Mrs Galawesh, her face lit up and she said she would do her utmost to be there. She seized my hand and asked me where I had learned Arabic. Mrs Galawesh was smiling too, looking from me to Christine to Mrs Nahla, and now that I was closer to her I could see the tiredness in her face. I caught a sudden glimpse of the burden these women carried, with their domestic responsibilities and their role as MPs, and I felt ashamed of having thought them frumpish earlier.

* * *

The Shireen Palace was comfortable and spacious, and had once been quite grand. Now the red carpet was worn down in places and the lavatories leaked, but it was the best hotel Arbil had to offer. Most foreigners who passed through the city stayed here. It had a telephone that worked, the men on reception were good at taking messages and the proprietor was said to know everything that was going on in the city.

We were 12 for dinner that night. We set up the table so that David and the lawyers sat at one end, Christine and I sat with the women MPs at the other, and Jill and Lilian, who didn't particularly want to talk to either group, sat in the middle. Their role was to be a buffer, so that Mrs Nahla and Mrs Galawesh would feel able to talk freely, out of earshot of the men. I wasn't too sure how Jill and Lilian felt about talking to each other, but I had other things to worry about. I was next to Jill and, in the rare moments when my attention wandered, I caught whiffs of their conversation, in which the inadequacies of British men seemed to be the main theme. They were both getting quietly drunk.

Nahla and Galawesh arrived together, accompanied by Nahla's eldest son, who was nine years old. She told us that she had brought him because he wasn't feeling well, but from what I had heard the real reason may have been that Kurdish women, even if they were MPs, were not expected to go out at night without a male chaperone.

Nahla spoke fairly good English, so Christine sat next to her, while I sat next to Galawesh with the idea that we would talk in Arabic. I was feeling very tired and doubted whether my Arabic was up to a detailed discussion of the position of Kurdish women, but somehow I rose to the occasion and the evening flew by.

As we sat down Christine leaned across the table and said to me in a low voice, referring to Galawesh, 'She lost her husband. He was taken away.' Christine had met the women in the lobby of the hotel and apparently this was one of the first things they had said to her. She was telling me to prevent me putting my foot in it by immediately asking Galawesh about her family, but Nahla overheard and didn't feel there was any need to be discreet.

'She is a widow and she has two children,' she confirmed loudly in a matter-of-fact tone. 'They killed her husband.' It reminded me of the way Palestinian women would often speak when informing strangers of the most painful things in each other's lives. Personal tragedy usually had a political interpretation and so became public information. Christine hadn't intended her comment to be taken up like this and she flinched, but I thought that if Galawesh had understood, it would probably be OK with her.

Galawesh had indeed understood and she nodded calmly. She had changed for the evening into a dark brown stripey suit and she was carrying a large leather handbag. Her hair was still tied back, but more loosely than before and I noticed that it was streaked with grey at the sides. Close to, her face was much softer than Nahla's and I felt drawn to her.

'How many children do you have?'

'I have two boys, the older one is ten and the little one is eight.' She smiled at me with real warmth and I was struck by the combination of strength and sadness in her face. I knew then that she had been through something really terrible and suddenly I felt tears coming to my eyes.

'I have four children and my husband teaches at the university!' Nahla piped up from across the table. 'And you, Teresa, you are a lawyer? In what field of law do you practise?'

Nahla went on like this for the first half hour, trying to engage both Christine and me, and translating for Galawesh when she couldn't follow. The waiters brought plates of salad and tangy green olives, which we ate as we talked. We spoke about the differences in social freedom between women in Kurdistan and women in Britain, and the difficulties of combining a career with bringing up a family. Nahla said that we were very lucky to be able to travel on our own and to have careers, but she wasn't sure that she would like to live 'the Western lifestyle'. I was expecting that at any minute she would ask Christine and me if we were married, but the question never came. Nahla told us that her husband was very good, he supported her being an MP and he helped her as much as he could in the home. But it wasn't like that for a lot of women, she added, often they had to give up work when they got married.

Eventually Christine raised the subject of women in the *peshmerga*. She was fascinated by the idea of Kurdish women dressed in traditional men's clothing, carrying Kalashnikovs in the mountains, and was hoping to find some to photograph.

Nahla and Galawesh seemed surprised at Christine's interest.

'Yes, there were women in the *peshmerga*, of course. Hero Talabani, the wife of Mam Jalal, was in the *peshmerga* for many years. But most of them didn't fight. They were all married women, who went to the mountains with their husbands. Single women didn't go.'

'Mam Jalal' (Uncle Jalal) was the nickname of Jalal Talabani, the leader of the PUK.

'And did they wear the traditional *sharwal*?'

'Yes, they wore *sharwal*, because it's easier to walk in trousers in the mountains.'

'Teresa and I love the trousers!' Christine exclaimed. 'We want to buy some to take home.'

Nahla was taken aback.

'You can get them in the *bazaar* if you like ... but why don't you buy the traditional woman's dress? It will look beautiful on you.'

For festive occasions Kurdish women wear colourful bloomers which peep out beneath a long, often gauzy overdress, typically with voluminous sleeves tied at the wrist and a bolero waistcoat or jacket on top. Bright colours and fabrics that glitter and shimmer in the sunlight are traditional, so that the women look like beautiful tropical birds.

Christine giggled and winked at me, 'I don't really wear dresses in London...'

We had both agonised for a long time about what sort of clothes to bring on this trip. I had brought mainly dresses, long-sleeved below-the-knee garments left over from my year in Palestine. They were cool to wear and I liked to confound people's expectations of me as a Western woman by looking 'respectable' according to the Middle Eastern dress code. Christine hated dresses and had only brought one skirt. She was wearing it this evening, in honour of our guests. I had watched her walk across the bar earlier and thought she looked decidedly awkward.

'Are there still some women *peshmerga*?' I asked.

'No, there are no women in the *peshmerga* now. Now we hope to have peace and women do not want to be involved in fighting. Our role is to help build the new society...'

'But if they did want to, are women allowed to join the new Kurdish army that is being formed?'

'Well, yes, actually there is a plan to include women in the army. It has been proposed. But it is not clear yet whether or not it will go through.'

'So which groups give the main opposition to reforms concerning women? Who, for instance will put up the most opposition to your demands for change in the personal status law?'

Nahla looked quickly at Galawesh. 'Why, the *mullahs* – the Muslim clerics!'

'There are *mullahs* in parliament?'

Nahla raised her eyebrows and opened her eyes wide, implying this was a foolish question. 'Of course! There are seven *mullahs* in parliament, that is our main obstacle.' She wrinkled up her nose. 'The PUK has five women and two *mullahs*; the KDP has five *mullahs* and two women!' She grinned as she said this, with a trace of wickedness. She and Galawesh were PUK.

After the main course arrived, of chicken tikka and chips, it became easier to hold separate conversations on each side of the table, and Galawesh and I began to talk. She asked me what I had been doing during my year in Palestine and I told her about my research with Palestinian women who had been interrogated.

'And what were your conclusions?'

'Well, it was bad, they are treated very badly by the Israelis, but I suspect there is no comparison with the way the Iraqis treat women prisoners here. There is a lot of sexual harassment, but no Palestinian woman has been raped in an Israeli prison in the five years of the *intifada*.'

Galawesh stopped with her fork in mid-air and looked me in the eye.

'I mean, I imagine it's much worse here,' I went on.

She put her fork down and nodded. 'Really, what happens to women in prison here is very terrible. I know the Palestinian women suffer, but I'm afraid here it is much worse.'

Suddenly I felt sick. I had been thinking for so many months of talking to Iraqi women about their experiences in prison, but now that I was faced with a woman who, if she hadn't been in prison herself certainly knew what it was like, I wasn't at all sure if I could handle it.

'I know, I've heard about what happens here,' I replied, meeting Galawesh's gaze. I badly wanted her to know that I had an idea of how awful it was, perhaps because I didn't want her to start telling me now, in the middle of this restaurant, but also because I wanted her to feel that my heart was with her. And it was. I had my hands over my eyes because part of me couldn't face what she might have to tell me, but my heart was with her nevertheless. Ever since the weeks after the war, when the papers were full of stories told by Iraqi men who had been liberated after years in government detention centres and about women and children being tied to the front of government tanks as they charged the rebels during the uprising, my mind had been wandering in those subterranean prisons and wondering what happened to women there. Having sat and talked to so many Palestinian women about their interrogations, it was a natural enough thing for me to think about. And it wasn't difficult to work out that a regime which would treat male prisoners so terribly and which unhesitatingly slaughtered female civilians would be horrifically cruel to women prisoners.

Just before leaving London I had read Kanan Makiya's *Cruelty and Silence*,[1] in which he spoke of finding an index card for an employee of Iraq's General Security organisation in the security building in Sulaymaniyah which gave the man's 'activity' as 'Violation of Women's Honour':

[1] *Cruelty and Silence: War, Tyranny, Uprising and the Arab World*, Penguin, 1994.

'Were you ever in prison?' I asked Galawesh.

'No, thank God I was not, but my husband was.'

Privately I felt relieved. 'In Baghdad?'

'Yes, in Abu Ghraib prison. Actually he was arrested many times, but the last time, they took him to Abu Ghraib.

'We are from Kirkuk but we were staying at a friend's house in Chemchemal at the time. It was in 1986, my children were small then. It was afternoon and my husband and I were out in the garden with the children, talking to the neighbours. First some planes flew over, very low. They circled in the air above the houses.'

'Did they shoot?'

'No, they were just trying to frighten us. When the children saw the planes coming they began to cry. We knew something was about to happen.

'The planes circled overhead, and then the *mukhaberaat* came, the secret police, in cars, and took my husband away. The planes were there to make sure nobody tried to resist. There was absolutely nothing we could do.' Her voice tailed off.

'Your husband was active politically?'

'Yes, of course.'

She smiled at me with an effort.

Galawesh never saw her husband again. She learned that he was taken to Abu Ghraib and then, some months later, that he was dead. After his arrest she was advised to leave Kirkuk for her own safety. She stayed in Chemchemal for a few years and then, after the uprising, she settled in Arbil. I asked her if she lived alone with the children.

'Oh no, I could not live alone. Usually when a woman from our society loses her husband – if he divorces her or if he dies – she goes back to live with her parents. My family wanted me to go back,' she smiled and looked up at me, 'but I felt I couldn't. I was too used to living my own life. So instead my uncle came to live with me. He is single and he loves my children a lot, and they love him. And also my little brother, who is 12, lives with us. You see, the rest of my family are in Kirkuk, which is under government control. I can't visit, they would arrest me immediately.

'It is very difficult. But I have my uncle and my brother and my children. And I have my work. Sometimes people say to me, "Look, you are young, you should remarry," but I have finished with all that. My husband and I were very happy and I wouldn't want to be with anybody else... It is enough for me to concentrate on my work and on bringing up my boys.'

'Do you like your work?'

'Oh yes, I do. Before, I was a primary school teacher, but now because I am an MP they have given me a sabbatical for as long as I remain in the parliament. And they have put me in charge of the Committee which works with the *Anfal* widows, because with my situation I am able to understand what it is like for these women. I understand their problems very well.'

I nodded slowly. Galawesh's expression was sad but warm.

'Teresa,' she went on, 'I have a question, about your research in Palestine. When they are interrogating a male prisoner, do they ever bring his wife?'

I thought for a moment. 'I think they may do. I've certainly heard of cases where they threatened to do that. Why?'

'They did that with my husband. The first time they arrested him, many years ago. They tortured him for days and he refused to speak, and then finally they threatened him that if he didn't speak they would bring me to the prison and he would have to witness what they did to me. He immediately told them what they wanted to hear. He told me afterwards, that that threat was the worst thing for him, worse than any of the physical torture they had put him through.'

Nahla interrupted now, wanting me to explain to her our domestic violence legislation in Britain. Christine had been telling her that many men in Britain beat their wives. Nahla was surprised, saying she had thought British men would be more 'advanced' than to do that.

'On the contrary,' I told her. 'When I first qualified as a barrister I spent my life going to court to get domestic violence injunctions to protect women! What about here? Is it a big problem?'

'Oh yes, there are men who beat their wives and their children. But I thought in Europe that sort of thing didn't happen...'

Nahla's son was falling asleep and she and Christine got up to carry him between them to a couch a few feet from the table. I turned back to Galawesh. Her story had really touched me and I was thinking about Ayad, and how painful it had been when we separated. I still wasn't completely over that experience, and listening to Galawesh had brought it back.

'Do you miss your husband a lot?' I found myself asking her.

'Of course.' She lowered her voice and as I leaned towards her, I saw that there were tears in her eyes. 'He was a very good man and I loved him a great deal.' She looked up at me. I wanted to put my hand on hers, but was too shy.

'Sometimes,' she went on, 'when I feel really bad, I sit down and try to write. Not exactly poems, just little pieces. And other times I paint.'

'Does it help?'

'Oh yes, it helps. Sometimes it is the only thing that can make me feel all right inside.'

chapter six

A GRANDMOTHER'S STORY AND A WOMAN PESHMERGA

One morning we visited the Kurdish Human Rights Organisation office in Arbil and I asked if they could arrange for me to interview some women who had been in prison under Saddam. 'That's easy,' said Darseen, the tall thin young lawyer with whom I spoke, 'there are many women.' We arranged that the next day they would take me to meet an old woman who had been imprisoned during the *Anfal* campaign.

At nine the next morning Darseen came to the hotel accompanied by Masoud, another lawyer who spoke excellent English and would translate for me. He was big and handsome, the sort of man who would have gone down well in Hollywood in the 1950s. His brown eyes danced under heavy black eyebrows and he seemed to be brimming with energy. He was wearing black trousers and a neatly pressed short-sleeved white shirt, and his hair was parted at the side and pressed down with bryl-cream. 'I don't like to work as a lawyer anymore,' he told me, wrinkling up his nose as if he could smell something bad. 'Being a lawyer here is not like in your country! I prefer to translate for foreigners.'

A young woman called Nermin, whom we had met the day before, had come with Masoud and Darseen. I felt uncomfortable at the idea of so many of us turning up at the old woman's home, but I didn't say anything.

Darseen advised me to bring a guard along, so I asked Mohammed, the *peshmerga* I had talked to at Saddam's palace a few days earlier. We had had several snatches of conversation since then and had taken a liking to one another.

It was a warm, sunny day. Masoud had rented a car for us, a small dented white Passat which he drove himself. Darseen sat beside him in the front and Nermin, Mohammed and I rode in the back. As we pulled out into the traffic outside the hotel I experienced a passing twinge of insecurity: this was the first time I had separated from the rest of the group. Now I was entirely in the hands of these three people from the KHRO whom I had only just met and a single guard. I was glad that I was sitting between Mohammed and Nermin, less visible than if I had been by the window, and I was glad that Mohammed had a pistol in the waistband of his jeans.

The light was bright and the streets were busy: dilapidated buses crammed with people roared along, battered white taxis with orange panels darted through the traffic, and men and boys swarmed the sidewalks. In the distance the walls of the *qala'a* were pale brown in the morning sun. While we were standing at traffic lights a child hawker came up to Masoud's open window selling bead necklaces. Masoud gave the child a coin and took one. He turned round, smiling his dazzling smile, and said, 'This is for you, Teresa, a souvenir of Kurdistan!'

Mohammed took the necklace and very carefully lifted it over my head. It was made of cloves, strung together on brown thread with tiny red beads between them. I gathered them up and held them to my nose. The smell was strong and fragrant.

'Beautiful,' Nermin grinned at me. She was 24, a student and worked in her free time at the KHRO. She was bundled up in a heavy black leather jacket despite the warmth of the day.

We drove a long way across the city to a residential district on the outskirts. Here we turned off the main road onto an unsurfaced side street, on either side of which stood low white-washed concrete houses. The car jumped and heaved over ruts in the surface until we stopped by a white metal gate.

Darseen got out and knocked, then beckoned to us. A young girl in a pale green *dishdasha*, the full-length cotton shift worn at home all over the Middle East, was holding the gate open for us. She was murmuring a string of greetings in Arabic and Kurdish and smiling shyly: '*Salaamu a leekum, chonin, chakin, bi-kher-bay, hosh bit*' – 'Greetings, how are you, welcome, you are welcome.' I didn't know if Darseen had informed the family in advance that we'd be coming or whether, as in Palestine, people who had been through traumatic experiences were simply accustomed to foreigners turning up on their doorsteps wanting to interview them.

We took off our shoes in the doorway and followed Darseen into a small room where a fine-looking old woman was seated cross-legged on a rug on the concrete floor. She welcomed us warmly and we all bent down and shook hands with her, one by one. She had long white hair, a thin, wrinkled, rather lovely face and large green eyes. She was small and delicate, in long black robes with a cardigan on top and a black band tied around her forehead.

'She is apologising for not standing up,' Masoud explained in a soft voice. 'She cannot walk.'

The young girl brought a mat and Nermin, Darseen, Masoud and I sat down cross-legged with our backs to the wall, facing the old woman. Another girl came in with cushions for us to lean against. The room was bare except for the mats and it was pleasantly cool. Mohammed squatted on his haunches near the door.

Masoud faced the old woman and explained in Kurdish who I was. She responded by nodding at me and touching her hand to her forehead several times, repeating, '*Bi-kher-bay, spass, bi-kher-bay.*'

'She says you are welcome and thanks you for coming to see her.'

I nodded back at the old woman and smiled, wishing I knew enough Kurdish at least to greet her and thank her for talking to me.

'Can you say I'd like to make some notes while she is telling her story and does she mind if I write about her when I get back to England?'

'Yes, you may write about her and it's OK to take notes,' Masoud confirmed after another exchange in Kurdish with the old woman. He spoke to her in a very relaxed, direct way and she replied in a similar manner, looking him straight in the eye. It was as if they knew each other, but he had told me in the car that he had not met her before.

Masoud addressed the old woman again and she began to speak.

'My name is Roopak Murad Khan. My family is from Jalamord, a village two to three hours' drive from Chemchemal. We were captured in the *Anfal* in the spring of 1988. One day when we woke up,

47

the village was surrounded by army and *jash*. We tried to escape, but we couldn't go very far, because we were surrounded. The *jash* were people from our village. All the families of the *jash* had their own vehicles and when they were rounding us up the army allowed these families to escape.

'I was with my husband, one of my two daughters and her husband, his mother, my son and his wife, and two grandchildren, both still babies.

'The army put us in trucks and drove us away. We stopped at a military fort at Tahla, where soldiers wrote down our names and we were put into new vehicles. By the evening we reached the military camp at Topzawa. At sunset they divided us into three groups: young women and children; young men; elderly men and women.

'My daughter and daughter-in-law were put into the first group, with their babies, as was my son-in-law's mother. My son and my son-in-law were in the second group.

'My husband and I were locked up in a hall in the camp with the other old people. There was no food and no water, and we hadn't eaten or drunk anything all day. They wrote down our names, but they wouldn't tell us what was going to happen to us. We thought, "This is Saddam, he will throw us into the river or shoot us!" '

Roopak fell silent for a moment and stared blankly at Masoud. Her eyes were huge. Then she continued, 'The next day at 6 a.m. they put us old people into a big bus without windows. I saw five buses altogether but I don't know who was in the other ones. We still weren't given any food or water.

'At sunset we arrived at Nugra Salman prison, in the south near the Saudi border. It's four hours from the nearest town, Samawa, and is like a military camp. There was a big courtyard surrounded by long two-storey buildings with windows very high up. There was a gate at either side of the courtyard, used by the police.

'They took us to the first floor of one of the buildings. They wrote down our names again and herded us in and locked the doors. We could sit on the floor, but there wasn't enough space to lie down. We slept leaning against each other. And we were still not given any food. By now we had gone two days and nights without food or water. We were tired of being alive!

'The next morning they wrote down our names yet again. They gave us one piece of bread each, three times that day, and warm water to drink. It was unspeakably hot inside the building. The one window was very small and it was closed. After two more days, people started to fall sick.

'We stayed at Nugra Salman for quite a few months, living on three pieces of bread a day and warm water. There were no sanitary facilities... It was a kind of torture. They told us we had come here to die and would not be going back home.

'The guards were police and security men, and all of them treated us badly. The worst one was a man called Captain Farouk. He wore green fatigues and had three stars on his shoulder.

'At noon they used to bring us down to the courtyard and make us stand in the sun for two hours. It was terribly hot. First they would make us sit facing the sun and not allow us to move. Then they would beat us. They beat the men first, but they also beat women. One old woman was flogged to death with a cable, for nothing.

'Then they would bring a tank of water into the courtyard. We were given buckets and told to queue up to collect water. And as we queued, they beat us, both men and women, with sticks and rubber cable.'

As I struggled to write fast enough to keep up with Roopak, I was feeling increasingly shocked. This was much worse than I had expected: it sounded like Auschwitz.

'Many people died at Nugra Salman: I think about 1,500. I don't know how many people were there altogether, but there were a lot of two-storey buildings like the one my husband and I were in. I think there were several thousand of us there altogether.

'At first we were all old people, but later they brought in people who had left Halabja after the chemical attack in the flight to Iran and had come back to Iraq when an amnesty was announced. They were arrested at the border. They were people of different ages, men, women and children.

'The guards told us that we had been arrested because we were *peshmerga* supporters and deserved to be tortured. They referred to the *peshmerga* as "the saboteurs".

'They tormented all of us in different ways. Sometimes they took the men away to be interrogated. When they returned they didn't tell us what had happened, but we saw that they had been tortured.'

Masoud glanced at me and said in a low voice, 'She was badly beaten herself. Let's see if she will tell you about it.' He said something to Roopak.

'Yes. One day when I went to fetch water, they beat me with a stick and injured my right arm. And because I had to sleep on the concrete floor without covers and didn't eat properly for all that time, I lost the use of both my legs. I don't know if it's a kind of rheumatism ... I've been to see several doctors in the last five years, but they've not been able to help me. Before all this happened, I could walk well. I used to walk down to the river in my village when I was taking care of the cows.

'One thing I remember: when people died, the body was left for 24 hours, then we would tell the police, who allowed our menfolk to take the body out of the building and bury it in a shallow pit and cover it with sand. Dogs used to come and dig up the bodies and eat them.

'Another thing I forgot to tell you: the main gate of Nugra Salman had written on it "This place is hell" in Arabic. It was written up there so that people saw it when they arrived.'

Masoud and I exchanged looks. 'I think it's true,' he murmured. 'I have heard this from many people.'

Several small children had crept into the room while we were talking and were sitting close to Roopak on the rug. One, a little boy, was leaning against her with his head at the level of her waist. His eyes were fixed on me. I asked how Roopak came to leave Nugra Salman.

'After we had been there for several months, there was an amnesty for *Anfal* prisoners. The police who guarded us heard the government announce it on the radio. They told us that because of the amnesty, they were going to release us. We were happy to hear that we were going to go home and from that point on they stopped beating us. The next day they began bringing vehicles and taking prisoners out in groups, in big buses with windows and seats. My husband and I were taken out in the last group, 40 days later.

'It was raining at the time we were released. It was autumn. I don't know exactly how long we'd been in Nugra Salman, but it must have been about six months.

'They took us to the town of Samawa, where we stayed for five days in a special centre which had been prepared for us, like a hospital. We were able to wash and the men shaved and they gave us good food to eat. The idea of this was so that it wouldn't be obvious from our appearance what had happened to us. They didn't want our families to find out and they told us that anyone who told what had happened would be executed.

'From Samawa they took us back to Topzawa for one night, in a big convoy of buses, to the same military camp where we were separated from our children. The next day we were driven to Chemchemal, where they took us to the courtyard of a government building and wrote down our names again. Then they told us we were free to go. Free, that is, to go anywhere other than to our own villages, which they said were now in a "prohibited area".

'We had no money. We sat in the courtyard until a relative came with a car and picked us up. He knew we were there because word had got out about the amnesty and everyone had seen the convoy.

'The relative took us to a town called Teynal, near Chemchemal, where my husband's brother lived. We stayed there for one month, then we came to live in this house in Arbil, with my husband's nephew and his family. We did try to go to our village at one point, but we were turned back by the army. Now, since the uprising, people are going back to the village. My husband went once, he found the whole place had been bulldozed into the ground. He couldn't even recognise the site of our house!

'When I got out I wasn't ill, just weak from the lack of food. I had a gash in the skin of my arm, where they had beaten me... I still have stiffness in my fingers from that beating, to this day.' She lifted her left arm and slowly moved her wrinkled brown fingers.

'I haven't seen my daughter since the day we were separated in Topzawa, after we were captured in the village; nor my son, nor my son-in-law. I haven't seen any of them, not his mother, nor my daughter-in-law, nor the children.'

Roopak's tone was matter-of-fact, but her eyes were glazed and it wasn't difficult to guess at the pain beneath the surface. Tears were welling up in my eyes.

At this moment the door opened and a very old man hobbled into the room. He was bent forwards from the waist, dressed in baggy trousers with a red and white keffiyah tied round his head in a turban. He murmured a greeting, nodding at us all, and sat down a couple of feet from Roopak and the little boy.

'This is the husband,' Masoud whispered.

After a few seconds Roopak began to speak again, in a different tone of voice, looking from me to Masoud and back at me.

'Please, can you make some enquiries about what has happened to my children? Can you try to find out where they are?'

I had been half expecting this. I asked Masoud to tell Roopak that I could write about what had happened to her and publicise it, but I wasn't part of any organisation and I didn't think I could help her find out where her children were. I thought it was very unlikely she would find out what had happened to them before Saddam was ousted, particularly if they had been taken to the south and killed there, like so many of the other 'disappeared people' of the *Anfal*. Masoud translated what I had said and Roopak nodded in resignation. Her eyes were huge.

I asked if she wanted me to use her real name when I wrote about her.

'What has happened to the Kurds is unique,' she replied. 'It's all right to use my name. Nothing worse can happen to us than what has already happened...'

I was struck by how quiet the children were, grouped around Roopak and her husband on the rug. Although these must be the children of the nephew, it felt as if Roopak's tragedy had affected them deeply too, casting a shadow over the entire extended family. I asked if I could take a photo and they agreed. The two girls reappeared, wanting to be included, and posed behind the old people sitting on the ground with the children. Everyone froze while I fiddled with my camera. I would have preferred something more natural, but when I got the film developed a couple of weeks later, I saw that the picture really captured the pathos of their predicament.

It was time to leave. I knelt down to shake hands with Roopak and she seized my hand and kissed it. I was very touched, wishing that I could express to her in Kurdish how shocked I was by what she had told me. I asked Masoud to tell her for me.

* * *

As I was leaving the hotel the next day I was given a message from Shireen, who was visiting relatives in Arbil. When I called her she told me that her old friend Bachshan Zinganeh was in town, and that I might like to talk to her about the Iraqi Communist Party, of which she was a long-standing member, and about her experiences in the *peshmerga*. She had spent 12 years up in the mountains.

Bachshan and Shireen met me at the hotel the following afternoon. Bachshan was small and attractive with bobbed blond hair. She was wearing a knee-length dress and I was struck by how Western she looked compared to most of the Kurdish women I had met. We shook hands, I kissed Shireen on both cheeks and we went upstairs to the restaurant, where we ordered tea and sat down at an empty table in the window. My fellow Brits had gone out to explore the *qala'a*, leaving me with just one silent guard who sat smoking at a table by the door.

I told Bachshan that I was interested in hearing about her life as a woman in the Iraqi Communist Party. She nodded, smiled shyly and began to talk.

'At the time of the 1958 Revolution, the CP was very strong in Iraq. I joined in 1963 at the age of 16 or 17. My family, though not Communist, had politics not so far from those of the CP. My great grandfather was from the tribe of the Zinganeh in Germiyan. My grandfather was a Kurdish nationalist; my father was a liberal and a democrat. My father worked in an office, he was middle class and I didn't suffer economically as a child. But I felt uncomfortable about class divisions. We had servants, as did most middle-class families at the time.'

The British mandate over Iraq ended formally in 1932, but Britain dominated the country indirectly through the maintenance of military bases and vast economic interests until the revolution of 1958. In July of that year, the Free Officers' Coup led by Qasim ousted the pro-British government and put an end to the British-installed monarchy. In the next five years Qasim made the British evacuate their military bases, withdrew Iraq from the Baghdad Pact and negotiated a greater share of oil royalties with the foreign-dominated Iraq Petroleum Company. In 1963 Qasim was overthrown by a short-lived alliance of the Ba'athists and Nationalists, who sought to suppress the CP.

'After Qasim was killed, thousands of Communists were executed in Baghdad. There were a lot of women in the CP then; we worked in our own separate section. We were in groups of six, and when security was very difficult, groups of three. During the repression in 1963 our role was to help to hide the men, to prepare safe houses, carry messages, organise demonstrations and so on.

'Later in the 1960s my role was to write, to organise and to encourage people. I tried to educate myself about Marxist ideas and the social sciences. I was studying physics at the College of Education and my political work had to be done in secret. My family had an idea that I was doing something and when I became very involved they tried to pull me back. I spent six years in dormitories in Baghdad studying at the university. I was always afraid, but I was never captured! There were lots of women students in the CP. There were many great women.

'Of course the role of women within the party was influenced by the social attitudes pertaining then in Iraqi society. Officially there was no discrimination between men and women in the party, but in practice women's roles were restricted. For example, women were not sent to work among the farmers in rural areas, because it would not have been acceptable to the farmers.

'The League of Iraqi Women had been founded in 1952 with branches throughout the country. It was not part of the CP, but most of the active women in it were CP members.

'In July 1968 the current Ba'athist regime came to power in another coup. From 1973 to 1978 the CP and the Ba'ath party were in coalition, and so we were able to do our political work openly. But by 1978 the Ba'ath party had become very strong in the whole country and they proceeded to crush the CP. I was married by then and had a daughter, who was born in 1977. She is my only child; by the time I finished being in the *peshmerga* it was too late to have more children. In 1978 I had to leave my daughter with my mother because I knew that there was going to be a purge of the CP and that if I stayed in Sulaymaniyah, I would be killed.

'I travelled to Baghdad, Mosul, Arbil and other places in disguise, sometimes with my husband, sometimes alone. Sometimes I disguised myself as a villager, other times I wore heavy make-up. People helped me a lot. Then, at the end of 1978 I joined the CP *peshmerga* in the mountains.

'Leaving my daughter to move around was very difficult. Sometimes in the evenings in the mountains the women sat around talking and we used to say to each other that our children will never believe that we lived like this.

'Women *peshmerga* suffered a lot. There were no baths, no special rooms for us. We lived sometimes in tents, sometimes we built rooms. We wore *sharwal*, like the men. There was no sanitation. Sometimes we had to walk for half an hour to find a place to pee!

'Most of the women were with their husbands, but some were single. Many of the single women later married men they met while in the mountains.'

I could see it was a painful subject for Bachshan, but I was curious to see if there had been any option other than leaving her child behind, so I asked if any of the other women had had their children with them.

'Yes, a few of the women had their children with them…But they suffered a lot. The winters were very cold and the only source of heat was wood fires. In the summer there were snakes. It was hard being separated from my daughter. Sometimes I looked at a chicken with her chicks and envied her. She had her babies with her, but I did not!

'I didn't see my daughter at all in those years. Once I came to Sulaymaniyah in secret and telephoned my father's house. My daughter picked up the phone and said, "'Allo, 'allo." I put the phone down. When I dialled again, she cursed me – this stranger who had called twice without speaking. I put the phone down again, but I was very happy because I had heard her voice.

'My family used to get lots of visits from the security people because of my activities, although I was long married and away from home. They even went to my sister's. But, thankfully, no one was arrested on my account. My mother avoided any close contact with my friends because the security people were always watching her.

'Once when I was in Syria I stopped outside a shop and looked at a little girl's dress and asked the friend who I was with if it would fit my daughter. She said, "No, Bachshan, your daughter is bigger than that now! She will be at school by now."'

'How did your mother feel about you leaving your daughter with her?'

'My mother was happy that my daughter was safe, but sad that I wasn't with her. I have three sisters. One is 22 and the other two are married. Yet even now my mother is asking me to have another child! Like all mothers, of course she would have preferred me to be around.'

'What about the women who had their children with them in the mountains?'

'Oh, it was very hard. Some even gave birth in the mountains. One friend of mine gave birth in a cave, with only her husband to help her. It was pitch dark, so they couldn't see the colour of the baby's eyes! And they were afraid it would die of cold.

'It was a terrible life for the children,' Bachshan went on. 'War was going on around us constantly, people were being wounded and fear was always with us. It was no real childhood. We tried to teach the children ourselves, as there was no school; but we were constantly moving on from one place to another.'

'Were you all together, or were there several camps?'

'There was one main base for the leadership and then there were many separate fighting groups.

'We were fighting, on and off, most of the time. We were subjected to almost constant shelling and bombardment by the Iraqi army. It was very hard when people were killed. When the men came back to the camp from a battle we would see them coming from far away. We would see what state they were in and we could tell from the expressions on their faces if someone had been killed.

'There was a huge range of people in the CP *peshmerga*: lawyers, doctors, university teachers, farmers, workers, but most of all it was peasants. And we were both Kurds and Arabs.'

'Did women fight?'

'I didn't fight very often. I used my gun a few times, one time I helped a man to fire an anti-aircraft weapon, but mostly women did the servicing – carrying messages, carrying weapons, propaganda, nursing. You see, in our society it is difficult for women to carry out certain tasks. I'll give you an example. In D'hok in the north, which as you know is a conservative area, a group of *peshmerga* went to arrest a man who was in the *jash*. A woman *peshmerga* went into the man's home first. His wife jeered at him because he was being arrested by a woman.

'A few of the women fought, but not many. There was an Arab woman who was with us in the mountains, a woman from Nasiriyah in the south, who used to fight. She was martyred in '86, in the Badinan.

'I was in the mountains until 1990, when I came back and worked in secret in Sulaymaniyah during the build-up to the Gulf War. I didn't come to my family then because it would have been too dangerous. I was moving around between the big cities – Arbil, Sulaymaniyah, Baghdad. I was constantly moving, concealing my identity, and I couldn't feel normal.

'After the war started in January 1991 I felt much freer. Just before the ceasefire on 28 February we began to move through the centre and south of Iraq, distributing leaflets remarkably freely. We started to make plans and to destroy portraits of Saddam Hussein. I came to Sulaymaniyah to prepare for the *rapparin*, the uprising. I still feel a thrill when I think about it!

'On 6 March there were Iraqi army weapons on all the high buildings in Sulaymaniyah. It was obvious that something was about to happen; the smell of blood was in the air.

'That day, I visited my family for the first time in many years; the next day the *rapparin* began.

'On 8 March we celebrated International Women's Day. On the ninth there were still some military in the area near our house. But on the tenth I went out of my door feeling free – it was wonderful!'

'Come and see me when you visit Sulaymaniyah,' Bachshan suggested as we said goodbye. 'I am less busy when I am there and I will be happy to talk with you again.'

* * *

We set off for Sulaymaniyah the following morning. We spent our last four days meeting women activists and making trips to Halabja, the border town of Penjwin and the collective town of Shorsh, which was home to a large number of *Anfal* widows. Then, before we knew it, we were heading back towards the Turkish border on the first leg of our journey home. We were all exhausted, but it felt much too soon to be leaving. I had not begun to digest half of the stories I had heard or the encounters I had had. The only way I could console myself for having to leave Kurdistan so abruptly was by deciding that I would return in the autumn for a much longer visit. I had discussed this with Masoud and several of the women activists I had met, and they had made it clear that I would be very welcome to return for as long as I wanted.

PART TWO

chapter seven

ZAKHO, SEPTEMBER 1993

Dawn was breaking as Sarah and I boarded the 7 o'clock flight to Dyarbakir from Istanbul's domestic airport. We had flown in from London the previous evening and sat up all night in the airport lounge. A soft red band ran along the flat horizon of the airfield, its colour bleeding gently into the pale blue sky above, promising a warm day and clear, pure light. It was just like the dawns I used to love in Palestine and Cyprus, and as I stood in the queue, swaying from lack of sleep, I whispered to myself, 'I am back in the world of beauty at last.'

The flight was only half full, but there was a group of Iraqi Kurds who would be travelling to the border on the same road as us. We were sitting some way away from them, but when I walked down the gangway to the toilet they looked up at me and smiled, and I felt reassured that we were not alone.

We were nervous about the road journey from Dyarbakir, because during the previous month the PKK had been kidnapping Western tourists in southeastern Turkey at the rate of several a week. The PKK launched their war of liberation against the Turkish state in 1984, calling for the creation of an independent state of 'Greater Kurdistan' which would unite Kurds from the five countries. I didn't know a great deal about the PKK, but I didn't like what I had read and heard. While it was clear that the Turkish state operated very brutal policies of repression against their Kurdish population, including the destruction of villages, torture and extra-judicial executions, the PKK were also known for brutality. In particular they had a reputation for killing Kurds who refused to support them, including women and children. Kurdish villagers were caught between, on the one hand, being terrorised by the Turkish army if they so much as expressed Kurdish nationalist views and, on the other, being terrorised by the PKK if they failed actively to assist them.

I thought that if the PKK stopped me, I could probably persuade them that I wasn't a tourist, but I didn't relish the thought of being in their hands. Relations between the PKK and the Iraqi Kurds were not always easy, and I wasn't sure how impressed the PKK would be if I told them I was a British lawyer writing about Iraqi Kurdish women.

I was also anxious about returning to Iraq; I was going for a longer period this time, seven or eight weeks in all, and I was going to be alone. I was travelling as far as Arbil with Sarah, who was an aid worker, but once there we would part company.

Because of our worries about the PKK, Sarah and I had tried to find some Kurds to travel with. A Kurdish organisation in London had asked us to escort a Kurdish boy who had been in England for medical treatment and was going home. We thought that being with a Kurd, even a child, might make us safer, so we agreed to take him.

It turned out that Burhaan, who was ten, had been run over by a military vehicle during the uprising in Zakho in 1991 and had suffered abdominal injuries leaving him with no bladder and no bowel and he was dependent on colostomies. The poor boy, although feisty and strong in spirit, was physically frail, and the journey had been an ordeal for him.

During the flight one of the Kurds came over and chatted with us. His name was Sami Jabbar, from Halabja, and he had been in the UK for eight years. He had been a *peshmerga* in Kurdistan and was now working as a computer programmer for a big firm in North London. He was on his way to Kurdistan for his first-ever visit home, impelled by the fear that if he didn't go soon his ageing mother might die without seeing him. Sami cracked jokes at first, but in the course of the next few hours began to admit to deep ambivalence about going home. He and his wife had left Iraq secretly in 1985, via Iran, and he was uncertain about how safe he would be in Kurdistan.

When we landed in Dyarbakir it was hot. Dazzling light and a wall of hot air hit us as we came down the steps of the plane. Sarah had arranged for a taxi to meet us and we persuaded Sami Jabbar to travel with us. I had the feeling he would have preferred to go with the other Kurds in their hired minibus, but perhaps his sense of duty to two unaccompanied women and a sick child constrained him to accept our invitation.

Sami sat in the front with the driver, and Burhaan, Sarah and I shared the back. Burhaan was exhausted, bad-tempered and smelly by now, refusing everything we offered him, whether it was water, a sleep on Sarah's shoulder or a bar of chocolate, sucking his teeth disgustedly in the idiosyncratic Kurdish gesture that means 'no'. The drive to Khabur was long, hot and uneventful. We saw small tanks by the side of the road and many more army checkpoints than when we had come this way in May, but to our relief there was absolutely no sign of the PKK.

Although it was 4 September, it was still high summer here in the east; by mid-morning the sun was bleaching the colours out of the arid landscape and I was less captivated by its beauty than I had been in May. All conversation between us had fizzled out by now, and Sarah and I were drifting in and out of sleep. At one point I opened my eyes and saw that it was 90°F on the temperature gauge on the dashboard of the car; all the windows were shut except the driver's, because none of us could bear the hot wind blowing on our faces. We had come through the hilly country and were spinning along on the long, straight stretch of road beside the Syrian border at 75 miles an hour. Shimmering flashes of silver lay on the road ahead like pools of water.

I had sent faxes from England trying to arrange for a couple of the *peshmerga* who were with us in May to travel with me as guards on this trip and was hoping they would be at the border to meet us. Having guards I knew and trusted would make the trip so much easier.

We reached Khabur in the blazing midday heat. A gaggle of young men were crowding round the Turkish immigration post and child hawkers were strutting around in the road with their beat-up polystyrene ice boxes trying to sell Pepsi-cola and Fanta. Few places are quite as male as a Middle Eastern border, and Sarah and I got our fair share of stares, but the formalities went smoothly and we changed cars into a local taxi for the quarter mile ride across the bridge.

By now my stomach was churning; I so much wanted to see a familiar face waiting for me on the far side. For the last hour in the car I had had a clear picture in my mind's eye of the wiry figure of Mohammed standing waiting on the bridge in his turquoise T-shirt and jeans.

But it was not to be. We stepped out of the car on the far side of the bridge into another crowd of men, all of whom were unfamiliar. Before I had time to think, a tall thin man in a khaki *sharwal* stepped forward and, holding out his hand, said, 'Teresa? Sarah? I am from the PUK Foreign Relations office in Zakho. You are most welcome in Kurdistan! My name is Nabaz Hussein.'

He was in his late twenties and was unusually tall and lanky for a Kurd. He had small, melancholy brown eyes and looked hurt when I said we had been expecting somebody different to meet us. He explained in good English that he had been sent by the PUK and had been waiting on the bridge since 8 o'clock that morning. One of my faxes must have got through, although there was no explanation of why it was he who had come and not the people I had asked for. Nabaz was accompanied by a small, flirtatious-eyed driver, who shook our hands excitedly and opened the back doors of their ex-Iraqi *mukhaberaat* Landcruiser.

It was 1.30 in the afternoon and the sun was beating down mercilessly. I was anxious about getting into a car with complete strangers, but there didn't seem to be much option. Sarah couldn't see what I was worried about and thought my hesitancy rude. Nabaz and the driver were piling our bags into the vehicle as if we were newly arrived relatives while we stood in the road, arguing in low voices, bidding farewell to Sami Jabbar and trying to take in the fact that we were once again standing on Iraqi Kurdish soil.

Nabaz, we found out later, worked for the PUK Foreign Relations Department as a translator. He stood very straight and tall, and in his khaki-coloured *sharwal* gave the impression of a military man, but he told us he had never been a fighter. He had studied English at Mosul university and now spent his life meeting foreigners at the border and escorting them on the first leg of their journey into Kurdistan. We asked to be driven straight to the Qandil clinic in Zakho, to which we were to deliver Burhaan, who had hardly spoken since we had left Dyarbakir. In the bright sunlight his skin was yellow, and he seemed terribly tired and listless.

The Qandil clinic was a grey concrete building in a residential area of Zakho, not far from the headquarters of the Military Command Council where we had met Bill Bennett in May. A fleet of new-looking Landrover-ambulances stood idle in the yard.

The clinic gate was opened by a Liverpudlian in shorts, who seemed surprised to see us but greeted Burhaan warmly. He invited us into a large dirty reception room where he and an Indian doctor were sheltering from the oppressive afternoon heat. I sat on a sofa beside the doctor and Burhaan collapsed on an armchair. The Liverpudlian tried to chat with him but Burhaan had clearly had enough and wasn't going to make conversation with anyone. His trousers looked damp and he was clutching at his crotch as if worried his colostomy was about to overflow. I wished they would drive him home to his village without further ado, but instead they offered us tea and asked if we had had any problems on the road from Dyarbakir to the border.

The Liverpudlian was a paramedic and spoke as if he had been in Kurdistan for years. He was about 40 and balding, and reminded me of hardened ex-pat aid workers I had met in Palestine and South America, people who had lived abroad for so long that it was hard to imagine them ever being able to settle again in the UK. He spoke of the hardships of daily life in Kurdistan with a hint of pride in his voice, and said 'we' when referring to the Kurds. I sensed a certain disdain for fellow Brits like me who were, in his eyes, 'just passing through'. Doctor Pali was a very different character. He didn't speak until the Liverpudlian had left the room to make the tea. He was a small, plump man of about 28, with an anxious look in his eyes.

'I am Indian but I studied in Britain,' he smiled shyly as he replied to my question. 'I am the only qualified doctor working for the Qandil project here in Zakho.'

I got the feeling he was quite pleased to have some contact with the outside world.

'Have you been here long?'

He sighed. 'Nearly a year now. Really it is very difficult. Are you familiar with the situation here?'

'Broadly speaking. I was here earlier this year, in May.'

'Yes, well, I don't think you will see any improvement since that time. The electricity has been off in Zakho and D'hok since August – it's all right for us, we have a generator here in the clinic. But most people do not, of course, and without electricity there are no pumps to pump water to the houses – so you can imagine the difficulties with hygiene, from a medical point of view. You see, the electricity supply for Zakho and D'hok comes from inside the government-controlled area. Saddam cut it off in August, just to make life difficult, and there's no knowing when it will come back on.

'You can imagine the difficulties having no electricity creates. Water is our biggest problem. The water supply was never clean, but now people fetch their drinking water from the river…'

'Is there cholera?' I asked. I had read about a new and particularly virulent strain of cholera which had started in the Indian sub-continent and was expected to spread to the Middle East within months.

'No actual cases yet, no. It is a worry, of course, because it is carried in the water supply; but I have not heard of any cases yet. You must be very careful, though, about what you eat and drink while you are here. On no account drink the water! You absolutely must stick to bottled water. And I wouldn't eat in restaurants. Where are you staying? If you want, while you are in Zakho, you can eat with us here. You see, it is all a question of hygiene, and if you eat in hotels and restaurants you don't know what you're getting. Much better to stay somewhere you can cook for yourself, or better still eat in the houses of people you know.'

This was alarming. I hadn't anticipated having to be that careful and it would be impossible never to eat in a restaurant. I wondered if Dr Pali was a bit of a worrier.

'What about the security situation? Has that improved?'

'Well no, really, I would say the security situation is very serious. They are still making attempts against foreigners; and there are car bombings and shootings.' He looked uneasy and shook his head. I felt sorry for him and wondered what inspired him to stay on, if he felt the situation was so fraught with difficulties.

The Liverpudlian came back in with a tray of glasses of fizzy lemonade.

'Sorry, ladies, this is all we could manage. Our gas cylinder has run out.'

His legs beneath the shorts were skinny and white. I wondered if he wore shorts in public, and, if so, what the locals thought.

'Have any more foreigners been killed?' I was pretty sure I would have heard if they had been, but felt I had better double check.

'Not since Vincent was killed. You know about him, I take it?'

I nodded. Vincent Tollet was the young Belgian aid worker who had been killed in March near Sulaymaniyah.

'But there have been attempts. There is an American doctor who has been here for about two years. They have tried to kill him twice. The last time was only 10 days ago. It has been disastrous, he has had to send his team home, all of them. Only he remains now, with his family.'

'Is he in Zakho?'

'Well, he works in the Badinan, which is this part of Kurdistan, yes.'

'So how are you enjoying being here?' I smiled at Doctor Pali, hoping to lighten the tone of the conversation. What he had just said was frightening, but I was feeling a bit dazed, a bit numb, and I saw my own situation as very different from that of aid workers who had committed themselves to remaining in Kurdistan for long periods of time. Right now the thing that bothered me most was not being given a cup of tea.

The doctor raised his eyebrows and shook his head. 'Really it is very stressful working here, very stressful. It is not easy...'

Shortly after this the tall languid form of Nabaz Hussein reappeared in the doorway. We got up to leave and bade goodbye to Burhaan, who was to be driven home by the Liverpudlian. He staggered out into the yard, bending forward from the waist in discomfort, but he grinned his wicked grin at me as I said goodbye.

Out in the street, Nabaz suggested that Sarah and I spend our first night at the PUK guesthouse in Zakho. We had planned to go on to D'hok, to the hotel I had stayed in before, but we were both exhausted and we accepted gratefully.

chapter eight

GUESTS OF THE PUK

The PUK guesthouse was only one street away, a white-washed villa set in a tiny garden with a pomegranate tree. There was a swing-seat with a canopy under the tree and a rickety table at which a group of PUK officers were sitting smoking. A path of baked earth had been trodden across the lawn to the door.

We were the only women at the guesthouse and the only real guests, although six or eight men from the PUK Foreign Relations seemed to eat and sleep there regularly. An old man who was referred to by everybody as *al doctor* – the doctor – showed us to a room with two beds; when we said we'd prefer separate rooms if possible, they turned a sleeping guard out of the room next door. I felt embarrassed, but the young man got up off the bed without a murmur of complaint.

The rooms were large, bare and dirty. Mine had two single beds and a mattress on the floor. A single, sweat-stained sheet covered each bed. I had forgotten to bring my sheet sleeping bag, but I sensed it would be pointless to ask for a clean sheet in this all-male environment where water had to be fetched from the river. Rolls of fluff lay in the corners of the room and the air was hot and stale. Torn mosquito mesh curled back from the curtainless window, which looked out over a low wall onto a strip of sandy wasteland. Rather exposed, I thought, and imagined diving to the floor if some-body fired a shot through the window.

A metal fan with three blades was fixed to the centre of the ceiling. I tried the switch on the wall, just in case, but nothing happened: the fan hadn't moved for a month. I looked at the huge metal blades hanging impotently from the ceiling and felt uneasy: their immobility brought home to me Saddam's massive power and the Kurds' extreme vulnerability.

I am not good in excessive heat and I wondered vaguely how long I would be able to cope without fans and with only very limited supplies of water. I took off my shoes and jeans and lay down on the bed under the window. My head was hurting from the long, sleepless journey and from standing out in the sun at the border.

A mosquito whined above my head. 'Why have I come here again and how on earth am I going to survive for eight weeks?' I wondered. 'What if I'm not strong enough?' I had been feeling very tired even before leaving England. 'One swig of dirty water now,' I thought, 'will lay me out completely.'

At around 6 p.m. Nabaz and the driver came to collect us to go out in search of bottled water. We climbed into the Landcruiser and drove for five minutes across the centre of Zakho. Dusk is a busy time in Kurdish cities and the streets were crowded with people: dozens of young men walking arm in arm, talking and calling out to each other, and the black triangular figures of women covered from head to foot in *abayas*, the long cloaks traditionally worn in public. They walked in twos and threes, carrying wicker baskets and dragging small children by the hand.

The sun was sinking and the light glowed orange on people's faces. There weren't many cars, but we had to drive slowly because of the men thronging the road, and I longed to get out and walk. It felt very remote to be sitting on the back seat of the Landcruiser, a newly-arrived foreigner being driven by a chauffeur. My eyes were glued to the windows and when I stared too long people looked up and caught my eye. I could tell that they saw, instantly, that I was foreign. Several people smiled, and I smiled back, quickly, shyly, still unsure whether it was a good thing to be noticed.

Nabaz directed the driver to a street lined with stalls displaying tall pyramids of Pepsi-cola cans. We crawled along, searching for a stack of the blue plastic bottles of mineral water I had drunk last time, but there were none to be seen. Finally I decided that Pepsi would be better than nothing, so we drew up at a stall and I leaped out of the car before Nabaz could tell me not to. He followed me, looking surprised at my waywardness but saying nothing. I asked the stall keeper in Arabic for six cans of Pepsi. It was exhilarating to be out in the street and I felt irritated when Nabaz insisted on repeating what I had said in Kurdish. But the cans were ice cold and it was a relief at last to have a supply of something safe to drink.

Back in the car we left the market area behind, turned a corner and drove alongside the river for a few hundred yards. It meandered through a canyon in the whitish golden rock the town was built upon. There were palm trees growing near the water, their foliage a deep green in the dusky light. The water too was a strong, bright green. For a moment I was delighted by the beauty of the fast flowing water, the glowing rock and the seemingly ancient palm leaves which hung so utterly still in the warm air; then I took in that the mud at the water's edge was crowded with barefooted women and children, filling old tin cans with water and carrying them away on their heads.

We spent the evening sitting in the garden of the guesthouse, talking to the local PUK leadership while 'the doctor' cooked dinner by a paraffin lantern in the kitchen. He was small and fat and he cursed as he worked. He wore a very old, very dirty *sharwal* tied at his waist with string and a stained white shirt with the sleeves rolled up. His job was to cook single-handed for all the guests and to make tea whenever people wanted it. Meanwhile the leaders in their pristine outfits sat out under the stars in the jasmine-scented garden, smoking and talking politics. There was almost complete darkness around us, apart from a building across the street which had lights in its downstairs windows. The intermittent roar of a generator drifted into the garden.

Sarah and I had an insatiable thirst for tea that evening, and we kept creeping into the kitchen during gaps in the conversation to persuade the doctor to put the kettle on again. He was puffing around the kitchen between the gas fire, his chopping board and a polystyrene box on the floor which contained a huge block of ice. He would get down on his knees, lift up the block – which was obviously heavy – and pull out from underneath a bloody piece of raw meat or some chicken legs. He would ignore us while he finished what he was doing and then he would look up, with beads of sweat on his forehead and a look of one who was anxious to please but exhausted, and say, '*Tchai?*'

We offered to make it ourselves, but he wouldn't have that. We were guests and foreigners, and it was his duty to run round after us, however much he resented it.

Out in the garden, the politicians were keen to talk to us. It must have been a novelty for them to have foreign women as guests and they rose to the occasion by treating us like honorary men. We were offered cigarettes and beer, and asked about the work we were planning to do in Kurdistan. When I said that, among other things, I was hoping to interview some Kurdish women, the response was enthusiastic.

'It is very good that you are interested in our women,' one man said. He was large and fat and had been introduced as the head of security for Zakho. His round face was boyish and I decided he could not be more than 30, some six years younger than me.

'Their lives are very hard. You will see, they work much harder than we do!'

In the back of my mind I thought of *al doctor* slaving away in the kitchen – presumably in the role of an honorary woman.

'Dilshad!' the security man called out. 'Bring us some water, will you?' He half turned round in his seat as the doctor appeared in the doorway, in a patch of lamplight. 'Water, please.' The doctor grunted noisily and disappeared inside the kitchen.

'His name is Dilshad, but we call him the doctor because he has a PhD in cooking! He is an excellent cook. You will see, shortly.'

The security man had a kind, open face and I warmed to him in spite of his job title. When the subject of torture came up later on in the evening, curious to see what he would say, I asked naïvely, 'Is torture ever used nowadays?'

The security man's shirt was double-breasted and stretched tightly across his large tummy. He chuckled and his black eyes glanced at me warmly as he replied, 'Why, no. I was imprisoned and tortured for four years myself, how could I wish torture on other people?'

'Of course not,' I replied. I was feeling sharp enough to see that there was no logic in his comment, but my inclination was nevertheless to believe him. He was warm and round and young and he didn't look like the sort of person who would order people to be tortured. (I know now that my inclination was wrong. Research done by Amnesty International and published in 1995 established that torture and ill-treatment were indeed practised by the Kurdish security services during this period.)

The man sitting on my left had been introduced as Rebwar Farraj, the deputy head of the PUK in Zakho. He was well-built and beautifully turned out in an olive green military-style *sharwal*, which he wore with ease and grace. He was very good looking, with large almond-shaped eyes, a long nose and perfect skin. There was something soft in his face, and thoughtful.

We began talking in Arabic and I found I could understand his accent quite easily.

'Can I ask you a question?' I ventured.

'*Ittfaddali*,' he replied. 'Please do.'

'What do you think's going to happen, with Saddam? Do you think he's going to try to come back into Kurdistan?' It felt cruel in a way to bring up the subject, but Rebwar Farraj looked intelligent and I really wanted to know what he had to say.

'Well,' he began, 'this is of course the question which we keep asking ourselves.' A shadow had fallen across his face. 'I think you know what the situation is. To be frank with you, I am very worried. It is now more than two years that we have been in this state of semi-independence. My personal view is that very soon we will see some movement from Saddam.'

'You mean he is going to try to retake Kurdistan?'

'I think he is going to start to try things. Now, in these next two months, I think we will see some action by him. There may be raids into the Kurdish-controlled areas, yes. No one can predict exactly what he will try to do, but I think something is going to happen.'

Rebwar Farraj's face had a look of tragedy as he spoke and I felt I had pulled back a curtain covering an abyss.

'Do you think the Allies would do anything if he tried to come back in?' I went on.

'Well, that perhaps is something you can answer better than I!' He smiled sadly. 'What is your view?'

I raised my eyebrows. 'I have big doubts, I'm afraid. Look at what has happened in Bosnia. Bosnia is in Europe, but still the Western powers have talked a lot and done virtually nothing. I am very worried that they would not do much to protect the Kurds, if Saddam tried to return.'

'Yes, we too are very worried.'

Despite the security man's predictions that dinner would arrive shortly, it was after 10 o'clock by the time it was served. I was so tired by then that I could hardly stay upright on my chair, but our hosts clearly expected us to eat with them and seemed to have forgotten that we were at the tail end of a 36-hour journey.

Dishes of rice and salad and a kind of soup with meat in it were carried through the darkness to the wobbly table by the doctor and one of the youngest-looking PUK men. We were eight by the time everyone took their places. The food wasn't delicious, as promised, and we couldn't see what we were eating, but it was hot and I knew that I had to appear to eat in order to be allowed to go to bed.

Within minutes of swallowing my last mouthful I pushed my chair back from the table and mumbled that I was very tired and I hoped they would excuse me.

'Of course, of course!' cried the security man. 'Go to sleep now. Of course you are tired from your journey. We will see you tomorrow!'

I borrowed a box of matches from the doctor, who was still grumbling away to himself in the kitchen, and stumbled through the empty house to my room. I wanted to sleep for 24 hours at least, although I had a feeling that sleep might be slow in coming. My head was turning with a million thoughts and I had been awake for so long that perhaps my body would not remember how to fall asleep.

It was stiflingly hot in the room. I undressed, took a grimy sheet off the spare bed and carefully laid my money belt under my pillow. I had just pulled the sheet over my naked body when the door, which had no lock, burst open and in trooped the youngest PUK man carrying a paraffin lantern, followed by the doctor. Instinctively I called out, half in Arabic, half in English, 'I'm asleep!' but they took no notice and advanced towards me like a couple of night watchmen.

'I don't want anything!' I yelled, but decorum seemed to require that they ignore me. The PUK man stopped by my bed and bent down with the lantern, while the doctor laid something on the floor with a clanking sound.

I was astonished. Never, in all my travels in the Middle East, had one man, let alone two, marched into my bedroom uninvited, without even knocking. It was against the most basic code of proper behaviour between the sexes. I was so surprised that I pulled the sheet over my head and pretended to be asleep, although I had called out to them and obviously wasn't. When I heard their footsteps recede and the door shut, I threw back the sheet and struck a match. On the floor by the bed was a plate of deep red chunks of watermelon and a glass of tea in a tiny saucer.

chapter nine

A NIGHT ON THE ROOF

We decided to spend another day in Zakho to rest up before making the six-hour road trip to Arbil. We pottered around at the guest house in the morning, drinking tea and chatting with the doctor, and in the afternoon Nabaz Hussein suggested a trip to the waterfall at Sharanish. It was only half an hour's drive from Zakho, a little way into the hills, and the one place, he said, where it was possible to get away from the heat. The idea of being near water, even if we couldn't swim in it, was powerfully appealing and we accepted.

I put my swimming costume into my bag, although I knew women didn't swim in Kurdistan and my reputation would probably be ruined if I were to appear in it. But I was feeling disgustingly sticky and desperate for a shower, and even to pretend to myself that I was going swimming made me feel slightly better.

Leaving the town behind we drove for 20 minutes along a straight road through a flat sandy landscape. The light was intense and there was little to see. Then we turned off onto a smaller road and began to climb into much a greener, hillier country. There were cypresses and fruit trees, and in the valley below the road I saw water sparkling. After about 15 minutes the road petered out and the driver pulled over and parked. Nabaz told us we would have to walk the last quarter mile to the waterfall, but mercifully the air up here was a few degrees cooler than in Zakho. Sarah and I climbed out of the Landcruiser and followed the two men down the rough red track to a little brook which flowed across it.

We were in a wide, shallow valley, the bottom of which was thick with trees, bushes and a tangle of growing things in many different shades of green. It was more lush and fertile than any other place I had seen so far in Kurdistan and because it was enclosed by hills it felt like a secret place. Behind us the red surface of the road snaked along the hillside before zig-zagging across the valley to the place where we had parked and the waterfall was hidden in the folds of the steep hill in front. We jumped across the little brook and followed Nabaz and the driver along a path and up some steps cut into the rock, and suddenly we could hear the sound of a colossal volume of water crashing down. After a few more steps we saw it: a great cascade of white spray, like the train of a giant wedding dress, falling from near the top of a 100-foot cliff into a deep pool at its foot. The water rushed out of the pool in a wide flashing stream, carving a bed for itself in the rock and running down towards the valley. Now, from 20 yards away, we could feel moisture in the air and the spray was almost touching us. We spread out and advanced towards the pool in awestruck silence.

The air was chilly at the foot of the cliff, stirred by a damp-smelling breeze created by the force with which the water fell. The four of us stood gazing up at the frothing white torrent, the glistening black rock face and the green ferns that clung in its crevices, catching the cooling spray on our faces and bodies.

The light was beginning to slant and bathe everything around us in orange as we drove back towards Zakho and the inferno of the plain. The waterfall had had a calming effect and nobody spoke in the car. We had filled some old Pepsi cans with water from the rushing stream, and I sat in the back pouring little drops down my chest and holding the can against the back of my neck. The ice-cold water on my hot skin felt delicious.

Ten minutes outside Zakho we passed through a village of low sun-baked mud houses by the side of the road. A herd of goats was being driven along the road in front of us and we were forced to slow to a walking pace.

Women and girls dressed in *dishdashas* in blue, yellow and cerise were collecting water from a sluggish stream, their garments luminous in the evening light. They were filling bright yellow cooking oil cans and carrying them away on their heads. Their strong, shapely necks were darkly tanned by the sun.

*   *   *

We reached Zakho about seven and I went out into the garden and sat on the swing chair while the doctor made us tea. There was no one around and I put my feet up on the seat and swung gently to and fro on the rusty metal frame, savouring the rare moment of solitude.

When the doctor brought the tea Sarah and I persuaded him to sit down and tell us about his family. He had six daughters, who lived with his wife in a town some hours east of Zakho. Times were hard, and it was very difficult to feed and clothe a family adequately, on top of which he rarely got to see them. He complained bitterly about how hard he had to work in the guesthouse, shopping and cooking for all the guests and no one ever helping him.

Nabaz had already told me that the doctor 'admired' me, so I knew he wasn't complaining about us personally. (Later that evening, when he gave me my last glass of tea of the day, the basis of his admiration became clear. He had asked me several times during the day if I had any *jurab* with me, and when I finally told him I didn't know what the word meant he had pointed energetically to his stockinged feet. 'Socks!' I had exclaimed. I did have a few pairs of socks. In the evening, as I thanked the doctor for my glass of tea, he said, 'The tea is for you, but tomorrow you can give me a present of some socks for my daughters, okay?')

There was something very likable about the doctor. I enjoyed the way he wore his filthy brown *sharwal* tied round his waist with string, as if to emphasise to his smartly clad superiors that he didn't have the time to wind a cummerbund round his waist, if indeed his wages permitted him to buy one. And I liked the way he grumbled, usually with a flicker of mirth in his eye, as he was talking to me. It made me feel he was treating me less like an important foreigner and more like a fellow human being.

As we talked in the garden, the subject of mosquitoes came up and the doctor told us we should try sleeping on the roof. He said the mosquitoes would bother us less on the roof than indoors, because it was cooler up there. I was enjoying the stillness of the garden, but he immediately heaved himself to his feet and lead us into the house and up a flight of stairs onto a large balcony, then up a second flight of external stairs to the very top part of the roof. There was a water tank in one corner and a washing line, and a 3-foot high concrete parapet ran round the circumference.

'Look, I will make you beds up here and you will sleep very, very well. It is just for you, this roof. The men all sleep on the balcony below. They can't even see you up here. Come, look.'

He led us to the parapet and pointed to a collection of bedsteads and rolled-up mattresses on the balcony below us. It was true that if we bent double when we were close to the parapet, nobody would be able to see us.

Sarah was in two minds about de-camping from the relative familiarity of her room downstairs, but I was keen to sleep under the stars and the doctor was already halfway down the stairs, searching for blankets and mattresses to bring for us. Within 10 minutes he had built us a cosy little 'bedroom' in an alcove of the roof, walled in by the parapet on three sides. He laid blankets on the concrete floor and thin foam mattresses on top, and then he brought up our sheets from downstairs, and several blankets apiece which he said we would need in the early hours of the morning. At the foot of the beds he rigged up a blanket over the washing line, so that we had virtual privacy.

The doctor puffed and wheezed as he worked, but would not allow us to help. I felt bad because he was so much older than us and obviously found the stairs a strain; but what could we do in the face of his determined mixture of fatherliness and gallantry?

When the work was done he disappeared downstairs and I wandered over to the parapet and leaned out. It was getting to be dusk and the view was extraordinary. The sandy plain spread out around Zakho and the deep green river wound through the town, and about 3 miles away in all directions a ring of low rocky hills surrounded the town, gleaming orangey-yellow in the fading light. The trees by the river – figs, cypresses and pomegranates – had turned a deep, blackish green, without the interference of electric lighting to distort their colour. To my eye it was extremely beautiful, and I longed to stay here and paint. For a long moment I regretted having come to Kurdistan in the guise of a researcher with a million questions to ask, and wished that instead I had set things up so that I could just *be* here. I would have loved to have spent a month of evenings standing up on this roof watching the changing light.

After a while I tore my eyes from the greens and oranges, turned and walked to the far side of the roof. Stars were beginning to twinkle now in the soft inky-blue sky and on the horizon, perhaps 10 miles away, a line of bright electric lights sparkled white. They were enormously bright, like searchlights. Suddenly I remembered that the Iraqi army line was about 10 miles from Zakho, and to the west, the direction in which I was looking.

We had told Nabaz that we wanted to go on to Arbil the next day, and he dropped in before supper to tell us that Rebwar Farraj was going too, and that we could travel with him if we liked.

'He is a *peshmerga*, so if you travel with him I do not have to send guards with you. Otherwise I have to find guards to send specially.' Nabaz regarded us in his languid, melancholy way, his eyes pleading with us not to make his life difficult, and we readily accepted to go with Rebwar Farraj.

After Nabaz had gone I wandered back out into the now dark garden and headed for the swing chair, which was my favourite place apart from the roof. As I sat down I realised that someone else was already sitting at the far end of the seat. I nodded and murmured, '*Salaamu a leekum*, peace to you.'

Through the dusky light I made out the man's moustache and realised he had been present at supper the night before, although he had not spoken.

'Good evening,' the man replied with the trace of a cool, very Western smile. 'Did you have a good day?'

His accent and the clipped way in which he spoke told me immediately that he was either German or Dutch. I told him that I had had a very good day and asked where he was from.

'I am from Holland. I am a freelance journalist. My name is Jan, how do you do?' He reached out a hand with a shy grin and as I shook it we both giggled. There was something absurd about shaking hands in the dark on a swing bench in the PUK guesthouse garden.

Jan told me that he had spent the previous four months – through the heat of the summer – travelling slowly through Iraqi Kurdistan, conducting many interviews and writing copious notes. Until recently he had worked as a residential social worker in

Utrecht and this trip was his bid to get out of the rat race. When he got home he was planning to write up his material, publish as much of it as possible and then set off for somewhere else.

'Have you had a good time?' I asked curiously.

'Oh yeah, oh yeah, very good. They are wonderful people, the Kurds! They are very good to foreigners. I never felt so welcome in my life!'

Jan had spent more than two months in Sulaymaniyah, and offered to give me names and addresses of people to look up there. He could even recommend a couple of women interpreters, who were a rarity in Kurdistan. I was planning to spend my first two or three weeks in Sulaymaniyah, as I had met some women on the previous trip who were very active in a women's organisation there.

'When you are in Sulaymaniyah, one of the things you should investigate is the problem of the refugees from Kirkuk,' Jan remarked thoughtfully. 'The ones who are living in the Red Security Building.'

I was swinging the seat gently to and fro, pushing with my bare feet on the baked earth beneath it.

Jan looked at me steadily and spoke in a low voice. 'It is really a scandal what is happening to those people,' he said. 'I spent a lot of time talking with them. I think you know their problem: they cannot go back to Kirkuk because the Iraqi government is there and anyway most of their homes have been destroyed in the crushing of the uprising. So they are stuck in Sulaymaniyah and nobody wants to know.'

'Doesn't the Kurdish government help them?'

He shook his head. 'No. The local people don't want them there at all and the Kurdish government, as you know, has no money – that is what everybody will tell you, anyway – and doesn't want to make itself unpopular by helping the Kirkukis when it doesn't help the people of Sulaymaniyah, and so they stay there, in terrible conditions, and nothing is done. It seems there is a kind of prejudice against the Kirkukis, born probably out of desperation. There is a feeling that there are not enough resources to go round, not enough food, not enough housing or petrol or electricity, and that these people who are from Kirkuk should "go back where they came from" – which of course they cannot do without risking their lives.'

After another late supper in the garden with the PUK officers, I carried my little 'notebook' computer upstairs to the roof, tucked it into the foot of my bed, undressed and lay looking at the stars. It was much cooler up here than in the house, cool enough to cover myself with one of the heavy, coarse grey blankets Dilshad had provided. There were still some mosquitoes and I got bitten, but certainly no more than I had the night before, and I slept deeply and well. I felt more secure up here than downstairs, knowing there was a ring of men sleeping on the balcony below, between me and the level of the street. And despite the fact that our 'bedroom' was under the stars, there was more of a feeling of privacy than there had been in the house. I woke at 4 a.m. to a bright moon shining on my bed and tiptoed downstairs to the loo, past the sleeping bodies of the men, curled childlike under blankets with their Kalashnikovs on the floor beside them. The doctor was stretched out on his back on a bare bedstead, fully clothed.

When I came back up to the roof I stood at the parapet and looked down at the moonlit streets. It seemed strange that such a vulnerable city could afford to go to sleep.

A cock was beginning to crow and I wondered if I should stay awake. But the next time I opened my eyes it was 8 o'clock and the sun was warm on my face. We were leaving for Arbil at 9 with Rebwar Farraj.

chapter ten

'MY HEART IS NOT ALLOWING ME TO MARRY'

We reached Arbil on Monday night and I said goodbye to Sarah and booked into the Shereen Palace hotel. Rebwar Farraj was staying in the city for a couple of days and told me I should call him if he could assist me with anything. My plan was to stay in Arbil just long enough to renew some contacts from my previous trip, arrange guards and spend a day visiting the Barzani widows in Qushtapa. By Friday at the latest I would set off for Sulaymaniyah.

I called Masoud, the lawyer I had met on my previous journey to Arbil, and he came to the hotel. We had dinner and talked for a long time. I asked him about going to Qushtapa and he said he was free to come with me on Thursday. He would hire a car and pick me up at the hotel at 9.30.

On Tuesday and Wednesday I met two more of the women MPs: Kafia Sulayman, who was Minister of Tourism and Municipalities, and Hero Talabani, who was an ex-*peshmerga*, very active in the Kurdish Save the Children organisation, and married to Jalal Talabani, leader of the PUK. Both women were welcoming and offered to help in any way they could. When I told Kafia Sulayman that I was planning to go to Qushtapa, she introduced me to her secretary, Leyla, and to a friend of hers, Saajda, saying that they would be happy to accompany me. Saajda was co-ordinator of the Arbil branch of Zhinan, the Union of Kurdish Women.

In 1983 a large proportion of the Barzani clan, of which KDP leader Masoud Barzani is now the head, were living in two *mujama'aat* outside Qushtapa, about half an hour's drive south of Arbil, to which they had been transferred from their home town of Barzan by the Iraqi government in 1980. *Mujama'aat* – 'collective towns' – are the soul-less housing estates to which the Iraqi government transferred the Kurds whose rural communities it destroyed in the scorched-earth policies of the 1970s and 1980s. They were generally built close to main roads, for ease of surveillance by the army.

In July 1983, at the height of the Iraq–Iran war, KDP units helped the Iranians to capture the border town of Haj Omran in Iraqi Kurdistan. In retaliation, the Iraqi government sent troops to Qushtapa, with orders to round up all the Barzani men and boys they could find. The men were taken away in trucks at gunpoint, leaving the collective towns of Qushtapa inhabited almost exclusively by widows and their children.

It was a very hot day on the Thursday. After collecting Leyla and Saajda we left Arbil at about 11.30 and took the straight road south across the plain which leads to Qushtapa. On either side of the road, flat scrubby fields stretched to the horizon and the light was bright and harsh.

The two collective towns attached to Qushtapa had been named by the Iraqis as 'al Qadissiya', after the historic battle in which the Arabs defeated the Persians and converted them to Islam, and 'al Quds', the Arabic name for Jerusalem, which means 'the Holy'.

As Masoud turned off the main road down the dirt track which led to al Qadissiya, a thick cloud of dust billowed around the car. Peering through the window I could just make out the sprawling shape of a mud brick and concrete block shanty town built on barren sand. It was desolate.

'You see,' said Saajda, 'there is nothing for the people here: very few clinics and schools, water and electricity only some of the time, and no work whatsoever.'

Heat hit us as we climbed out of the car; heat and the smell of rotting garbage. We followed Masoud to the end of the street, pursued by a big crowd of children, to a plot of land surrounded by a mud brick wall. Masoud shooed the children away and we stepped through a door in the wall into an impressively neat courtyard-garden.

The house consisted of a series of mud brick rooms built around the courtyard. I was struck by the contrast between the lush green of the few plants growing in the dry flowerbeds, the deeper green leaves of a fig tree and the pinky-brown of the mud walls, which were the same colour as the earth from which they had been dug. A neat ridge had been sculpted in the soil around the perimeter of the garden, like a kerb, and a raised path crossed it from one side to the other. There was a sense of order, of things being well cared for.

The family were eating in a long, narrow room which opened onto the courtyard. Ten lean, beautiful women dressed from head to foot in black, their hair hanging in braids which came to below the waist, sat cross-legged on the floor around a long narrow mat on which their food was spread. To my hungry eyes it looked like a banquet. There were huge round metal platters laden with *dolma*, the traditional dish of aubergine, onions and tomatoes stuffed with spiced rice; little dishes of diced tomato and cucumber salad and piles of wafer-thin Kurdish bread.

Initially we politely refused the women's invitation to join them and went to wait in an empty room on the other side of the courtyard. But, after they had finished, three of the women brought us a platter laden with *dolma* and bread, and we caved in gladly.

When we had finished the women served us tea in *piyalas*. By now a crowd of little boys had dribbled into the room and it was so crowded that I felt awkward about asking questions. I suggested that we might go somewhere else to talk and the women took us to the room next door, which was empty and pleasantly cool.

Masoud, Leyla, Saajda and I sat on mats on the earth floor with our backs to one wall, and the three women sat facing us leaning against the other wall. The two younger-looking women leaned against each other, their arms touching, while their older relative hovered by the door. They had indicated that they were willing to answer my questions, but I sensed that they had a highly developed, almost aristocratic sense of dignity and preferred to remain at some physical distance.

The younger two, Raz and Awaz, were sisters-in-law; both were about 27. The older woman, their aunt, was 50. Raz was single and Awaz's husband had been taken by the government in 1983, leaving her with three small children.

I asked Awaz to tell me about what had happened in 1983. She started to talk, but her manner was aloof, as if she suspected my motives.

'It was night and we were asleep. In the morning we found the whole area had been sealed off. Special Forces soldiers woke us and told the men to gather in Qushtapa for a meeting; they said they would start shooting if they didn't come. There were Popular Army people there as well and two helicopters hovering in the sky.'

The Popular Army was a people's militia under Saddam's regime in which all Iraqis were obliged to serve for a period of time.

'We women followed the men. The helicopters fired at us and four or five women were injured. One lost her foot.

'When we got to Qushtapa the men were loaded into civilian buses with the windows curtained over ... and ... we haven't seen them since.'

She stopped speaking and a heavy, angry silence filled the room.

'Two months later,' Awaz began again, 'the Popular Army came back and this time they took the sick and the disabled men, and even men who were blind or mentally ill. They went from house to house, searching the beds to see if the people sleeping in them were men or women.

'For the next two years we had no water or electricity: the supply was cut off by the government. They surrounded us with military posts, and there were tanks and armoured personnel carriers in Qushtapa, and foot soldiers patrolling al Qadissiya and al Quds. The troops stayed until the uprising in 1991.'

'Were any women sexually harassed by the soldiers?'

'No, not as far as we know.'

Something in Awaz's face shut down as she said this, making it impossible for me to pursue the subject.

'So how did you cope after your husband was taken?'

She fixed her gaze on the wall behind me, and said, 'I was only 17 when my husband was taken. After they took him, I went out to work in the fields, on the tomatoes and cucumbers. The older women cared for the children and the younger ones went out to work. To begin with I found it very hard to have to work and I was always crying for my husband. When he was alive, you see, I never went out. I stayed at home with the children and did the housework and the baking, that sort of thing. I was very happy in those days!

'But the field owners were good to us. They weren't Barzanis, but they were Kurds and they treated us well. My friends still work in those fields. I have asthma, so I stopped working three years ago and now I stay at home. In those days the pay was enough to feed the children, but now it isn't – prices are so much higher. We have had to sell furniture to buy food. Some of our women are even working in factories in Arbil…'

'Once you got used to it, did you enjoy going out to work?'

Awaz looked surprised. 'No, we don't like working in the fields, but we have no choice! It's very difficult to do men's work, very hard!'

'And Raz? Do you work in the fields?'

Raz was friendlier than Awaz; she was shy, but was making eye contact with me and seemed more willing to talk. She was very fair-skinned and her pink cheeks gave her a young, soft look. 'I don't work in the fields because I do housework.'

'Are you going to get married?'

I thought this was an acceptable question because Kurds were forever asking me if I was married; but as soon as I had asked it, I regretted doing so. Raz blushed slightly and shook her head, so that her long braids swished against her dress.

'No, my heart is not allowing me to marry, because I lost my father and two brothers in 1983. And my mother died two years ago.'

Silence filled the room again. I racked my brains for what to say next.

'Is there anything you'd like to ask *me*?'

Awaz and Raz both looked at me as Masoud translated the question. After a pause, Awaz said forcefully, 'Yes, why is it that nothing has been done to discover the fate of our men? We have spoken so many times to journalists, and foreigners have come and taken our photo, yet still we have no news of our men! Why?'

*   *   *

I had heard a lot of stories about the repercussions that rape and harassment by Iraqi soldiers had had in the community of Barzani women. I had also heard that some of the women had taken to working as prostitutes in Arbil, out of economic necessity. The idea of the 'untouched woman' is very strong in Kurdish society, according to which a woman must have no sexual contact outside of marriage. If she does, the honour of her entire family, particularly its male members, is called into question. Traditionally the only way to 'wash away' the shame is for the male relatives to kill the woman.

A journalist who had visited Qushtapa had told me of cases among the Barzanis where unmarried women had become pregnant and had been killed by their own mothers, who, in the absence of husbands or fathers, were obliged to assume the role of head of the family.

The twin concepts of 'honour' and 'shame' permeate women's lives all over the Middle East in varying degrees. In some cultures the ideology is stronger than in others, and it varies between different religious groups, between rural and urban communities and between the uneducated and the highly educated, being strongest among the least educated rural communities. Contrary to popular belief, it is not unique to Islam.

Kurdish women have a reputation for going unveiled and for being permitted more freedom than their Arab or Persian counterparts. Some say that this is a myth; others that it contains a grain of truth, citing in particular the respect which Kurdish men show to their wives compared to the attitudes of, for example, Arab men. Whatever the true picture, the paramount importance of preserving family 'honour' and avoiding 'shame' is a constant issue in Kurdish women's lives.

There is a saying in Kurdish which translates as 'Everything a woman does is shameful.' According to Shanaz Baban, a Kurdish woman academic whom I met later on, the behaviour of Kurdish female children is monitored from early childhood and they are assiduously taught to avoid behaviour which could bring shame upon their families. It is not only overt sexual behaviour which is disapproved of. To speak loudly, to laugh a lot, to dress immodestly, to look a man who is not a relative in the eye, all of these are shameful acts for girls and women in traditional Kurdish society.

Virginity at marriage is seen as absolutely essential, but public *suspicion* about a woman's behaviour and morals is almost as bad as actual 'misbehaviour'. Thus a woman can lose her good reputation merely by being seen alone in the company of a man to whom she is not related.

A woman's reputation for sexual purity can be destroyed both by conduct in which she is a consenting party and by conduct in which, in the West, we would say that she is not, such as rape or sexual assault. Masoud explained the reasoning behind this as the belief that there is no such thing as illicit sexual activity to which the female partner has not consented. 'Is rape possible if the woman does not consent?' he asked me. 'We believe it is not possible. If there is rape, the woman has consented.'

In the most traditional circles, the ultimate penalty for a woman whose conduct has damaged her family's honour is death. 'Honour killing', as it is called, still happens in traditional, mainly rural, communities in Kurdistan. At the other end of the social spectrum, in urban communities and among the educated, attitudes are more relaxed and punishment for conduct which brings shame on the family is more likely to be restriction of the woman's freedom of movement.

The Iraqi Ba'ath party was very clever at exploiting the ideology of honour and shame to the full as a means of humiliating its political enemies. The stationing of large numbers of Iraqi troops and security men in the collective towns of Qushtapa after the Barzani men had 'disappeared' was probably aimed, at least in part, at damaging the honour of the remaining men of the Barzani clan and thereby deeply demoralising them.

It wasn't until my second visit to Qushtapa, in mid-October, that I found a woman who was willing to talk to me about the problem of sexual harassment and the terrible consequences it had had for her family. Her daughter had been raped while working in the fields and the woman had killed her to defend the family's honour.

Masoud went into several different houses before being directed to the one where he found this woman. She was a thin, wiry, middle-aged widow and once Masoud had explained what I wanted she agreed to talk to me, on the strict condition that I did not ask her name.

The woman invited us into a small dark storeroom, where we sat among sacks of straw on the earth floor, with the door ajar while children played in the yard outside. Another woman of about the same age sat on the floor by the door; both were dressed from head to foot in black. I was wearing a dress which came to below the knee when I was standing, but when I sat down on the floor my knees showed. I felt the first woman's eyes alight disapprovingly on my bare flesh and I tugged at the hem, wishing it was longer. She had a hard, unsmiling face and although she was courteous I didn't warm to her. We got down to the business of the interview swiftly, without formalities, and the woman talked virtually without prompting.

'I lost 14 husbands in 1983, when the government took away our men. My daughter was very beautiful. She used to work in the fields.'

'She means 14 men from her family,' Masoud explained. 'This is a form of expression they use here, it's a sign of the pride they take in their male relatives. She means 14 men, one of whom one would have been her husband.'

'As I said, I lost 14 husbands. I had two very young sons, who were not taken; and six daughters.

'I was afraid of my god,' she added, looking fiercely at Masoud, by way of explanation of what she had later done to her daughter. 'This is my religion.' She glanced at me and back to Masoud, perhaps hoping he would explain to me how as a Moslem she had felt obliged to do this. 'We did it for the honour of the 14 men.'

I felt uncomfortable in the presence of this woman in a way that I had not during any of my other encounters with Kurdish women. Whereas usually I had a good idea of what the person I was talking to felt about what had happened to them, it was unclear to me what this woman's feelings were about the death of her daughter.

'We killed her six years ago, maybe more. She was 23 then, the eldest of my children. She was working in the fields at the time to earn money. She married in 1979, at the age of 15. In 1983 her husband disappeared, when the government took all the men. It was four years after that that I killed her. She had two children. The daughter is 10 now and the son is 12.'

As she spoke a little girl wandered in through the open door and hid behind the woman.

'She was working in the fields and the man she was working for raped her. We didn't know him. Like I said, she was very beautiful.'

This last thing seemed to be said by way of explanation.

'I couldn't accept it,' the woman went on, 'because of my god and my religion.'

I searched her smooth, tanned face for evidence of some emotion, but could detect none. To look at her, you would think she was talking about some routine event that had happened to somebody else.

'Since we are the nation of Mohammed, we should protect the honour of our religion. And the honour of the 14 men.'

At the time, I accepted the woman's attempt to explain what she had done in terms of Islam. When I thought about it afterwards, however, it struck me as strange. The ideology of 'honour' and 'shame' did not originate in Islam but rather is a feature of Middle Eastern society which cuts across religious differences. I wondered then if the woman had referred to Islam because she thought a foreigner might accept it as an explanation.

My eyes had been wandering uneasily from the face of the grandmother to that of the granddaughter, who was clearly listening to what was being said. When I could stand it no longer, I asked Masoud to ask the woman to send her outside. The woman clearly thought it an odd request, but she complied.

After the child had gone I asked, 'Does she know?'

The woman shook her head. 'She doesn't know. She calls me "mother", she thinks I am her mother.' She smiled faintly, unperturbed. 'Sometimes children in the street tell her that I am not her real mother. But she doesn't know any better. She doesn't remember her real mother.'

I found that very hard to believe, but said nothing.

'How did you find out that your daughter had been raped?'

'My daughter told me about it.'

'It's the man who should have been killed!' Masoud suggested.

'May God kill the man!' the woman agreed. 'My daughter was crying and upset and angry. She told me the same day that it happened, but I could not accept it. She said, "Mother, don't kill me, for the sake of the children!"'

The woman shook her head.

'When my daughter told me about the rape, she knew that I would kill her. She told me because she was afraid that if she didn't tell me, someone else would.'

'Did you think she had somehow wanted the man to rape her?' I asked, trying to fathom out the thinking behind what she had done.

'Look, we are Barzanis and we respect our honour,' the woman replied through tight lips. 'Of course my daughter did not want this man to rape her!'

There was a pause.

'So how did you kill her?'

The woman looked at me and said with a very faint smile, 'She was asleep and I killed her with electricity. But I can't talk about it.'

I wasn't going to ask any more, but the other woman, who had not spoken till now, lifted her black-veiled head, pointed to the front of her neck and said, 'She applied the electricity here: a lot.'

The first woman went on, 'It was seven days after she told me about the rape. I killed her here, in my house. Her younger sisters were very upset and they cried. But I had to make the decision about what to do. I did it because of my religion. We are all going to die eventually ... and I am the head of the family now.' Her tone was philosophical.

'How do you and your family live?' Masoud asked after a pause.

'We are living on charity. Masoud Barzani doesn't help us. My daughters try to work in the fields, but there's no work. Foreigners came and took our photograph, but nothing happened. Institutional aid doesn't reach us. We make bread by burning straw: we don't have any paraffin. We are waiting now for it to be distributed.' She sighed and then, with an air of pride, she went on, 'The government were very pleased that I killed my daughter. And the police, too, said that I did the right thing; so did the people. Honour is a great thing! Kurds, government, everybody was pleased with what I did.'

Masoud turned to me and muttered, 'Now she is talking rubbish, I don't believe she told the government or the police about what she did. She is trying to make it seem better.'

'Do your other daughters still work in the fields?' I asked, trying to change the subject.

'Yes, and we worry about them every day until they come home. The strain of it has made us weak and old!'

The woman looked frighteningly strong to me, but I nodded and shook my head, trying to appear sympathetic. Silence filled the dark room, in stark contrast to the cries of the children playing in the sun-filled yard. As I put my notebook away and zipped up my bag, the woman seemed suddenly embarrassed.

'We are very poor and when visitors come we can't offer them anything, because we don't have much.'

'It's OK, it's OK!' I replied, trying to smile at her.

'It's the same in Arbil,' Masoud added. 'No one can offer anything to their visitors. Don't be worried, please.'

chapter eleven

THE ROAD TO SULAYMANIYAH

On the Friday morning I packed my bags and sat waiting with Masoud and his neighbour Fareed in the restaurant of the Shereen Palace. Masoud had arranged for Fareed to drive me to Sulaymaniyah and remain there with me for two weeks as my driver. He was a small ageless man in a neatly pressed white shirt with the sleeves rolled up above his elbows and his hair cut squarely round his face. He sat back in his chair with his wrists just touching the table and the index finger of his right hand pushed tightly through his key ring. He had nodded politely as Masoud introduced us but had difficulty with my accent when I spoke to him in Arabic. He nodded a lot and smiled nervously, but asked Masoud to translate into Kurdish.

The question of guards had turned out to be tricky, as I had been told by the PUK that the *peshmerga* who had travelled with us in the spring were not available. I had been promised that two new men would be sent to the hotel on Friday morning and had been preparing myself to set off to Sulaymaniyah in the company of strangers. I was surprised and delighted, then, when the little figure of Mohammed came bounding through the swing doors of the restaurant, grinning at me. I trusted Mohammed, I knew he liked me and on the last trip I had observed that he was an alert, sharp-witted guard. I knew he would take good care of me, both in terms of keeping me out of danger and fending off any unwanted male attentions that might be directed at me as a woman travelling alone. Mohammed held out his hand, shook mine and murmured, 'Later, I'll explain later.'

Masoud had advised me to travel in a small, old car in order not to draw attention to myself. 'These foreigners who travel in convoys with dozens of guards simply make themselves vulnerable. If you move around in a new Landcruiser, you are very conspicuous and everyone knows there's either some big political figure or a foreigner travelling in it. Whereas if you are in a small dirty old car like everyone else, nobody will even bother to look through the window.'

I had seen the force of what he was saying and readily accepted to go with Fareed in his family car. But now, as we came out of the hotel, I was taken aback to discover that Fareed's car was an unusual shade of dark chocolatey brown. I had imagined it would be white, like almost all the old private cars on the road. It was old and battered and would not draw attention from its condition: but anyone who saw me getting into it wouldn't have any difficulty following us.

It was just after 10 when we finally set off, with Omar, the second guard, sitting in the front and Mohammed and me in the back, with my work bag with the computer in it between us on the seat and a pile of bottles of cold mineral water at our feet. I had bought these the day before and left them overnight in the hotel freezer.

Omar was from the same office as Mohammed and they had grown up in the same town. He was short and stocky, with a round belly which bulged under his olive green shirt, and short sturdy thighs, the muscles of which threatened to burst through the denim of his jeans. He had a big head set on a short thick neck, the back of which bristled with neatly clipped hair. On his left hand he wore a shiny new wedding ring. Try as I might over the next two weeks, I could not guess Omar's age. He might have been anything from 25 to 35. Eventually Mohammed told me Omar was 33 and that his bride of six months was still living with her parents within the government-controlled area, which meant he rarely saw her.

Omar's attitude was relaxed, casual and a little off-hand, as if he couldn't see what all the fuss was about in terms of foreigners needing guards. Later on, when occasionally I asked him his opinion about whether it was safe to go to a particular place, he invariably clicked his tongue, smiled and said, '*Maku-shay*' – 'There's nothing to worry about.' He nevertheless went through the motions obligingly enough. That morning he was wearing a pistol in his waistband

and had slung a Kalashnikov on the floor of the car beside his seat, the long thin muzzle of which pointed recklessly at Mohammed's thigh.

It was very hot by the time we set off. I went to wind down my window, but in the place where the winder should have been there was just a hole. Once we were through the last checkpoint on the outskirts of town, I put on my dark glasses. Masoud had warned me about dark glasses the first day I met him. 'Only foreigners wear dark glasses,' he had said. 'If they see dark glasses, even when they don't see you, they know it's a foreigner.' He hadn't needed to explain whom he meant by 'they'.

Southeast of Arbil the flat, scrubby landscape soon turned into low sandy hills. The colours were bleached by the relentless sun and it wasn't interesting to look at. The road surface was good and there was little traffic but we had to stop at a checkpoint every 20 minutes or so. Sometimes it was just a painted oil drum in the middle of the road and a youth with a Kalashnikov. Other times there was a tent or a shack beside the road and a couple of red-and-white planks laid across alternate sides of the carriageway with a little interval between, so that the car had to manoeuvre slowly around them. There would be a couple of young men in pale khaki police uniforms with white armbands and black caps, and other men in *sharwal* sitting outside the shack, drinking tea and smoking, their rifles propped beside them.

We always drew to a halt beside the guards, and they invariably noticed me and stuck their heads in the driver's window. After a while I developed the habit of taking off my dark glasses as we approached the checkpoint and leaning forward to allow them to get a good look. Invariably they smiled and nodded, asked the driver with intrigued curiosity where I was from, and waved us on without hesitation. Sometimes they even touched their foreheads as a mark of respect.

Often as we pulled out of the checkpoint we would pass a line of plastic petrol cans guarded by barefooted boys whose eyes would focus expectantly on Fareed, hoping for a sale. Petrol was smuggled into Kurdistan from the government-controlled areas and was in short supply.

After we had been travelling for about an hour and a half on a road which zig-zagged through the bare sandy hills, a small town came into view: a collection of low whitish buildings, trees and a couple of minarets.

'Koysanjaq,' Mohammed murmured. 'We'll go and have lunch at my aunt's, OK?' He leaned forward and said something to Fareed.

At the end of the main street we turned down a narrow, unpaved side road. The car lurched round a corner as Mohammed gave directions to Fareed. The street sloped steeply downhill and the surface was very rough; I worried about the tyres. Part of the deal with Fareed was that I paid for all minor repairs that might be needed to the car. We drew up beside a group of little boys and Mohammed opened the door and called out to one of them. The child looked surprised, stared past Mohammed at me and then pointed down the hill without speaking. Mohammed leaned out of the car, pinched the boy's cheek and then threw himself back into the car as Fareed drove on. Twenty yards further down the hill we screeched to a halt.

In a matter of seconds Mohammed was out of the car and had opened a white-painted metal gate in the wall. He was kissing a large woman in a pale *dishdasha* on each cheek and gesturing towards the car. Leaving the door ajar he came back towards us, beckoning with a vigorous gesture of his hand. Mohammed was slightly built, but his neat figure and expressive physical agility more than made up for it. His thick, wiry black hair shone blue-black in the sunlight.

'*T'aali*, Teresa,' he addressed me in Arabic, opening the door for me and picking up the bag with the computer in it. 'Come.' '*Wara*,' he said to the others in Kurdish, 'Fareed, Omar, *fermo*!'

The metal gate led into a small yard in front of the aunt's three-roomed, single-storey house. Her name was Saywan and she was Mohammed's mother's sister. She stood there smiling broadly as if she had been expecting us, shaking hands with Omar and Fareed and kissing me on both cheeks. She looked about 40, which in Kurdish terms is respectable middle age for a woman. She had black hair tied back with a scarf, which seemed to be more a way of keeping it out of her eyes while she cooked than an Islamic headscarf. Her *dishdasha* was white with the faded remains of a flower pattern; it was unironed and her heavy body was very evident underneath.

Mohammed's uncle was sitting on the floor in the front room in pyjamas. It was Friday today, the Muslim weekend. He called out a welcome and struggled to his feet. He shook my hand warmly, saying, 'Welcome, welcome,' as if there were nothing unusual about a Western woman walking into his living room.

We were invited to sit on a couch and chairs while the uncle resumed his spot on the floor. He sat with one leg stretched out and the other bent at the knee, his big rough hand resting comfortably on it. Fareed sat shyly in an armchair in the corner, his index finger pressed tightly through his key ring and his short legs only just reaching the floor, but Omar was soon well into conversation with the uncle and another man who had arrived just after us. The aunt, meanwhile, was standing in the doorway, eyeing me from top to toe across the room and talking to Mohammed in a low voice.

'*Zor jwana*,' I heard her say. It was one of the few Kurdish expressions I had picked up, and it meant 'very beautiful'. I chuckled to myself silently. It wasn't the first time I had been paid a compliment in Kurdistan. Since I didn't get them very often in England, I had decided that it was my 'otherness' which made me something of a beauty here. Being tall and very pale-skinned made me the opposite of most Kurds.

It did cross my mind to wonder what else the aunt and Mohammed were saying to each other, as she continued to stare at me, but I couldn't pick out any more familiar words and I decided to turn my attention to looking round the room, while quietly enjoying the innocence of non-comprehension.

The floor was of bare concrete and the walls were a faded cream. A clock designed like a giant watch with a gold plastic wrist chain hung on one wall and an oversized set of wooden worry beads hung on another. Beside me, on a little glass table, a bunch of paper flowers sat tiredly in a pot. A large colour television was the focal point at the end of the room, standing on a gleaming steel frame. It was tuned to 'PUK TV', but the sound was turned down. A group of men in traditional dress stood in a green meadow with a mountain back-drop, gustily mouthing a song.

When lunch was ready Saywan and her teenage daughter brought a couple of rugs which the men unrolled on the floor. A white plastic sheet was laid between them and the women spread the food upon it. There were three large plates of rice, some small bowls of stewed okra in tomato sauce, a plate of chicken joints, bowls of finely chopped tomato and cucumber salad and folded sheets of wafer-thin home-baked bread.

'*Fermo*! Help yourself!' cried the aunt, and we all took our places cross-legged on the floor. All, that is, except for the teenage daughter, who drifted away in the direction of the kitchen.

It was the first time I had eaten lunch with a real Kurdish family, sharing dishes and using bread and a spoon for cutlery. It was to be the first of many such meals: one of my best memories of Kurdistan is of sitting knee-to-knee with a large group of people and sharing whatever was available, however simple. Mohammed's aunt and her husband were relatively well off, but later on I ate in many homes where meat was a rarity and vegetarianism was forced on people because of the economic situation.

After we had finished, with many encouragements to me from the aunt to eat more than I wanted, the dishes were cleared away and the plastic cloth, now stained with tomato juice and littered with sticky grains of rice and discarded corners of bread, was rolled up and taken out to the yard to be cleaned. The teenage daughter reappeared, carrying a tray with a little brass tea pot, seven tiny glasses and a bag of sugar. She ladled at least three teaspoons of sugar into each glass before filling it to the brim with pale gold cardamom-flavoured tea.

It was 2.30 by the time we set off, the hottest part of the afternoon. The aunt had invited us to stay longer, to sleep for a couple of hours at her house, but we decided to press on to Sulaymaniyah.

We had only been driving about half an hour when the car began to make coughing sounds. A mile further on, the engine started to shake; we were on a long, empty stretch of road which wound through deserted, open country. There was no shade from the scorching sun and if we broke down we couldn't be more vulnerable to attack.

Fareed was shaking his head and muttering discreetly to himself, as if hoping I might not have noticed there was a problem. Omar began muttering, too, and after a few more yards Fareed pulled over to the side of the road. I made to open my door and get out, but Mohammed motioned to me to stay put. Fareed opened the bonnet and his small figure disappeared under it; Mohammed and Omar got out, lit cigarettes and stood in front of the car. Omar had slung the Kalashnikov casually over his shoulder.

After a few moments Fareed opened the door and asked me for a bottle of mineral water for the engine, then disappeared again under the bonnet.

I sat in the back studying Mohammed and Omar's posture through the windscreen. Body language has always fascinated me, and in Kurdistan the vocabulary of the way men move and stand is different from in England. Mohammed had a way of standing with his arms dangling loosely from his shoulders and his legs a couple of feet apart, which made his slim frame seem bigger and more powerful. Omar's short body was very clearly power-packed, but he was slouching now with his weight on one leg and a hand on his hip, inhaling sharply from the butt of a cigarette, looking very casual.

I knew it was mostly an act, and that if anyone tried seriously to attack us Mohammed and Omar would be unlikely to be able to prevent them, but I found their nonchalance and physical self-confidence reassuring; and I didn't doubt that if anything happened they would risk their lives trying to protect me. As time went on, and I became more fond of them, that prospect bothered me increasingly; but there wasn't much I could do about it.

It felt very odd to remain sitting inside a car while a bunch of men tried to figure out what was wrong with it. Part of me felt irritated with being told to stay put, while another part was inclined to enjoy the luxury of letting others do the worrying. Besides, it was very hot outside and if I stood around with the men that would make us conspicuous, whereas if I stayed in the car, passing drivers would see just another bunch of Kurds whose car had broken down. Given the shortage of spare parts and decent petrol, it was a common sight. We had stopped in an area of semi-desert, with rocky, whitish gold hills over to the left, in the direction in which the road was leading. To the right the sand and scrub sloped down gently to a barren plain, and about 100 yards from the car a collection of bushes and a weedy sapling grew along the line of a dried-up ditch.

Suddenly the bonnet smacked down, dead cigarette ends were thrown into the road and the three men jumped confidently back into the car.

But 200 yards down the road, the juddering and shaking began again. Fareed pulled over once more, swearing now in a soft undertone. Again the chocolate brown bonnet went up, again the three men got out. This time I lent back against the seat and shut my eyes against the intense glare of the mid-afternoon light.

'Water,' Mohammed opened the door beside me. 'Leak in the radiator, that's the problem.'

I reached down and passed him a second bottle of warm mineral water. There were two left and I decided to take a swig before it was too late. The water was almost hot enough to make tea. I forced some down and shut my eyes again. I found the emptiness of this nameless place, the lack of shade and the lack of water mildly threatening.

When Fareed started the engine again it sounded better and we drove slowly for half an hour before having to stop again to empty the third bottle into the radiator. We were well into the rocky hills by now and, as we set off, Sulaymaniyah became visible in the distance, an indistinct shape 20 miles away on the pale gold plain.

A deep hush reigned in the city as we drove in, it being late Friday afternoon when most people were at home sleeping. We pulled up outside the familiar rose garden of the Abu Sana hotel, where I had stayed the previous May. But the Abu Sana was full, Friday being the night for parties and weddings, so we made bookings for the following night and checked into a smaller hotel near the centre of town called the *Funduq Salaam*, the 'Hotel Peace'.

It was a four-storey 1930s-style oblong box of a building, with a large, dark, dirty lobby and a garden at the back with tables and chairs set with stained white table cloths.

As we stood at the reception desk trying to establish the price of the rooms with the smooth, somewhat cagey, be-suited manager, I made out the shapes of a few traditionally dressed men sitting smoking and staring at me through the gloom. Unlike the Abu Sana, I sensed that this was a hotel where foreigners did not usually stay;

and I could tell from the atmosphere that I was the first woman to set foot in the place in years.

'Yes, we have rooms for you on the top floor,' the manager replied in English to my question in Arabic. I always found that slightly unnerving: it was like a rejection, a refusal to allow me to have any power in the exchange between us.

'So, you are from Britain? Very nice. May I see your passport?' He smiled a testy, faintly lecherous smile which I met with a glower.

'You her guard?' he asked Mohammed. 'OK. Rooms 403 and 404, these are the keys.'

He handed Mohammed two heavy wooden templates with mortice keys attached and ordered a boy hovering near the desk to carry my bags. Omar and I took the lift, a tiny cubicle with a cracked glass panel in the door, while Fareed and Mohammed walked.

The landing on the fourth floor was large and empty, carpeted with old dusty red rugs. There was no one about except a middle-aged man in a white *dishdasha* who peeped at us from behind a half-open door and shut it again. I took the room at the end in the corner and the three men would share the room next door.

When my bags arrived I locked the door behind me, went to the window and opened it. At the edge of the city the beautiful mountains of Sulaymaniyah rose gold and greyish blue in the late afternoon light, and below me lay low, flat-roofed concrete houses with trees in their gardens and green lawns and flowers. It was so much more attractive than airless, tree-less, trafficky Arbil. There was even a slight breeze moving the leaves on the tree below the window.

I turned back into the room and sat down on a chair to take in my surroundings. There was a faint smell in the still, stuffy air. Three large beds took up most of the floorspace, a huge dark wardrobe stood against one wall and a metal fan hung from the ceiling. Everything was covered with a layer of dust.

After supper I put a chair by the open window and sat down to write my journal. The electricity was off and I lit a candle. After a few minutes I heard a soft knock at the door.

'*Meen?*' I called out. 'Who is it?'

'*Ani,*' Mohammed's voice replied very softly. 'It's me.'

I walked over to the door in my bare feet and unlocked it. Mohammed was standing outside holding a shapely glass oil lamp and a box of matches.

'Come in,' I said, and stood aside. He glanced both ways down the corridor before stepping into the gloom: it would not do for him to be seen entering my room.

He smiled at me a warm, shy smile and I pulled up another chair by the window. He sat down, put the lamp on the window sill and lit it. The small flame burned a pale yellow, giving off a faint smell of paraffin.

'What are you writing?' he asked, nodding at my journal which lay open on the floor.

'Oh, all sorts of things. Everything that happened today... Can you read English handwriting?'

Mohammed could read printed English better than I could read Arabic. We always spoke with each other in Arabic, though, as my spoken Arabic was more fluent than his English.

I watched his face as he pored over my journal by the weak light of the lamp. He had been to the barber's the day before and his hair was clipped smooth on his neck. It was strange how his face looked so different at different times. Sometimes it was the face of a very young man, just out of boyhood, and at other times it expressed a haggard weariness and a depth of feeling that seemed to belong to someone much older. He was in his mid-twenties but in his short life he had experienced things that I and most people I knew would never go through. He had lost his beloved older brother in combat when still a teenager; taken his place and gone to be a fighter in the mountains; spent six months in the Iraqi army; fought against Iraqi troops in hand-to-hand combat in the suppression of the uprising, in the course of which he saw scores of people killed; and lived for six months in a refugee camp in Iran. All this he had told me briefly in snatched conversations during my first visit to Kurdistan. I had thought about his life while I was back in England and there were a thousand questions I wanted to ask him.

*　　*　　*

I went to sleep at 11, but was woken later by the sounds of a factory next door to the hotel where they were working in the yard at gone midnight. In the garden below my window a party of 10 men were having dinner. The clinking of their cutlery and the rise and fall of their voices disturbed me.

It was hot in the room and I remembered the fan, a huge three-bladed contraption like a bird of prey, hanging heavily from the ceiling. I got up in a stupor of sleepiness and pressed the switches by the door. I thought the electricity would be off, but slowly the fan began to turn, creating the beginnings of a breeze. It turned faster as I got back into bed, getting louder all the time.

Suddenly I pictured the propeller of a helicopter hovering above me and imagined the wings flying off and slicing into me. I dragged myself up once again, went to the door and switched it off.

chapter twelve

THE MAN WITH NO HANDS

We left the Hotel Peace early the next morning and took our things to the Abu Sana. I was wondering what to do first in Sulaymaniyah, when Omar and Mohammed suggested we go to the Red Security Building to talk with the refugees from Kirkuk.

Of all the Kurdish towns and cities that rose up against the government at the end of the Gulf War, nowhere was the violence and destruction greater than in Kirkuk. The uprisings began in the south of Iraq in the Shi'i city of Basra on 28 February 1991, the day of the ceasefire, when a column of tanks fleeing from Kuwait rolled into Sa'ad Square and the commander at the head of the column stopped in front of a giant mural of Saddam and climbed onto the roof. He denounced the dictator as responsible for the humiliation and defeat of the Iraqi people, climbed back into the tank and began to blast the portrait with shells, to the delight of the assembled crowd.

Within days, turmoil had spread to Karbala, Najaf, Hilla, al-Nasiriya, al-Amara, Samawa, Kut and Diwaniya – all the larger cities of southern Iraq. On 4 March rebellion erupted in the Kurdish north, beginning in the town of Ranya to the northwest of Sulaymaniyah. It spread so rapidly that within 10 days the Kurds were in control of every city except Kirkuk and Mosul. The Kurds' greatest moment came on 20 March, when they succeeded in capturing Kirkuk.

But the success of the uprisings both north and south was short-lived. In the south, the government regained control of all but a few areas by the end of March, inflicting indescribable suffering in the process and seriously damaging the holy Shi'a sites at Karbala and

Najaf. This left loyal army units free to turn their attention to Kurdistan.

Kirkuk was retaken by 28 or 29 March, D'hok and Arbil were taken on 30 March, Zakho on 1 April and Sulaymaniyah by 3 April. There followed a mass exodus by the civilian population, who feared the renewed use of chemical weapons against them. By 5 April it was reported that up to 3 million people were on the move in Kurdistan, some heading east for the Iranian border and the rest heading north for Turkey.

In the south of Iraq the force of the uprising had been increased by the participation of large numbers of soldiers whose disillusionment with the government led them to side with the rebels. In Kurdistan much of the *jash* collaborator militia defected and fought alongside the *peshmerga* and the people. In both the south and the north the rebels attacked security force headquarters, brutally killing large numbers of their personnel in revenge for the suffering of countless past torture victims. Prisons were sacked and large numbers of prisoners released, many of whom saw the light of day for the first time in more than a decade.

Kirkuk is a city with over a million inhabitants. Traditionally its population has consisted of a majority of Kurds and a sizable minority of Turkomans. It has an important oil refinery and is a city over which Iraqi central government has never been willing to compromise with the Kurds: for this reason it was left out of the definition of 'Kurdish areas' for the purposes of the autonomy agreement in 1970. In the following decade, large numbers of Kirkuki Kurdish families were forced out of their jobs and homes and resettled elsewhere. Arabs were then made to move to Kirkuk from the south, as part of the government's 'Arabisation' programme.

In the second week of March 1991, suspecting that the Kurds of Kirkuk would soon join the uprising, the Iraqi army increased street patrols in Kurdish neighbourhoods and placed many of them under curfew. Ali Hassan al-Majid was put in charge of the city's security and a door-to-door operation began in which several thousand boys and men aged from their early teens to their fifties were arrested. They were transported to military camps and compounds outside the city, where they were held in appalling conditions for the next five weeks. When the majority were finally released, they were forbidden to return to Kirkuk.

Having put many of the men out of action, the army was then sent in to demolish large numbers of houses in the Kurdish neighbourhoods, using dynamite and bulldozers and putting families out on the streets. Army patrols drove past houses that were still standing, calling out on megaphones to the 'heroic masses of Kirkuk' to surrender their weapons to the Ba'ath party.

Despite these measures, *peshmerga* were advancing on Kirkuk from the north and on 18 to 19 March Kurdish neighbourhoods began to fall under their control. By 20 March the *peshmerga* were in control of the entire city. Journalist Gwynne Roberts, who reached Kirkuk shortly afterwards, wrote in the *Independent*:

> Kurdish rebels were using bulldozers to clear the streets of Kirkuk of Iraqi corpses ... I saw several bodies of security officials sprawled in the mud, one of them with live rounds of ammunition jammed into his mouth. A local Kurd said: 'That bastard was a torturer, and God knows how many men, women and children he persecuted. He deserves what he got.'

Peshmerga lined up government officials and security police against walls and machine-gunned them by the dozen. Regular soldiers were spared because it was known that they had been forced to serve in the army.

Few civilians had been hurt in the *peshmerga* seizure of the city, but a counter-offensive by government forces began almost immediately. By 21 March, tanks to the southwest of the city began shelling residential areas day and night, and helicopter gunships flew over the city firing rockets and dropping napalm. Scores of residents were killed daily and some began to flee the city.

After a week-long bombardment, Kirkuk fell to the government. On 27 March, loyalist troops including Republican Guard assault units, paratroopers and special forces entered the city. One of their first acts was to attack Saddam Hussein hospital with tanks and helicopters. They then entered the wards, which were crammed with injured *peshmerga* and civilians. Scores of patients and medical staff were shot dead and some patients were slashed with knives or thrown out of windows.

As they consolidated their hold on the city, the government troops ordered the remaining Kurdish population, which was predominantly women and children, to leave the city within 24 hours. Soon a stream of refugees was fleeing north and east in the directions of Arbil and Sulaymaniyah, while troops looted their abandoned homes.

Before the uprising the Red Security Building was Sulaymaniyah's main security police building. People were tortured in cells in the basement, hundreds of women were raped in the 'Raping Room' and many people died there. During the uprising it was stormed by the people of Sulaymaniyah and in the course of a long battle the security personnel were all either killed or driven out. Now, two years later, the basement cells were full of water and unusable, and 230 refugee families from Kirkuk had made their homes on the ground and upper floors.

The battle for the Red Security Building had left some of the walls and most of the windows missing. The building was constructed on three sides of a courtyard in which, as I walked in with Omar and Mohammed, children were playing and women were making bread, doing the washing and cooking on open fires. The scene was strikingly colourful: the building itself was of pinkish-red concrete and the women and children were dressed in bright *dishdashas* and headscarves in greens, yellows, blues and dark pinks. The building was crawling with people. When they saw my camera, every window cavity and every doorway on the upper floors filled with figures, and children stuck their heads through holes in the walls and waved at us.

As I hadn't found an interpreter yet, Mohammed offered to translate for me into Arabic. As soon as we walked into the courtyard I caught sight of a woman we had met when we came before in May. Christine had taken a photo of her and I felt as if I was recognising an old friend. She invited us to come and sit in her room, which was on the ground floor near the entrance and had one wall entirely missing. It was about 20 foot square and the gaping opening onto the courtyard was partly covered by a large sheet, suspended on a washing line.

We left Omar chatting to an old man in the courtyard, and went in.

The woman's name was Asmar Brahim. A crowd of children gathered around her as she spoke. She was wearing a stained yellow *dishdasha* and her reddish brown hair was matted and dirty, pulled off her face with a scarf.

A girl of about eight dragged a mat towards me and Asmar motioned to me to sit down. I put my bag on the ground and sat cross-legged, trying to wave away a trio of flies that were buzzing round my head. It was hot now and the sheet-wall did not prevent the sun coming into the room. Mohammed squatted a few feet away.

A man had wandered in and was hovering behind Asmar. I wondered if he was her husband, but something told me that he was not. He was dressed in jeans and a yellow check shirt and both his arms ended in stumps above the elbow. He had thick black hair, a bushy beard and lively, intelligent eyes.

'It must be very cold here in the winter,' I said to Asmar. 'How do you keep warm?'

'If there were paraffin we would use it for heating,' the man replied dryly, 'but there isn't any.' He squatted down beside Mohammed, then dropped into a cross-legged position.

I asked him if the people had work. The man knew Arabic and didn't need Mohammed to translate the question into Kurdish. He twisted on his haunches, leaned one truncated shoulder towards me and said, 'The men here don't have any work. They try to work as porters in the *bazaar*, but they are not allowed to officially by the Kurdish administration, because there are too many porters. The UN brings us oil, rice, sugar and flour, but only once every three months. It's not enough.' He exhaled the words with a mixture of despair and disgust. 'What we want is for the Iraqi government to leave Kirkuk, so that we can go home.'

I asked what he thought of the Kurdish administration. Before he could answer, Mohammed said something to him which I didn't understand but felt sure wasn't a repetition or clarification of my question. They were sitting close together and the man glanced at him and murmured a reply before turning to look at me steadily. I was trying hard to read his expression, but unsure of the signs.

'The Kurdish administration has no money, they can't help us. They are in a desperate situation. What they say to us is that we should go back to Kirkuk and push the Iraqi government out. You see, we are a big problem for the Kurdish administration. There are refugees from Kirkuk all over southern Kurdistan. Altogether there are over 100,000 Kirkuki refugees in the Kurdish-administered area.'

'Look,' he jerked his head around Asmar's room, and his torso rotated with it, 'you can see how we're living! Two families to one room, no bathroom, and the water supply is shared between men and women, which isn't right.' He seemed to be referring to the toilets. 'And the health situation is very bad: we have malaria, tuberculosis and dysentery.'

I nodded slowly. I was surprised at myself for not being more frightened or repelled by the man's stumps. His energy came across powerfully, as did his expectation that we could and would communicate.

'Do you get help from anyone except the UN?' I asked.

The man glanced at Mohammed then turned to me. 'The political parties bring food,' he began, 'but only once every six months or every year. Otherwise, all our food comes from the UN. But the UN gives the same amount of food to families who have money as to the ones who don't.'

'Are you politically affiliated?'

He smiled, half to himself.

'I'm with the KDP. Mullah Mustafa Barzani is the only one who has ever helped Kurdistan.' He glanced at Mohammed in an easy, brotherly way, and then at me. 'Come and meet my family. We live in the next bit of the block.'

We got up and said goodbye to Asmar, who had already faded towards the high tiled walls of her three-sided home and was making preparations for lunch. She thanked us for coming, said we were welcome and that she hoped we would come and see her again. If she felt it, she didn't show any resentment that the focus of my attention had switched from her to the man with no hands.

We followed the man back out across the courtyard and into a narrow low-ceilinged corridor which led to a small room. The floor, walls and ceiling were covered with petrol-blue tiles. It was empty except for a few cooking pots in one corner.

'*Fermo*,' our host announced, 'come on in, this is my home. It used to be a bathroom!'

There was no window and we sat down on the clean, cool tiles in the semi-darkness. After a few moments a young man came in with an illuminated bulb attached to a wire, which he hooked over a nail on the wall.

'My nephew,' said the man with no hands, nodding at the young man. 'Welcome to you both,' he added as he turned back to us. 'My name is Mustafa al-Hussein – and yours?'

We introduced ourselves. Mohammed had already told Mustafa that I was a lawyer from Britain.

'I am Turkoman, from the old city of Kirkuk,' he announced, smiling with reserved pride. 'I am a glazier by trade.' He glanced at the stumps of his arms and added 'before this happened'.

I reckoned the room measured about 12 foot by 10 and I asked how many people lived in it.

'In this room, we are two families. My wife and I, we have two girls and a boy.' As he spoke, a little boy of about four ran into the room and placed himself in the cross of his father's legs. 'Then there is my brother's family: my brother, his wife and their four children. So, you see the conditions we live in!'

It was appalling to imagine 11 people all trying to sleep, eat and live in this tiny space, and with no natural light. It had one advantage, though, over Asmar's room: it would be much warmer in winter.

'Do you always have electricity?' I asked, pointing to the bulb.

'It comes on and off, just like everywhere else,' Mustafa replied. He had some movement in the stumps of his arms, and he waggled one of them at the light bulb as he spoke. 'It's free, the electricity. That is one good thing: the government pays for it.'

Mohammed lit a cigarette and held it to Mustafa's lips. He took a deep drag, nodded at Mohammed and slowly exhaled.

'I was in the Iraqi army when Kuwait was occupied. You know, before the Gulf War. I was taken prisoner, and held in Saudia.'

'Is that how you lost your arms?'

'No, I lost my arms in the uprising, in Chemchemal. I was fighting as a *peshmerga* for the KDP. I'll tell you the story.' He accepted another drag on the cigarette and went on: 'I came back from the war zone four days before the uprising started. I was in Chemchemal when it began. When the government tried to come back, the *peshmerga* were still in control of the town and the government troops surrounded it. There was a big battle. I got my injuries in a TNT explosion, a building that was blown up. It wasn't just my arms, it was my head as well. I was evacuated to hospital in Sulaymaniyah: my family were here already. The doctor told them one night at midnight that I would be dead by 3 a.m. – but I didn't die! After 12 days in the hospital, I began to get better. When I came out of the hospital, everyone was fleeing from Sulaymaniyah, so we went too. We went to Iran and spent six months in a camp.'

A thin girl of about 12 in a green *dishdasha* had come in and was squatting on her haunches by the wall.

'My daughter,' Mustafa said, nodding at her. He spoke to her and she left the room, returning a few seconds later with a folded piece of paper, which she handed to me.

'Look,' said Mustafa. 'This is from the Kurdish government. Read it, I think it's in English.'

I unfolded the paper. It was headed 'The Iraqi Kurdistan Regional Council of Ministers – Ministry of Health and Social Affairs'.

It was a short medical report confirming that Mustafa al Hussein Ramadan was examined on 22 April 1993 and that he needed to travel abroad to have artificial limbs fitted. The cost, it estimated, would be $5,000. It said that he had also suffered injuries to his right eye and ear.

'You see, they came to examine me a few months ago. I need to go abroad for treatment. Of course I don't have the money. Five thousand dollars! That is what I need.'

It went through my mind that Mustafa might be hoping I would help him.

'Look, I can't arrange medical treatment for you, but I can write about your situation, if you want me to,' I told him.

'Write about me, of course! Write about me!'

chapter thirteen

IN THE BAZAAR

The dining room at the Abu Sana was a vast, gloomily-lit hall with four rows of tables running the length of the room, which was as long as the building itself. It could easily seat a couple of hundred people, although the most I ever saw there was about 30. When we got back from the Red Security Building, Mohammed and I chose a table near the double doors leading out to the garden.

The most unforgettable thing about the Abu Sana was the carpeting. The floors throughout the entire hotel were covered in what looked like artificial grass, as used on greengrocers' stalls in England to display fruit and vegetables. But unlike the brilliant green of greengrocers' matting, the Abu Sana carpets were the pale yellowy-green of a field in summer which has been over-pastured by sheep. In the mornings as I walked down to breakfast I would see the *shar-wal*-clad cleaning women bent double with their dustpans, brushing the horrible plastic strands.

Mohammed and I sat down facing each other in the heavy wooden armchairs with upholstered seats. Mohammed took his gun from his waistband, lifted up the stained white tablecloth, slipped it underneath and patted the tablecloth back into place. I was to watch him do this 100 times before it finally dawned on me to ask him what the reason was.

'*Choni?*' I asked playfully. '*Chaki?* How are you? How's things?'

Before Mohammed could answer, the waiter came over and was asking what we wanted to eat. There was very little left in the kitchen, so we ordered *fasoulia* (beans) and rice. I was paying and I tried to persuade Mohammed to order meat, but since I wasn't having any he refused. It would be a long time before people would accept that my vegetarianism was from choice, rather than economic necessity.

While we were waiting Mohammed took his left hand in his right and pulled out his knuckle joints one by one, looking me in the eye as he did so. They clicked as loudly as the safety catch on his pistol being released.

'So,' he began, 'you see how the Kirkukis live?' He searched my face, wanting to be sure I had taken it all in. Mohammed was originally from Kirkuk, although he had moved as a child to Touz Khurmatu, a town about an hour to the south. Touz, like Kirkuk, had remained under Iraqi government control. Being a *peshmerga*, Mohammed couldn't go there and his family only rarely made the difficult journey through the Iraqi army checkpoints to visit him in 'Free Kurdistan'.

'It's terrible,' I replied. 'I've never seen people living in such appalling conditions. But what I don't understand is, why were they so uncritical of the Kurdish government? Mustafa, for instance, seemed to think they couldn't expect any more help than they're getting.'

Mohammed signalled to me to lean forward across the table so that he could speak in a very low voice. 'Look, you know when you asked Mustafa what he thought of the Kurdish government? Remember I spoke to him before he answered? I know Turkish and I told him in Turkish to be careful what he said to you.'

'Why?' I was taken aback.

'Because you're a foreigner and he doesn't know who you really are. It's not on, here, to go criticising the government to foreigners. People have to watch their backs!'

'But I can write about him without identifying him.'

'Exactly. You can, and you must. I know that, and I know that you're good, but I didn't want the guy to feel he had compromised himself.'

The *souq* in Sulaymaniyah was roofed over, a warren of alleyways dimly lit by roof lights and, when the current was on, electricity. I walked close behind Mohammed, unable to forget the specific warning I had heard that *souqs* were dangerous places for foreigners, but equally unable to resist the fascination that all *souqs* hold for me.

'We say *bazaar* in Kurdish; *souq* is Arabic,' Mohammed had said, gently reminding me that although Arabic was our common language, he spoke it with me to be helpful and not from preference.

The stalls on the outer fringes near the street sold fruit. Black grapes were in season now and pomegranates and huge dark green watermelons. One trader had hacked a watermelon in half and was selling it by the dripping red fleshy slice, offered on the point of a dagger knife for a quarter of a dinar.

Further in we passed strings of plastic shoes hanging from the roof like onions, alongside clusters of handmade wicker baskets and wooden spoons. In the twilight beneath, women's headscarves were laid out on a trestle table: black wool squares embroidered with gold thread, spangled with green and purple sequins or hung with gilt tassels. The stall holder emerged from a dark corner and watched patiently while I fingered them. I chose one with tassels for 75 dinars.

'Come, you wanted to see the fabric bazaar,' Mohammed beckoned. He turned down a side alley past a couple of money-changers' booths and stopped in a well-lit passage lined with open-fronted shops. Each one was crammed with bolts of extraordinarily glitzy synthetic fabric. 'This is what they make the traditional women's clothes with,' Mohammed said. 'There are tailors here, too. If you want we can order you a Kurdish outfit.'

There was chiffon in puce and mustard and lemon yellow, gauze in orange and green, lurex in emerald green and peacock blue and purple, and satin in red and gold. In rainy Britain these fabrics would look cheap and tawdry, but here with the strong sunlight they were perfect for making the women's clothes at affordable prices.

Round the next corner we came to a row of carpet sellers. Here most of the shops were glassed in at the front like little offices. We were the only customers in sight. 'Where is everyone?' I asked as we wandered into one of the shops. On the back wall I had spotted a handmade kilim in orange, red and purple with dark brown borders. Beside it hung factory-made Persian rugs with intricate patterns in darker colours.

'No one has any money these days,' Mohammed replied. 'Isn't that right?' He turned to the turbanned merchant who was sitting in a corner, flicking through a wad of 5-dinar notes.

The man looked up and nodded. 'Times are very bad,' he agreed, glancing at me with ill-concealed interest. 'What are you looking for, Madam?'

I protested that I was only browsing, but 20 minutes later and after two glasses of tea I had exchanged the kilim for a 20-dollar bill. I could have got it for less if I had bargained, but it seemed wrong to do so, given the current economic crisis and my relative wealth. The merchant was happy, having charged me somewhat over the going rate, and so was I, knowing that in Britain it would have cost me at least five times as much. He rolled up the kilim, tied it with string and shook my hand warmly. Mohammed heaved the rug onto his shoulder and we sauntered out through the pungent-smelling alleys of the spice bazaar into the dazzling sunlight.

Later in the morning I went with Zelda, a German photo-journalist staying at the hotel, to visit an orphanage for the children of *Anfal* victims.

The orphanage was run by Swedish Save the Children and was located in a quiet residential quarter where the villa-style houses had verandahs with small shrubs and flowers in pots. We arrived while the children were having lunch and Mohammed and I waited in the reception room while Zelda went into the dining room to photograph them. A young woman teacher came out and chatted with me in Arabic. She looked about 25, and although she was simply dressed, in a dark red skirt and yellow blouse, I was struck by something glamorous in her aura. Her dark, glossy hair was held back off her face with a gold plastic slide and she wore red lipstick. Her manner was friendly and she went out of her way to answer my questions, giving me the unnerving impression that I was being taken for somebody important.

Fourteen children lived in the orphanage, their ages ranging from five to twelve. All of them had lost either both parents or at least their breadwinner-father in the *Anfal*. The criterion for admission was that they should have no relatives who were able to take care of them. Kurdish families are large and close-knit, but sometimes, although relatives did exist, they were so poor that they simply could not afford to feed another child. There were thousands of children in this situation.

The children were fed and clothed by the orphanage and all their practical needs were provided for. The little ones did basic lessons in the mornings and afternoons, and when they were old enough they were sent to school.

Paintings by the children were pinned up around the walls, quite a few of which showed scenes from the *Anfal* and the uprising. In one, aeroplanes were dropping huge black bombs on a village and people were lying bleeding on the ground. Behind the village were V-shaped mountains, on the sides of which stood stick-figure *peshmerga* holding Kalashnikovs. In the next picture a black helicopter hovered above a house which was engulfed in red and orange flames. Stick figures stood beside the house, their arms raised in gestures of terror.

'Nowadays we try to discourage the children from painting *Anfal* scenes,' the teacher said quietly. 'We think it's time their thoughts moved on to happier subjects. It's been five years now.'

'What do you tell them about the fate of their parents?'

'Often we tell them that their mums and dads are in Baghdad.'

The teacher was called out to the kitchen and I turned to Mohammed. 'Did you hear what she said? D'you think that's the right thing to do?'

'No, of course it's not good,' he replied gloomily, 'but what are they to tell them?' I had noticed a dark cloud descending across his face while we were standing talking to the woman.

She returned a moment later. 'For the first year after we opened the orphanage, the children used to have frequent dreams about the *Anfal*. Sometimes they would wake up in the night screaming. Now that seems to have stopped, but sometimes a child wakes up in the morning and says, "I saw my daddy last night." '

The door opened and Zelda walked in, cameras round her neck, smiling delightedly. 'Come on, you really must have a look at these kids. They're so *sweet*! After they finish lunch I'm going to photograph them having a lesson.'

Curiosity got the better of me and I followed Zelda back into the dining room, where about 10 young children were seated round a table spooning rice and something in a tomato sauce into their small mouths. They carried on as Mohammed, Zelda and I stood looking at them, but their large eyes focused on us so that they appeared to be all eyes, spoons and mouths.

I glanced at Mohammed and saw that he was getting really upset. He had told me briefly about his sister's experience in the *Anfal*, and how he had spent his first year as a *peshmerga* trying to help threatened villagers escape over the mountains to Iran, ahead of the army operations. I suggested he wait for us outside. He threw me a grateful look and went out to the porch where Omar and Fareed were sitting smoking.

The lesson took place in a basement schoolroom. The children sat on low wooden benches facing the teacher, calling out simple figures as she wrote them on a blackboard behind her. I watched for five minutes and then left Zelda to it. She was crawling around the floor taking pictures from every conceivable angle.

When I rejoined the others on the porch, Omar gave me a chair and offered me a cigarette. I only smoke very occasionally, but he always offered.

Mohammed was a few feet away, squatting with his back to a low wall at the front of the verandah. A small boy with silky blond curls and a lost expression in his eyes was standing in front of him. He was fair-skinned and stood bare-footed in a pair of shorts and a grubby beige T-shirt, eyeing Mohammed cautiously.

Mohammed whispered something and looked into the child's eyes. The child didn't answer, but stared back at him. Then Fareed put his hand in his pocket, pulled out a 10-sided one-dinar coin, and gave it to Mohammed to offer to the boy. The child took the coin hesitantly, squeezed it in one chubby hand and continued to eye Mohammed, still unsure. Mohammed reached out and gently laced his fingers together round the boy's back. He kissed him on either cheek and whispered to him again.

'He lost his father and his mother in the *Anfal*,' Fareed turned to me and said by way of explanation, as if any child who had lost his parents had an established right to be loved and paid attention to by any adult who came into contact with him.

'He can't talk very well, he's a bit behind. But he told us just now, while you were inside, that his daddy's in Baghdad. He thinks he'll be coming back for him soon.'

I nodded slowly. I didn't really want to talk, I just wanted to sit and watch Mohammed and the curly-haired boy. It was as if all Mohammed's pain about the *Anfal* was going into the love he was offering to this child.

chapter fourteen

SAHAD THE SINGER

I had arranged to meet some women at Zhinan, the Union of Kurdish Women, in the afternoon. I had visited the Sulaymaniyah branch of Zhinan on my previous trip. It was a lively place, housed in a pleasant modern building that had once been a Ba'ath party guesthouse and had its own rose garden and lawn. The rooms were set up now as workshops and classrooms and thronged with a healthy social mix of women, some in headscarves and *dishdashas*, others in skirts and blouses, along with a couple of foreign volunteers in jeans and T-shirts. A small bunch of educated women ran it, providing literacy classes and craft workshops where *Anfal* widows and other poor women came to learn a trade such as weaving or dress-making and were then given help in setting themselves up in business. Nazaneen, whom I had met in May, was one of the moving forces behind it and the main fund-raiser. She was a strong feminist, spoke good English and had become an expert at obtaining funding from the various NGOs operating in Kurdistan. Sirwa, her great friend, was less involved as she worked full-time as a headmistress, but she too had been one of the founders of Zhinan. Both women were in their mid-forties and unencumbered by husbands or children.

We arrived a little after four in the still intense afternoon heat. Most of the Zhinan activities were over for the day, but a handful of women remained, chatting and hanging around on the stairs and answering the constantly ringing telephone. Some of the women remembered me and greeted me with kisses and welcoming words. Mohammed shook hands with several of them, surprisingly at ease in this all-female environment, and then retreated discreetly to the garden to talk and smoke with the Zhinan guards while he waited for me.

Sirwa appeared a few minutes later, looking more relaxed and less tired than when I had seen her in May, when she had been in the middle of the high school exams. She was a small, lean woman with a delicate bone structure and prominent, beautiful eyes; her skin had the coarseness which comes with heavy smoking. I had found her fascinating when I met her before, and was looking forward to spending time with her and getting to know her while I was in Sulaymaniyah.

'Nazaneen too will be so ple-eased to see you!' she cooed. 'She is in Penjwe-en, she will be so cross with herself when she finds out you are already he-ere!' Sirwa always elongated her English vowels. 'Why didn't you tell us you were coming?'

I protested that I had faxed them before leaving England, but the fax had apparently not got through.

The Zhinan staff had chosen a woman who had been in prison to talk with me. Sirwa offered to translate and took me to an upstairs room where the woman was waiting. She was a country woman with a robust, strong look; her name was Sahad. Her hands were calloused and her face was lined, and at 34 she had born nine children. She was gutsy and warm and her brave spirit soared out of her. She wore her shoulder-length black hair loose and uncovered, and something in her bold, friendly expression told me that she no longer felt like a young woman. Marriage and motherhood, surviving a chemical attack and, above all, her experiences in prison had combined to make her no longer think of herself as a sexual being; and that, I got the feeling, was a relief and a liberation.

She sat down next to me on a little sofa and Sirwa sat to one side. Sahad had not met either of us before but was not the least bit shy. I asked her a few questions to get her going and she talked freely and openly, as if she were only too happy to find someone who was interested in what had happened to her. More than any of the other women I talked with later about their experiences in prison, Sahad saw it all in acutely political terms and made it clear that her commitment to Kurdistan was what had sustained her and seen her through.

'I was in prison for four months at the end of 1982 and beginning of 1983. I was held in a security building outside Sulaymaniyah, which is known as the Tawara'a. They arrested me after I took part in some student demonstrations against Saddam's refusal to allow the students to study in Kurdish. Some of their books had been translated into Kurdish, but the government was insisting that the students should be taught in Arabic. At that time I was involved in helping the *peshmerga*, hiding their guns and clothes in my house. I was already married by then, with three children. The security people came and found the guns and clothes and took me to the Tawara'a. When they came, luckily the children were at my mother's and my husband was out. He is a *peshmerga* for the PUK.'

Suddenly Sahad sat forward in her chair, beamed at me and said, 'I want to sing you a song which I used to sing in prison, OK?'

She took a deep breath and began to sing in a high-pitched, beautiful voice. Although I couldn't understand the words, I heard courage and defiance in her voice and it brought tears to my eyes. The way she used her voice made me think of someone singing on a mountainside, projecting the sound over a great distance. It was astonishing to think of a woman singing like that in the depths of an Iraqi prison.

When she had finished Sirwa paraphrased the song for me in English. It was about being in prison and the world being on fire and the singer's determination that Kurdistan would survive.

'When I arrived at the Tawara'a,' Sahad said, picking up her story where she had left off, 'they beat me with an iron rod. Then they gave me electric shocks on my arms and legs. They beat me on my back with an iron bar which had nails sticking out; and on my buttocks and my arms. They also hit me on my chin with a knife – look, I still have the scar.'

She stuck her chin in the air and pointed out a raised area of skin.

'Every now and then they gave me tablets – something like valium – and water to drink. Then they would start to torture me again. They tortured me about 15 times altogether, over several days. They were asking me for information about the *peshmerga*, and why I had the guns and clothes in my house. I didn't tell them anything, in all that time!

'When they were going to torture me they would take me to a big room with special equipment. They made me take my clothes off. One time they put something like a giant pair of scissors round my neck, and said, "Give us the names of the *peshmerga* you know."

'I felt dizzy all the time. They brought a Kurd to interpret because they didn't know Kurdish. He was a collaborator and told me I shouldn't work for Kurdistan. The interrogators said that if I told them what they wanted, they would give me a house and a car.

'Sometimes they touched my breasts, even bit them. And they used electricity on me, I still have the marks.'

She pushed down the neck of her *dishdasha* to reveal a bare breast, which looked like it had fed a lot of children. There were dark purple marks on the underside.

'Sometimes they dosed me up with valium so that I fell asleep. I didn't feel anything, but when I woke up I realised that they had raped me.' Sahad looked from Sirwa to me and back again. She spoke in a matter-of-fact tone, as if she had long ago lost any feelings of embarrassment or shame, but there was anguish in her eyes and I felt that something in her was asking for our support.

After a moment Sahad smiled at us bravely. 'All the time I was thinking of the day I would be free! My father is a *peshmerga*. I was feeling strong.'

She paused, then added in a more wavering tone, 'But now, I am always thinking of the time I was tortured ... My head still hurts from where they hit me.

'I was kept in a room with a lot of other young women. Most were students. There were eight of them and me. They were all Kurds and all from Sulaymaniyah. In the end all eight of them were executed, all except for me. I kept saying I knew nothing and in the end they believed me.

'When they gave us food, it had shit and pee in it. They threw it into the room I shared with the other women and shut the door. We ate it, but we were sick afterwards. When we asked for water they gave us pee to drink.

'We were not allowed to wash at all. My hair and body became very dirty. And I couldn't walk because my body hurt so much.

'In winter it was very cold, there were open windows near the ceiling, although most of the room was underground. There was one Kurdish woman in our cell who we knew was actually a spy. We used to talk among ourselves about why we had been arrested – mostly for having husbands who were *peshmerga*. But because of this woman I always used to say I didn't know why they had come for me.

'Then one day they just decided to release me. They took me out in a car and dumped me somewhere far from Sulaymaniyah. I walked all the way home.'

'Who had been taking care of your children while you were in prison?'

'They were cared for by my mother, but I was very worried about them. The smallest was three months old and the other two were toddlers. I couldn't sleep for thinking about them. I used to write poems on the walls of the cell for my children and I sang songs for them.'

I looked at her admiringly. 'You are very strong, Sahad!'

She smiled proudly. 'I will do anything for Kurdistan.

'When I came out my children were OK, but over the next few years I had several more children and we moved to a town in the Balisan valley which was attacked with chemicals in 1988. Two of my daughters died and two are still sick now from the effect of the chemicals. I too was affected. The skin of my forearms was already sensitive from the electric shocks and the chemicals made it worse.' She shook her head, more with disgusted anger than self-pity.

'You know, my husband is angry with me about what happened to me in prison. He knows the reason I was arrested was that I was working with the *peshmerga*, but when he is feeling angry about his own situation, having no money and no job, he says bad things about me to my face. He says I have damaged his honour.

'My mother says I should bring the children and go to live with her. But I don't want to, I can't take my children away from their dad, and I feel I ought to listen to my husband rather than to my mother, and anyway he is sick from the effect of the chemicals.'

I nodded slowly, half disappointed that Sahad felt she couldn't leave her husband, half amazed at her willingness to endure.

'How do you feel now, about your time in prison?'

'I am always thinking about what happened to me. Even when I see someone killed in a movie on the television, it reminds me of it.'

I caught a glimpse of her hardworking day-to-day life being overshadowed by painful memories which she rarely shared with anyone.

'But I am a *peshmerga*! As a *peshmerga*, you put your hand in the fire but you don't feel the pain. If you feel the pain, you are not a *peshmerga*.' She beamed at us forcefully again.

'In 1991, when the *peshmerga* came here to Sulaymaniyah on 4 March, I wanted to sing! My heart was very hot!'

Tears moved again behind my eyes.

'Sahad,' I said, 'if I write about you in my book, do you want me to use your real name, or to make up a name?

'Use my real name! I am not afraid of Saddam. I want you to write about what happened to us. I want you to be with the Kurdish people!'

chapter fifteen

'IF I GIVE MY HEART TO YOU, WILL YOU HANDLE IT WITH CARE?'

I was bewitched by Nazaneen's beauty from the first time I met her. She was 46 years old, with the energy and physical presence of a woman in her prime. She was magnificent looking, with a full, goddess-like figure, a large nose, arching eyebrows and a head of luxuriant chestnut hair.

I was also fascinated by Nazaneen's self-confidence and independence. She was single and, besides being a leading light in the Kurdish women's union, Zhinan, she trained teachers at the Sulaymaniyah Institute of Education. She lived with her sister Drakushan in a small house next door to their brother and his family.

Nazaneen took it upon herself to receive and act as hostess to foreign visitors who came to Sulaymaniyah, particularly if they were female and interested in the problems of Kurdish women. She had a huge collection of visiting cards given to her by journalists, aid workers and development funders from Scandinavia, France, Germany, the US and Canada. When I had come to Sulaymaniyah the previous May, she had laid on a special lunch at Zhinan, showed us around the city and taken us to Halabja and Penjwin.

She had been very encouraging when I'd told her I planned to come back to Kurdistan later in the year. I sensed that she would take me under her wing and see to it that I got the support I needed.

'Naza', as she was known to those close to her, wore respectable, rather middle-aged Western clothes – high-necked blouses and full, calf-length skirts – as a woman of her age and position had to, in her society; but her exuberance bubbled through and she was attractive in spite of them. In a previous life, I thought, she must have been a

cabaret singer, for when she was in a good mood she would burst
into song at the slightest excuse. Frank Sinatra and Doris Day were
her favourite singers. She would seize the hand of the nearest person, twirl rapturously around in the centre of her living room with
her skirts flying out in a circle, and sing *'If I give my heart to you, will
you handle it with care?'*, closing her eyelids on the high notes and finishing by gazing into the other person's eyes.

Naza had studied history and sociology and was constantly
thinking about her Kurdish people and what they needed in order to
develop and move themselves forward, particularly the women. She
was always coming up with new ideas for income-generating projects for the *Anfal* widows. She spent a lot of time moving among the
staff of the foreign NGOs, going to meetings with them and writing
proposals for projects. She was adept at getting them to fund her
ideas.

As I got to know her better, I realised that Naza's one fault was
that she liked to be in control of everything. She often complained
that the other women at Zhinan wouldn't do anything on their own
initiative, that they lacked gumption and that unless she went down
to the office and got things going, nothing happened. Most afternoons she did go down and get things going; but then she was
unable to let go and would try to do all the work herself.

Sometimes Naza asked me to help her write proposals for new
projects. Her spoken English was excellent, but naturally I had a
better grasp of how to put ideas into the sort of language that would
appeal to potential funders. Most of her ideas were for projects to
help the *Anfal* widows. One NGO specialised in agriculture and we
wrote a proposal asking them to provide a couple of goats to each
woman in a particular area. The goats could be milked, yogourt and
cheese could be sold and they could be bred to build up a small
flock.

Zhinan already had a scheme to teach women rug-making.
When they had completed the course successfully, Zhinan tried to
provide each woman with a loom and an initial stock of wool; they
sold the rugs at their office in Sulaymaniyah, passing on most of the
profit to the women.

The house Naza shared with Drakushan consisted of three pleasant, cool rooms, a large kitchen at the back, a parched garden at the front and a flat roof where they hung out the washing.

The garden was adjacent to the verandah of their brother's house and there was a constant coming and going of teenage nieces and nephews who came to watch television and get away from their parents, and of neighbours who wandered across the street to borrow sugar or use Naza's telephone.

The two main rooms were cool, shady and well furnished. Naza's family had been comfortably off, and before the Gulf War she and Drakushan had lived well on their teacher's salaries. There were divans and armchairs, little tables and glass-fronted cabinets containing china and books. Most of the time the house was like a bus station, but on the rare occasions I found Naza and Drakushan alone it had a calm, quiet feel.

Drakushan was large and slow-moving, with long black hair. She prowled around the house in a dark red dress and bare feet, smoking one cigarette after another. She was less extrovert than Nazaneen and, although she intrigued me from the first, it took a while before we began to get to know each other. She taught Physical Education in a girls' school and did voluntary work with the Kurdish branch of Save the Children.

It was school vacation time when I was in Sulaymaniyah, and on mornings when she didn't have appointments, Naza would waft around the house in a long, pale pink Marks and Spencer's nightie which she had bought on a trip to England. I would arrive at lunchtime to find Drakushan frying 'finger-chips' on the gas stove, with a cigarette hanging out of her mouth, while Naza moved between a funding proposal she was writing, the incessantly ringing telephone and a couple of visitors, often foreign.

Naza would kiss me affectionately, greet Mohammed and introduce us to the visitors. We would leave our shoes at the door and help to set the lunch out on a plastic sheet on the floor. Sometimes when she had the time Naza made *lablabi*, a chick-pea soup; she knew it was my favourite Iraqi dish.

One evening Naza said to me, 'There's going to be a wedding here tomorrow, my neighbour's daughter is getting married and the family are coming from Baghdad.' She snapped her fingers, swung her hips and seized my hand. 'You like to dance?'

* * *

I arrived with Mohammed about 5.30, to find the whole street had been blocked off with two semi-circles of garden chairs. A glistening circle of young men and women were dancing in the middle, while their parents, grandparents and women with babies sat watching. I found Naza sitting quietly in a chair. She was dressed in a white blouse and slinky, pleated polka-dot skirt. She took my hand and led me into the neighbour's house, where the older guests were eating and drinking. As I was swallowing a small plate of rice and *dolma*, Drakushan suddenly appeared.

'Come, Teresa!' She led me through the crowd back to the street, broke apart the hands of two dancers and linked us into the circle.

'You know how to dance?' she asked me in her husky voice, beginning to raise and drop her shoulders in time to the music.

'More or less,' I replied, as the stilettoed heel of the woman next to me came down perilously close to my sandalled toe.

The *peshmerga* had taught me to dance the Kurdish *dibka* back in May, and I remembered the footwork. The tricky thing was the shoulders: they were meant to rise and fall rhythmically, as if you were a marionette.

Nazaneen's neighbour was rich and the young women in the circle were sleek and well groomed, some in brightly-coloured traditional Kurdish outfits, others in Western dresses with stockings and smart shoes. They all had thick, shining black hair which they wore in curls or bobs. In my jeans and cotton shirt I felt appallingly under-dressed, but I knew that as a foreigner I would get away with it. As we shuffled, shoulder-shaking, first clockwise then anti-clockwise, I caught the eyes of several of the young women. Naza's pretty niece Jwan smiled at me warmly, but in the haughty glance of the girl next to her I sensed a measure of reserve. 'Who is this foreigner in jeans?' her eyes questioned. 'And surely she doesn't know how to dance the *dibka*?'

From time to time as the circle rotated I caught a glimpse of Mohammed leaning against a tree by Nazaneen's gate. He had a can of Pepsi in his hand and was smoking pensively. I wanted to leave the circle and bring him over to dance beside Drakushan and me, but I knew that in the eyes of my upper-class hosts a guard was a guard and should remain in his place. What they would make of a foreign lawyer who took her *peshmerga*'s hand and invited him to dance beside her, I dreaded to think.

chapter sixteen

JWAN, A NURSE

I met Jwan one afternoon in the upstairs room at Zhinan. She looked much older than her 24 years. Her face was haggard and anxious, contrasting strangely with her chestnut hair, which curled softly around her neck. She wore an olive green skirt half covered by a long loose blouse and an old battered black plastic handbag hung from her shoulder. She looked poor but respectable, a young woman who had once taken a pride in her appearance but nowadays was lucky to have shoes on her feet. Later, at her home, Jwan showed me her wedding photos, in which she appeared as a strikingly beautiful young woman in a black velvet dress.

Jwan had told her story to many journalists. During our first meeting she told me that she still felt very angry about what had happened to her. She wanted everyone to know, both in Europe and in Kurdistan. She was particularly angry that when men survived abuse or torture at the hands of government personnel they were treated like heroes, but when it happened to women, she said, everyone recoiled from them. She had been rejected by her husband's family because of what had happened; they had tried to persuade him not to marry her.

At the end of our first meeting Jwan gave me a bundle of medical reports to take away and said she would like to meet again at her home the following afternoon. She gave directions to Sirwa and warned us that it was a simple place consisting of just one room. When she got up to leave she squeezed my hand with her own small, thin one, smiled and said, 'See you tomorrow,' in English. There was something very compelling about her delicate, fragile face and large green eyes.

The following afternoon Fareed drove us to a quiet quarter of Sulaymaniyah and stopped in front of a house. Washing was hanging outside in the yard, and Jwan appeared in a pale blue dishdasha at the top of the outdoor steps which led to her room. She looked very tired.

Sirwa and I climbed the steps and took off our shoes. Inside, the square concrete room was bare except for two thin mattresses on the floor and a large wardrobe in which all the couple's belongings were stored. Jwan gave us bolsters to lean against, put water to heat for tea on a tiny electric ring and began to tell us her story.

'During the uprising I was in Kirkuk, working as a nurse in Saddam Hospital. On 28 March 1991, the day the Republican Guard retook Kirkuk and the *peshmerga* forces withdrew, everyone tried to take what they could and run away from the town.

'I was trying to help the wounded *peshmerga*. At 9.30 a.m. we found the hospital was almost surrounded by Republican Guards, so we tried to help the *peshmerga* to leave. I called 11 of the men together to leave with me in a hospital car, but then I remembered I had not brought their medical files, so I went upstairs to get them and it took me a bit of time. When I came back down, the men had gone without me. My brother was among them.

'About 200 people remained in the hospital, which by now was in the control of the savage soldiers of the Iraqi regime. There were Arab, Turkoman and Kurdish doctors and nurses, but all the patients were Kurds.

'I had a pistol, because during the 14 days of the uprising, while the *peshmerga* had been in control of the hospital, we had searched the building and found weapons and I had kept one. I knew how to use it from my days in the Popular Army.

'When the Republican Guard found me I tried to defend myself. I shot a lieutenant, causing him flesh wounds in the arm and chest. Then I ran and hid in a storeroom in the basement of the hospital. Two or three of the people who had been working with us in the hospital were informers. So when the Republican Guard came, they already had my name and those of three others – all doctors – who had managed to flee. The security people would have had my name anyway, as someone who was organising to kill supporters of Saddam. I had been doing political work with the PUK since 1983, when I was 14.

'While I was waiting in the store room, absolutely terrified, I heard my name called over and over again by the soldiers as they began to search the hospital looking for me. Eventually one of the Republican Guard officers found me, but he told me he would help me to escape and that I should wait for him to come back. I waited, but an hour later I heard soldiers shouting that they would kill all the people in the hospital if they didn't find me, so I decided to go out and give myself up.

'When the officers saw me they began to taunt me with every bad name they knew. There were about a hundred Republican Guards in the hospital by then. A big group of them took me upstairs to the canteen and began to insult me. They showed me an execution order with my name on it which had been drawn up in Baghdad. They called me a "bitch", a "coward", a "spy"; they said I was a "prostitute" and had "sold myself to the enemy". I thought I was finished, that they were going to kill me there and then.

'The Commanding Officer came up and asked me if I realised I was going to be raped. I told him that he could not destroy my honour in the way he thought, that my honour is my land – Kurdistan. The verbal abuse went on and eventually I began to laugh at the soldiers. I thought my life was at an end and suddenly I wasn't afraid anymore. The officers told the Commander that they were going to kill me, but he said "Don't do that, I am going to take her to Ali Hassan al-Majid as a present."

'I was taken to the back of the canteen and left with two officers to guard me. After a while the two officers took me to a store nearby. One of them was very good to me. He was an Arab from Mosul and he said he would help me escape, if I promised not to give his name if I got caught. That night I was left alone to sleep and nobody interfered with me. The Mosulawi had said he would help me to escape at 7 a.m. the next day, but it didn't work out like that.

'In the morning I was taken back to the Commanding Officer, in a little office in the hospital. He asked me why I was so pale and said I must be feeling ashamed of myself. I replied that I was pale because

I had given blood to the *peshmerga*. I said I was not ashamed: I was very happy because Kurdistan had had a great victory.

'After a little while the Commanding Officer took me out into the road outside the hospital. There were dozens of officers there and he asked me questions in front of them. Meanwhile, some of the officers were preparing their guns to kill me, but he told them, "Don't kill her yet, we're taking her to Ali Hassan al-Majid."

'Some of the officers slapped my face and hit me on the head with their guns; others called me horrible names. I began to feel very weak. The Commander said, "Aren't you afraid of what they're going to do to you?" Again I replied that my honour is my land. He went on: "You Kurds shouldn't be making revolution, Saddam Hussein is a very good man. Why do you rebel?"

'I replied, "Because in Kirkuk we are not allowed to speak Kurdish, there are no Kurdish schools, we are not allowed to use Kurdish in any of the offices."

'Then I told him that if he had finished saying what he wanted to say to me, *I* had something to say to *him*. I raised my voice so that all the officers could hear, and shouted: "You are going to remember this day and you are going to tell your mothers and sisters about this, about what you did to me, a brave Kurdish girl!"

'After that I was taken back inside and left in the reception area of the hospital. I was unguarded so I decided to run for it. But after I had gone about 100 yards, two military cars came speeding towards me from each direction. They caught me, saying they had let me run away so that they would have the fun of catching me, and took me back to the hospital.

'The soldiers asked me where in the hospital I worked. I told them that I worked in the premature baby unit and they took me there. There was one dead baby left in the unit, but nobody else. I was left there with three soldiers to guard me. After a while, one of the soldiers said that he would help me to run away if I had sex with him. I spat at him, saying, "You can sell yourself if you want to, but I'm not selling myself!" The soldier pointed out that if I refused his offer, he could kill me with a single shot. He added that he would tell the other officers that I had insulted Saddam Hussein, an offence which is punishable by the death sentence. I replied that I wasn't afraid, I had already insulted Saddam in front of the other officers. The soldier said he would fetch someone else who would know what to do with me. After a few minutes he came back with the lieutenant I had wounded and two other officers, and they began to beat me up.

They hit me all over my body, using their bare hands and their army whips, which were leather whips with thongs. The lieutenant said that I had insulted his honour by shooting him, because I was a girl. They bent my right thumb backwards and my wrist broke; I was in so much pain that I fainted.

'Next they brought ECT equipment from the psychiatric ward and wired me up to it. They gave me electric shocks to my head, at very high voltage, several times. Each time I fainted, and each time they held perfume under my nose and threw cold water on me. The lieutenant and the two officers tortured me all day on the Thursday and through the night until the Friday morning. They hit me on the head with a cable until my eyes began to be affected.

'Then they made me undress to my underwear and tied me to a chair. First they burned my legs with cigarettes – look, I still have faint marks on my legs.'

She raised her dishdasha slightly and pointed to a mark on her left calf.

'Then they took off the rest of my clothes and the lieutenant raped me. The other two officers held my legs and my arms were tied to the chair. The lieutenant raped me four times and while he was doing it the others took photographs of me. When he finally stopped, I passed out. I don't know if the others raped me as well.

'When I came round I was lying on the floor, freezing cold, with my hands still tied to the chair. It was 2 o'clock in the afternoon and I was alone. Somehow I dragged myself over to a heater which we used to heat milk for the babies. I managed to light it to warm my hands and to burn the rope round my wrists. My hands got burnt a little, but I got myself free.

'At that moment, I wished I was dead. I felt terribly weak, not having eaten anything in two days, but all I wanted was to get out of there. I hadn't yet begun to feel the pain.

'I found some clothes belonging to a friend I used to work with and put them on. Then I opened the door, which led to a back staircase to the basement, and began to creep down the steps. When I opened the door at the bottom, by a strange chance I saw the officer who had offered to help me the first day. There were only a few Republican Guards left in the hospital by now, because most of them had gone on to attack Arbil and Sulaymaniyah.

'I told the officer that I was to be handed to Ali Hassan al-Majid when he arrived in Kirkuk that evening; so he should either kill me or help me. The officer took me to an office full of medical files and told me to stay in there and not open the door till he came back. After a quarter of an hour a soldier came, sent by the officer, with a spare Republican Guard uniform for me to put on. I put my hair up in the cap so that I looked like a man. Then he lead me through the basement of the hospital to a door into the yard outside. The soldier told me to get out of the grounds, take off the uniform and throw it away. So that is what I did; I had my friend's clothes on underneath.

'The officer had said the Republican Guard were advancing towards Arbil and Sulaymaniyah and that it would be safest for me to go to Baghdad, where no one knew me. The uprising had ended in Baghdad by now, the government were in control of the city and things were relatively calm compared to the situation in Kurdistan, so I decided to take his advice. The people of Kirkuk had mostly fled eastwards in front of the advancing Republican Guard and I saw almost no one on the way to Baghdad.

'I found out later that when Ali Hassan al-Majid arrived in Kirkuk, he knew about me and asked where I was. Luckily by then I was far away.

'When I reached Baghdad, I went to a hotel run by a very distant relative. When he opened the door to me, at first he was afraid. I told him I had come from Kirkuk and, reluctantly, he let me in. At first I told him lies, saying I had been sent by another relative whom I knew he was very close to. This set his mind at rest and he agreed to help me. The hotel was closed but there was a Turkoman soldier staying there and another man.

'Although I didn't tell them my story they must have guessed something had happened to me and they said if necessary they would hide me. I'm sure the torture showed on my face and hands. Once I had rested a little I began to feel the pain in my body and gradually it became so bad that I couldn't move from one chair to another.

'Eventually they told me I should show them my injuries, so that they could help me. They brought me a tube of ointment for the bruises on my legs and my face. They were afraid to take me to a doctor because it could have got them into trouble, but every morning before they went out they used to boil water for me to bathe, to soothe my body and help me to relax.

'I felt hungry and they fed me well, but I couldn't sleep at all.

'The Turkoman was older than the other two, about 40. He sensed that something awful had happened to me and wanted to know what it was. He said, "I am ready to help you in any way I can." He even offered to marry me, if necessary, to protect my honour. He was already married to a Polish woman and they had four children living in Poland. If it would help, he said, he would take me as a second wife and get me out of Iraq on his wife's passport. But I didn't want to go, because I was too worried about my family. I was constantly thinking about my brother and my father, who were both *peshmerga*.

'The Turkoman took me to see various doctor friends of his: an eye doctor, a skin doctor and a gynaecologist. They asked him who had beaten me up and he told them that my brother had done it; he said we had quarrelled about something. They were surprised and said my brother must be a savage. The eye doctor sent me to get a head X-ray. When he saw the results, he said that a part of my skull had been broken and that was why the vision in my left eye was affected. He said I had paralysis of the left pupil. I would have to go abroad for an operation and it ought to be done before I reached the age of 25 – I was 22 then. He said there was an 80 per cent chance of this operation restoring the sight in my left eye.

'When the gynaecologist asked me how I got all my bruises, I told him I had fallen down the stairs. The Turkoman had told this doctor that I was his wife. He did some tests and told me I was pregnant.

'This came as a terrible shock. I was very worried about my family's reaction. I thought my father would die if he found out and I didn't know what to do.

'I was always feeling dizzy at that time, and one day I fell down the stairs in the hotel, which brought on a partial miscarriage. But it wasn't complete and I went on bleeding afterwards.

'After nearly a month in Baghdad, I decided to go back to Kurdistan. The Turkoman took me to a hairdresser to have my hair cut short and dyed a light colour to disguise my appearance. He bought me new clothes, too, so that I wouldn't be recognised at checkpoints. Then we took a service taxi to Kirkuk. The Turkoman came with me and I got through safely. I felt very scared about being in Kirkuk, though, because everyone knew me there. When we arrived I said goodbye to the Turkoman and got a ride in a pick-up truck to Sulaymaniyah.

'When I reached Sulaymaniyah, the city was crawling with soldiers. I went to my uncle and his family. He let me in, but he made it clear that I shouldn't stay there: the army were looking for me.

'I heard that my family had fled to a place called Gokhlan near Penjwin, about two hours' drive from Sulaymaniyah. So I left my uncle's early the next morning and took a bus there. I also heard that my *peshmerga* brother had not been killed by the Republican Guard as I had feared, and I was overjoyed.

'By now the great exodus from the Kurdish cities to the border had finished, but there were a lot of people camping out in the mountains on the Iranian border.

'When I got to Gokhlan, I went to the *peshmerga* camp and asked for Zozik, a friend of mine. When he saw me he wept and embraced me, because he thought I had been shot dead. He tried to make me tell him what had happened to me, but I couldn't. Then a woman doctor came into the tent and I told her what had happened. She drew up some papers to send me to a hospital in Iran for treatment.

'I knew my brother was in the camp in Gokhlan, but I didn't want to see him. I was still in a bad state, my skin was inflamed, I had pain in my abdomen and I was still having difficulty walking.

'At the hospital in Iran the doctors told me that I was probably still pregnant and should have a pregnancy test and then might need an abortion. We didn't have enough money to pay for the abortion, so we went back to Gokhlan, to try to get help from one of the Kurdish political parties.

'Two days after we got back to Gokhlan, I met my brother. When I saw him, I collapsed. I was worried about what he might do to me, because he would feel his honour had been compromised by what had happened to me. Zozik had said that if my brother tried to do anything to me, he would defend me. But in a way I wasn't afraid of my brother trying to kill me, because I was feeling so awful that I didn't care what happened to me.

'My brother asked my friend what had happened and he told him everything. In fact, my brother's reaction was to blame *himself*, because he had left me behind in the hospital when he left with the group of *peshmerga*. To my relief, he didn't blame me for what happened at all.

'My brother raised some money and we went to Sanandaj in Iran, where I was given a dilation and curettage operation. Afterwards the doctors gave me some drugs to take and told me I needed to have three months' rest.

'When we got back to Gokhlan I was feeling really bad, so depressed and worthless that I decided to kill myself. I went to a high place in the mountains and tried to throw myself into a ravine, but Zozik stopped me.

'After this I went to Hero Talabani for advice, because I was in such a bad way emotionally. She suggested I go to Penjwin and work with Dr Runak, a woman doctor in the hospital there. I lived with Dr Runak and her family and she did her best to give me support; Zozik got a job in the hospital as a medical assistant. He and Dr Runak were very good to me and gradually I began to regain my confidence.

'It was at this time that I started giving myself pethadine injections as a sedative. Zozik tried to dissuade me, but I couldn't cope without them.

'After we had been at the hospital for about 15 months, Zozik and I got married and moved to Sulaymaniyah.'

The light was fading in the sky outside the window and it was almost dark in the room. After a pause I asked Jwan, 'And what about your family? Are you in contact with them?'

She was sitting with her arms wrapped round her knees, rocking herself gently to and fro. 'My relationship with my family has suffered a lot. My mother is always asking me what happened. All I have told her is that I was beaten on my hands and on my legs. One day I told a male relative the whole story, and he said, "Tell her, she is your mother and she will understand and forgive you." But I *can't* tell her. I can't even *look* at her!

'To begin with, I always felt ashamed when I saw people I knew. I wanted to be far away from everyone I had ever met. After a time, before I got married, I wrote a letter to my family and told them that I felt it was better that I shouldn't live with them any more. One of my sisters suspects what happened and keeps asking me. She says I have changed a great deal. I'm not afraid of her, because we're very close. Many times she has cried and asked me to tell her, saying it's better if I tell her so that if anyone says anything against me she can answer them back. But I haven't told her.

'My family are back in Kirkuk now, so I don't see them often. They have told the security people that they have disowned me as their daughter: they had to do this to protect themselves. They have to stay in Kirkuk because, as Kurds, they have no right to sell their house and shop, and if they left they would have nothing.

'I still give myself pethadine injections. When I can't get it, I feel bad and I get headaches.' She got up, opened the wardrobe and pointed to a pile of empty plastic phials on the floor. 'I must have given myself about 100 injections.

'Sometimes I wake up at night and can't get back to sleep and so I go outside and sit in the street till I feel better. I never sleep the whole night through; I wish I could. Every night for the first year after it happened, I saw the face of the lieutenant who raped me, lunging towards me in the dark.'

She was clutching her knees and rocking herself again.

'Nowadays I live in fear that my husband will leave me. His family are putting him under so much pressure.'

She paused and rested her chin on her knees. Her eyes were focused on the floor.

'My mother-in-law was very good to me until we got married. But she is a very traditional woman and she can't accept what happened to me. The thing I want most in the world is for her to forgive me.'

chapter seventeen

TWO VILLAGES:
BIYAARA AND TAWELLA

After meeting Jwan, I spoke with various other women who had been abused by the Iraqi regime. There was a lot of common ground between their stories. Only Skala and Jwan told me that they had been raped; but in the cases of two of the five other women I spoke to, their friends found the opportunity to tell me discreetly that they had been raped, although the woman herself had chosen not to tell me.

I talked with several women at Afretan, the KDP women's organisation. They had a large airy building on the same road as Zhinan, but about a mile out of the town centre. The feeling of the place was very different from Zhinan. The rooms were dingy and the walls were covered with portraits of Masoud Barzani, standing square and stocky in his brown *sharwal* and red-and-white turban. But the women were friendly and welcoming and very keen to ensure that I met as many of 'their' women as I did women I had met through Zhinan.

I was struck by so many posters of a male leader on the walls of a women's organisation. The office was dark and there was something about the way the Afretan women dressed – very conventionally and respectably, with a lot of the strong mustard yellow which is the KDP colour – which made me sense that their organisation existed mainly to support the KDP role in the nationalist struggle rather than to promote the interests of women. Whatever else may be said for and against each of the two main Kurdish parties, there is no doubt that the KDP is the more conservative on social issues. It was KDP policy not to support the proposed reforms to the family status law which were being put before parliament by women campaigners. The Zhinan women were strong nationalists too, and PUK supporters, but there was a distinct pro-women current in their activities and their thinking.

By the end of my second week in Sulaymaniyah I was feeling physically tired and emotionally drained. The city was like a hot sauna and I had been meeting two women a day, morning and late afternoon, only sometimes catching a siesta in between. Nazaneen was taking me to meet people most evenings and on my few free evenings I had either been at Sirwa's or had sat out in the hotel garden talking to Omar, Mohammed and Fareed.

I was exhausted by constantly trying to give my full attention to new people and by the often horrific things they were telling me; the torture stories, as they slowly sank in, were distressing me a great deal.

The night after meeting a woman called Nasreen at Afretan, I lay awake in the stiflingly hot room till long after midnight. She had told me how her torturers had tied her by her wrists to the ceiling fan and spun her round for up to 10 minutes at a time. Sometimes they had made her bend double, tied her hands and feet together and spun her.

There were two beds in my room and the fan hung in between them, motionless because the electricity was off. Now that I knew what the security people used fans for, I felt sick when I looked at it.

Always when I talked to women who had been tortured, I asked myself how I would have coped in the same circumstances. I am English and wasn't brought up in the culture of 'honour and shame' in which Kurdish women are raised; but English culture has its own concept of female shame, and I thought I could imagine roughly what it felt like to have been brought up as a Kurd. When I thought about the experiences of Nasreen, Skala and Jwan, a feeling of terrible darkness came over me. I had a sense of these women having their physical vulnerability as women twisted around their necks in a tight knot and I could imagine, in their position, wanting to die.

Torturers, whether they are Iraqis or Israelis, use their knowledge of where women are most sensitive emotionally and psychologically.

They know that 'shame' is a powerful weapon to use against women. They know that if they rape a woman she will feel dirty and worthless and that that feeling may never entirely leave her for the rest of her life, however much she washes her body and even if she doesn't fall pregnant with the rapist's child.

Both Afretan and Zhinan were still lining up women who had been in prison for me to meet and I was struck by how keen the women were to talk. I sensed they had a real need to be listened to, and wished I had the time and the energy to meet all of them. But I didn't have the time and I knew I was nearing the limit of what I could take.

On Thursday I woke feeling exhausted and queasy and decided to cancel the meeting I was meant to go to. I spent the morning sitting in a small patch of shade on my balcony writing my journal, and in the afternoon I slept. Mercifully the week was nearly over and Sirwa had suggested that on Friday we go on an outing to Tawella and Biyaara, two villages up in the mountains near the border with Iran, in the area her father came from. I still felt tired and sick when I woke on Friday morning, but I knew that it would refresh me to have a change of scene, and the air in the mountains would be cooler.

It was only just light when I got out of bed. The mountains behind the city were silhouetted darkly against the dawn sky. I had a shower and shivered as I was getting dressed, which delighted me: it was the first time I had felt cool since leaving London.

We drove to Sirwa's and found her waiting at the metal gate of her courtyard, mysterious and tired-looking in a calf-length black dress. She greeted us with her usual warmth and got in the back of the car beside me.

The streets of Sulaymaniyah were empty as we slipped out onto the road which goes southeast to the small town of Said Sadeq and then divides, one branch going to Halabja and the other to the mountain villages of Biyaara and Tawella. Both villages had been destroyed during the Iraq–Iran war and the inhabitants had been forced to flee. Now people were moving back and re-construction work was getting under way.

We reached Said Sadeq in half an hour; Fareed drove slowly down the main street, where the market was beginning to come to life and people were walking in the road. Donkeys were pulling carts and traders were laying out quantities of purple Halabja grapes on cloths on the ground, next to piles of green and purple figs and huge red tomatoes. I opened the window and caught a breath of cool air, mingled with a whiff of frying meat.

After Said Sadeq I began to feel more awake. We were climbing slowly and the small cultivated fields on either side of the road were full of shadows and subtle colour: yellowy-green grasses, deep blackish-green bushes and patches of brown dry earth. Water sparkled in a ditch and a little river wormed slowly between tall rushes. In the distance, in the direction we were heading, the grey-brown ridge of mountains was entirely in shadow. And the narrow white road catching the first rays of the sun was empty but for the occasional pick-up truck coming the other way, with black-clad passengers squatting in the back among sacks of flour and rice.

This was the first time I had been out in the country early in the morning, at the time when shadows still lay on the land. In a couple of hours the ferocious sun would chase the shadows away and bleach all real colour out of things. I was surprised by the beauty of this landscape, which until the uprising in 1991 had been part of a closed military zone stretching from near Sulaymaniyah to the Iranian border. Although we were climbing slowly, the land on either side of the road was flat, with little fields and small one-storey mud brick buildings here and there and the odd solitary figure standing very still. In the soft early morning light it was wonderfully lush and fertile.

Sirwa had nodded off to sleep beside me.

'So beautiful,' I murmured to Mohammed, who was sitting on my left. His eyes, like mine, were wandering across the rice fields and the corn, along the little paths beside the ditches, into the deep shade beneath a fig tree. 'Very...' he replied. 'Why don't you stay here, Teresa, in the countryside?' He was murmuring into my ear, very low so that no one else could hear. 'I'll build you a house, and buy you a cow and some chickens and a donkey...'

I smiled. At that moment I felt I could happily spend a year here, sitting out in these early morning fields, painting.

We were climbing quite steeply now and the road began to zig-zag towards Biyaara. It was eight thirty and I was ready for breakfast. Fareed parked the car at the top of the village and we got out, stretched and walked slowly down the main street. The light was pure and clear and the mountain air was deliciously sharp, piercing down into the bottom of my lungs. I blinked in the light after the relative gloom of the car.

The main street was lined with one-storey stone shacks housing shops and tea places, and teeming with squarely-built men in turbans. Wood smoke spiralled up through holes in the café roofs, scenting the air. There wasn't a woman in sight.

Omar led us into a tiny café where the air was alive with flies zipping round in mad circles. One side was open to the street from waist height, with wooden poles supporting a wicker roof. Omar ordered tea and gestured to Sirwa and me to sit on stools in an unoccupied corner. Male eyes fixed on us as the elderly owner filled our tiny glasses with sugar and melted it with scalding red tea from a large blackened kettle. He served us fumblingly, anxiously, laying wet saucers on a ledge in the wall, setting tiny teaspoons on them and finally the steaming glasses of tea. It was funny, I thought, how older Kurdish men rarely eyed me up but rather would fuss over me as if I were a rather fragile child and they my grandmother. Perhaps it was the legacy of feudalism and the sight of Sirwa and me in our Western dresses reminded him of some middle-class Kurdish household he had worked in as a boy.

Mohammed and Omar stood a little distance from us, nonchalant, drawing on cigarettes and sizing up the Biyaara scene with the reserve of newcomers in a strange town. Fareed had stayed with the car, feeling it was too risky to leave it unattended. This was Hawraman district, where the dialect was so different from the Sorani Kurdish spoken in Sulaymaniyah that they could barely understand what people said. Besides, Biyaara was a stronghold of the KDP, and Omar and Mohammed were *peshmerga* of the PUK.

From the shade of the café and through the cloud of flies I looked out into the pure morning light and watched the men of Biyaara going by. They were strolling up and down, standing in groups and squatting on low stools outside the café opposite, smoking and drinking tea. All were wearing the rich, chocolate-brown wool *shar-wal* which seemed to be the local costume and there were some striking faces among them. Very few appeared to have work to do, yet they stood and moved with the confidence of men who feel that the morning, and the world, belong to them. I wished I could make myself invisible and perch in that café with a drawing book for a couple of hours.

After we had drunk our tea we walked up to the mosque at the top of the village. It had been damaged in the Iraq–Iran war and was being rebuilt with Saudi money. The new shell of the building, on the original site, was white and full of light. There were new mosaics on the floor; an old man showed us the gravestone of Sirwa's great-grandfather, who was from Biyaara.

'You know, Teresa,' Sirwa said in her husky voice, 'in the old days people used to come to Biyaara for psychological and physical cures, from a sheikh who is now buried here.'

She gave some alms to the old man, for the mosque; in exchange he gave her four little strips of dark green cotton a few inches long. She gave one to each of us with a giggle, saying, 'It will bring you luck and protect you.' I took mine eagerly, hoping it would indeed protect us on the road ahead. Omar and Mohammed accepted politely but walked away smirking. They are cynical socialists, I thought to myself. I kept my little green strip about my person until the end of my stay in Kurdistan.

We got back in the car and continued on up the mountain road, reaching Tawella about 10.30. The hills up here were brownish green, round and dotted with ancient trees and the remains of old stone buildings. As we rounded the last bend before the village, Sirwa pointed out the tree-like figure of an Iranian soldier standing on the ridge opposite: that was the border, no more than 3 miles away.

Tawella was a thriving village of 5,000 people, built on a hillside with a stream running down the middle beside the road. Everywhere you looked you saw the legacy of war: breeze-block walls tilting at precarious angles under roofs that had cracked and collapsed in the middle; piles of rubble and buildings that had lost their top storey or one of their walls. But equally, everywhere you looked you saw the work of rebuilding being carried on with energy and love. There were people everywhere and, unlike in Biyaara, we saw women and girls squatting outside their houses baking bread and cooking on open fires. The displaced people of Tawella had started to trickle back here in 1991, so there had already been two years of reconstruction. Traditionally the houses were built of stone and timber with a mud and straw roof, but concrete was being combined with the old materials to build the new homes.

As we wandered up the unpaved road that was the main artery of the village, a woman in a red *dishdasha* called to us from her courtyard at the top of a steep bank. 'Sirwa! Come up and visit me!'

Her name was Yasar and she was the Tawella representative of Zhinan. Yasar and her husband had returned to Tawella in 1992 and had built themselves a two-roomed house with a view across the valley to the Iranian hillside opposite. They invited us in and we climbed up to the house and sat down in their new front room, the walls of which were raw cement with a large window cavity with wrought iron bars painted green. The air was cool and fresh and there were no flies: it seemed the perfect place to live in summer.

While our hostess made tea on a samovar, her husband brought handfuls of soft, bitter walnuts and a hammer to crack them with. We leaned against bolsters spread along the wall and Sirwa chatted with Yasar while Omar, Mohammed and I talked with her husband. He asked if I had a camera and we took photos of each other and of their sweet, sticky-faced, three-year-old daughter, who was lolling against her father's knees and eyeing us warily.

In a corner of the room stood an old-fashioned treadle sewing machine. Yasar worked as a seamstress when she could and was trying to set up a sewing workshop for other women in Tawella, to make garments which Zhinan in Sulaymaniyah would then sell. Earlier we had seen a man in the village weaving woollen cloth in a little workshop, producing a long strip of fabric about 8 inches wide on a traditional loom, while an old woman sat on the floor at his feet spinning the wool. Yasar's husband now showed us a new *sharwal* in grey wool which she had made from this kind of fabric. The narrow strips had been sewn together to give the voluminous width for the upper part of the trousers. I was fascinated to examine it and see how it was made. The legs were sewn together at a surprisingly wide angle, as if the legs of Kurdish men turned out like Charlie Chaplin's. It seemed a strange design to me, but when Mohammed tried it on over his jeans, the *sharwal* hung beautifully. He put on the matching tunic as well, which was slim-fitting, V-necked and long-sleeved, and wound a 15ft long flowery cotton cummerbund around his waist. Now I knew what he must have looked like when he was fighting up in the mountains. The sombre grey wool suited him perfectly, and when he moved the clothes looked as natural on him as his jeans and T-shirt had a minute earlier.

After leaving Yasar's we wandered back through the village, peering into a shop where espadrille-like canvas shoes were being made by hand, and buying a kilo of grapes from a man at the side of the road. We washed them in the stream and were about to get back into the car when Sirwa spotted some teachers from her school, who had come to Tawella for a Friday picnic. They had spread themselves under a group of tall trees at the entrance to the village and were finishing a large lunch of *dolma*, bread and salad. The group was all women, mostly in their thirties and forties, and they were clearly enjoying themselves. We went over to say hello and they immediately insisted we sit down and share the remains of their meal. After we had eaten there was tea served from a giant thermos flask and then the dancing began. I leapt to my feet and joined the line of women, holding hands and shuffling over the rough ground, while the others sang and clapped their hands.

chapter eighteen

DEMOCRACY IN KURDISTAN

In one corner of the hotel garden a semi-circular concrete stage with a strange sculptural backdrop spilled onto the lawn, from which in more affluent days bands had played nightly for parties and weddings. Now, in the evenings the waiters would carry a television set to the stage and often at midnight a handful of lonely men would sit facing it on chairs dotted around the garden. From my balcony the television looked ridiculously small in the centre of the stage, but the volume was often loud enough to prevent me sleeping.

The light began to fade at about six in the evenings, turning the mountains behind the hotel a gorgeous gold beneath the pale mauve sky and by seven it was completely dark. Little groups of men would gather at the tables scattered around the lawn, drinking beer, smoking and talking before they ate.

One night I had supper with Omar, Mohammed and Fareed at a table on the hotel side of the garden. As we sat down I glimpsed a group of smartly dressed, important-looking men conferring in low voices at another table. Their guards, heavily armed, sat smoking nearby. 'That's the Minister for – and the Minister for –,' Fareed told me in a low voice.

We had to wait an unusually long time to be served, and while we were waiting I noticed that all manner of delicacies and dishes which I had never been offered were being carried to the Ministers' table.

After we had eaten our meal of chicken, chips and salad and the dirty plates were piled up with raw onion and fragments of bread, we pushed back our chairs. Omar and Mohammed were smoking and picking their teeth, I was drinking tea and Fareed was telling me about his experiences during the Gulf War. From the war the conversation turned to class dynamics in Kurdish society, sparked by an occasion earlier that week when Sirwa had invited me to eat dinner at her aunt's house. The aunt was wealthy and lived most of the time in Baghdad, but kept a house in Sulaymaniyah for holidays. It had a flush toilet in the bathroom, at least five rooms and we had eaten sitting on chairs at a dining table.

When we were at her own house, Sirwa always offered Fareed, Mohammed and Omar food and drink, but on this occasion they had been left to wait for us in the car and the aunt had only invited them to come in and eat quite late in the evening after we had finished. I had felt bad about this, but being a guest with people I was meeting for the first time I hadn't felt able to say anything. Besides, I had been curious to see what the aunt would do. The men had politely but adamantly refused her belated invitation.

Omar was picking his teeth, examining the tooth pick and looking at me by turns.

'D'you understand why we didn't accept the invitation to come in and eat?' he asked.

'Well, it was a bit late to invite you, wasn't it?'

'Exactly. We would have accepted if they had invited us at the beginning, to eat with all of you, but what is this asking us only after they've finished, to have the leftovers?!' He clicked his tongue disgustedly. 'That's the *bourgeoisie* for you, Teresa. Do you know what "*bourgeois*" means?' It was the same word in Arabic as in English. 'It means people who have *everything*. In this country people who have nothing will always share with you what they have; but the rich won't!'

'That's the same the world over.'

'In Kurdistan the rich, and the big politicos, they're all the same. All *bourgeois*!' He jerked his head disgustedly in the direction of the important-looking guests seated across the garden. 'These so-called "ministers" and "MPs". They sit in their big houses and in smart restaurants eating the best food money can buy, while we *peshmerga* go out and give our lives for the Kurdish cause.'

'Do you include Talabani in this?' I asked after a moment.

Mohammed and Omar looked at each other. I could see that they were weighing up how frank they could be with me.

Omar frowned. 'No, not Talabani,' he said hesitantly. 'Talabani is good... He's OK.'

'Barzani, Teresa,' Fareed joined in, 'Barzani is *bourgeois*. Big, rich family, from years back. Like Margaret Thatcher's family. Same thing!'

I got the point and decided not to tell Fareed that Margaret Thatcher was the daughter of a grocer.

'Like the way this hotel is run,' Omar went on, spitting out the words with the energy of strong disgust. 'Abu Sana, the guy who owns it, you've seen him strutting round the foyer sometimes in the mornings. He's a very rich man, a millionaire maybe. And does he ever do a stroke of work? No way!'

I nodded. Abu Sana had said 'hello' to me once or twice and had graced me with a lecherous smile.

'And d'you know what the staff in the hotel get paid? We asked one of the waiters, you won't believe it. Five dinars a day! That's all!'

Five dinars was the equivalent of 10 pence. If they worked seven days a week it would come to 150 dinars a month, or a dollar – which would scarcely keep you alive in present conditions in Kurdistan.

'And board and lodging,' Mohammed added dryly.

'Oh yes, and board and lodging. But no, you can't call it "lodging". They have to sleep in the corridors, haven't you seen them, Teresa, sleeping on the floor in the corridors in the mornings?'

On days when I'd got up early I had indeed seen men rolled in blankets lying in the corridors in the upstairs lobby. They always had the blankets pulled over their faces and I hadn't appreciated that they were the men who waited on us in the restaurant during the day.

'And look, here on the bill.' Omar picked up the bill for supper and held it out to me. 'Ten per cent added on for service, right? Should go to the workers, shouldn't it? But does it, hell! It goes straight into Abu Sana's pocket. That, Teresa, is democracy for you in Kurdistan!'

chapter nineteen

'THIRTY YEARS OF WAR'

Sirwa dyed her hair jet black, was very slim and smoked quantities of long, thin cigarettes. We saw a lot of each other throughout the time I was in Sulaymaniyah. Sometimes I would go and sit with her during the long hot afternoons in the cool kitchen of the little house she shared with her sister. Once she said to me, 'How could I not smoke, after 30 years of war? So many people have died and I am still alive!'

Sirwa had a slow, thoughtful, expressive way of talking with a musical lilt in her voice. She elongated her vowels as she talked – 'smo-owke', 'yee-ars', 'stee-ill' – in a way that I loved to listen to. And she drew pensively on her cigarette as she spoke, sitting in her armchair with her thin legs crossed elegantly under her long black skirt.

Sirwa almost always wore black and it suited her well. She used to say, 'So many people die-ed, always wearing bla-ack, so why no-ot?', holding her head on one side, exhaling smoke and smiling faintly in resignation. 'Now I became used to it, I don't cha-ange no-ow!' She often giggled at the end of her statements, and as she did, sparks of light would crackle in her dark brown eyes. The giggle meant different things at different times: sometimes it was self-deprecating, sometimes it expressed amusement, sometimes it was a thin cover for despair.

Sirwa's family were from Halabja. She was indirectly descended from Lady Adila, a nineteenth-century aristocrat who had become head of her tribe after her husband's death and whose sons had been officials in the Ottoman administration. Sirwa's mother had worn traditional Kurdish dress. She showed me a black-and-white photo of her mother dressed in pantaloons, a long overdress and a jacket with a head-dress consisting of a scarf and various gold chains studded with coins hanging across the brow and down the sides of the head.

'All the time, my mother in the house, in these heavy cloth-es. Nothing to do, just giving orders to the servants!' Sirwa thought it must have been an awful life.

Sirwa's family had experienced a long series of tragedies and disasters since she was a child. Most of her relatives had died or been killed and they had gradually lost all their property, lands and wealth. Thirty-five members of the family had died in the chemical attack on Halabja in 1988.

'Thirty years of war,' she kept repeating. 'From 1961. In the sixties and seventies, the Kurds at war with central government. Then the Iraq–Iran war, fought on our doorstep. Then in '88 Halabja, in '90 the Gulf War, in '91 the uprising!

'We used to wish just to survive,' she had told me that morning, sitting in the office at Zhinan. 'Just to stay alive, that was enough. But now, since this freedom, we want it to go on! We want to stay with this freedom for as long as possible.'

As she spoke I could feel the incredible weariness in her spirit. I could see it, too, in her skin, which in bright sunlight looked yellow and wrinkled. She drew on her cigarette with its yellowy brown filter, smiling sadly with her beautiful eyes and looking into the distance somewhere in the middle of the floor.

'I always wanted to be a lawyer,' Sirwa confessed one night while we were drinking tea after supper at her house. She hadn't told me this before, but it made perfect sense; it was very easy to imagine her as a lawyer, even down to the detail of being a woman who looked good in black. She was clever, she was thin, she had a restless, energetic mind; she liked to argue.

'But my uncle wouldn't let me. He said I should be a teacher.'

'Why was it up to your uncle?'

'My father died when I was a child. He had a heart attack. It was very terrible, he loved me very, very much. After that it was for my uncle to decide, and he said I should be a teacher.'

'What would your father have said about you being a lawyer?'

' "Very good", my father would have said. He would have let me do anything I wanted.'

Every time I saw Sirwa she told me things that I wanted to write down: anecdotes, bits of history, stories about her girlhood, tales about being a headmistress in Sulaymaniyah during the 1970s and 1980s. What she said fascinated me, partly because she had lived through so much and was good at putting things into historical context, and partly because she was an aristocrat *manquée* who had become a socialist at an early age and whose life had been an extraordinary journey from wealth and power to relative poverty. A few days before I left Sulaymaniyah I went over to have lunch with Sirwa, taking my tape recorder. After lunch we went upstairs to her dark old-fashioned sitting room, and I asked her questions and she talked.

'Lady Adila was the co-wife of my maternal great-grandmother. As I told you, Lady Adila had two sons, Taher Beg and Ahmed Beg. Both of them were poets. Taher Beg was visited by Major Soane, the British traveller who travelled through the region in the 1900s disguised as a Persian peddler and who later wrote *Through Mesopotamia and Kurdistan in Disguise*.[1]

'My maternal grandfather had five wives. One of them was Jewish, and till now many of her relatives are living in Israel. My maternal grandmother died when my mother was a small baby, so she was brought up by the other wives. They all lived in one very big house, I remember it well, it had 65 rooms – it was a castle, not a house! The biggest house in Halabja. When Halabja was controlled by the British army in the 1920s, they made this house their headquarters.'

I found it hard to imagine a house of this size or age in the Halabja I had visited in May. We had approached the city down a long straight road which ran across a strikingly fertile plain. Weeds and wild flowers were growing waist-high in the verges. We passed rice

---

[1] *Through Mesopotamia and Kurdistan in Disguise*, London, John Murray, 1912.

paddies and orchards and fields where the growth was so abundant that nature seemed to be over-compensating for the poison that had been spilled on the land only five years before. But on the outskirts of the city stood derelict streets of damaged grey breeze-block buildings, with missing roofs, buckled metal girders and weeds growing in the window cavities. I saw rusting abandoned tanks and the carcass of a missile. It was the most recent and by far the worst war damage I had ever seen, and it chilled me. I was assuming that very few of Halabja's original population of 70,000 had returned to live here; but as we got nearer to the centre of the town, it became clear that many had returned. Although the wreckage had not been cleared away, the streets were alive with people and many of the less damaged houses were inhabited. Washing was hanging out to dry and small children were playing in the rubble.

'The big house was destroyed in 1959. At the time of the Iraqi Revolution in 1958, most of the revolutionaries were Communists, so they wanted to take away the property of the ruling class. Many times the Communists tried to attack the house and destroy it. So in 1959 my grandfather decided to destroy it himself, and he blew it up.

'My other grandfather had a very great house in Sergat. There were three parts to the house, one for guests, one for women only and the other for men only. In front of each part there was a great pool, and huge fir trees. It was a very nice place! That house was destroyed in 1979, when the Iraqi government wanted to make all the borders empty of people, and they gave us nothing for that, no compensation. We got nothing!

'I was born in Kirkuk in 1946. When I was a child we were always, always, moving from one place to another, because my father was an officer in the Iraqi army. When I was very small, we were transferred from Kirkuk to Basra. We were there for three years, then we came back to Baghdad and I started school, at a private school for army officers' children. They were teaching us French and English and all our teachers were nuns, some were French and some were Arabs from Baghdad. It was a mixed school, my brothers went there too.'

'When you were in Baghdad, were you conscious of being a Kurd?'

'Of course! Most of the other children were Arabs. Sometimes they were pulling the sleeves of our coats and telling us, "*Hawat shi-maal kullish kawi* – the wind of the north is very strong." '

'Meaning that there was a lot of revolution in the north?'

'Yes ... and then when I was in the fifth class in primary school we came back to Halabja again and I finished the sixth class there. That was a very nice time in Halabja, with my father, and all the house so busy, all these servants, and coming and going and coming always, as if it was not a house, but a hotel! The visitors used to pay me lots of attention and I was always on my father's shoulder. I was *very*, very close to my father! And when my father died, my uncle loved me very much, my great uncle, and he began to do the same with me. Both of them spoiled me!' Her voice lit up in delight.

'More than they spoiled your brothers?'

'Yes, they didn't like my brothers, I don't know why, but they liked me very much, I was the favourite... And I lost them all, every one of them!'

Sirwa's voice rose to a wail.

'I lost my great uncle, I lost my father, I lost my mother, I lost my grandfather. Now I have none, just only my brothers and sister... Thank God, till now we are a foursome, we are all still living!'

'Tell me about your father,' I asked after a pause. 'What were his politics? Did he want to be in the Iraqi army?'

'My father was a nationalist, a great Kurdish man, although he was working in the army.' Sirwa spoke with pride. 'He was speaking six languages fluently: Kurdish, Arabic, Persian, Turkish, English and French. He was made an officer because of the special relation-ship between the heads of tribes and the English administration. They always chose the officers from the sons of the heads of the tribes and these kinds of people. But he was a nationalist. He was a special friend of one of the Kurdish officers who were executed in 1946 for going with Barzani to Mahabad.'

In 1946 a group of Iranian Kurds established a short-lived Kurd-ish Republic in Mahabad in Iran. Mullah Mustafa Barzani, the father of Masoud Barzani and co-founder in the same year of the Iraqi KDP, led a group of fighters to Mahabad to provide military support to the rebels.

'My father died when I was 15, of heart attack. After that we lived on his pension; and our lands were still producing something. We had great orchards, of walnut trees and grapes and pomegranates. You know, in Hawraman there is a very nice walnut, we tried it in Tawella. We never used to buy these things, until the chemical attack on Halabja! Until '88 we had a lot of people working on the land. I had 36 sheep at one time! Every year they decided not to give me my share of the money, they used to say, "We are going to buy a sheep for you, in order to make the flock bigger." But all of the sheep were killed in the chemical attack, none of them was left. And all the land was poisoned...

'In the year my father died, 1961, the Kurdish Revolution began. Halabja was attacked for the first time by the Iraqi army in 1963. Jet fighters came and bomber-aircraft; *peshmerga* came to our house in the middle of the night and told us, "You should run away from here." We fled to the Iranian border, to a very small village called Hanagermala. We stayed there for three months: my mother, my sister, my brothers and I. When we came back to Halabja we found everything in our house had been completely destroyed by the army. Completely.'

The last word came out in a whisper.

'Although your father had been an officer in the army?'

'Yah, he was dead! And so they didn't care for anything... The walls were still remaining, but they had even burned my father's bedroom. The bedding was still on the bed, but it was smouldering! We decided to come to Sulaymaniyah and the army made documents for us to travel with them. If you go in normal times, it is only one hour from Halabja to Sulaymaniyah, but it took 15 days with the Iraqi army because they were searching for *peshmerga* along the way. At night we slept on the road or in the vans. It was winter and very cold.

'When we reached Sulaymaniyah we found most of our friends and relatives had been arrested. We had left our mother in Halabja, to take care of the few things we had managed to salvage from the house. My sister Saywan had stayed with her. So it was just myself and my two brothers: I was 17 and they were a bit younger. And when we reached Sulaymaniyah, we found no one there whom we knew. *No one.*

'I had a gold necklace which was decorated with King George coins and I had to slowly sell them. With each gold coin I bought 5 gallons of kerosene. It was a very severe winter that year, with 6 feet of snow on the ground in Sulaymaniyah. In the spring, in April, the government began to negotiate with the Kurdish leaders again, and they began to open the roads and to break the economic blockade which had been put on Kurdistan by Baghdad at that time.

'We travelled to Baghdad and reached my grandfather's house in late April. I enrolled in school, but the school year was nearly over – I don't know how I managed to pass the exam! We spent that year with my grandfather in Baghdad and came back again the following year to Halabja to see our mother. We decided with her to move from Halabja to Sulaymaniyah because there was always fighting in Halabja, guns and clashes and we children were still young. So we rented a house here in Sulaymaniyah and left Halabja forever.

'My uncle said I should become a teacher, so I went to study at the University of Baghdad, together with Nazaneen. I finished college in 1968, the year of the second Ba'athist coup. In 1969 I applied for a job and they sent me to Halabja to be headmistress of a school. At that time the KDP were strong in Halabja and the city was always being bombed. I was the headmistress of my school and I didn't know what to do.

'The school wasn't very big: 254 pupils, but I had never even worked as a teacher before. The reason they made me head was because they didn't have anyone else to be headmistress there. Halabja was my home town, and the law is that you should work in your home town for three years first, and then you can choose anywhere you want after that. Halabja was always under attack and nobody wanted to work there. It was very dangerous: people might be killed if they went there. But *I* could not refuse, so I went. Luckily, after three months they brought me back to Sulaymaniyah, and I began to teach "Principles of Teaching" at the Institute of Education. I had still never taught, myself! It's funny, no one does the job he wants. I very much wanted to teach, but they wouldn't let me.

'After I had been at the Institute for a year, they decided to close it, because there were so many teachers that they didn't know where to put them. Then I began to teach in four schools at once: one was the school I am in now, one was a boys' secondary school where I taught four classes, one was Nazaneen's school and the other one was Sulaymaniyah High School for girls. I was out from seven in the morning till seven in the evening, every day. I liked it, because you know I like always to be busy, not to think of anything, just to forget...

'At that time I was living with my mother. When I was teaching in all the different jobs, my mother was not so happy about it. She wanted me to get married. She was always saying to me, "Look at yourself, you are getting old, put on some make-up, wear this, wear that!"

Sirwa laughed.

'You know that here usually marriages are arranged. They go to the mother and tell her, "We want your daughter for our son." Sometimes when I came home from work I saw visitors sitting with my mother and, if I didn't know them, I knew that that was what they were there for. I would call my mother to me and say, "Tell them I am sleeping, I am not coming out!" It would be the mother and the sisters who came, not the young man. Usually the young man does not come until everything is arranged. And then, if you don't like him, it's too late!'

'What did you feel about getting married?'

'I wanted a love marriage, but I didn't find one. All my life I wanted that. Better to have no marriage than to have an arranged one.' Sirwa sighed as she spoke.

'You know, when I was still a young girl at school, I had a friend who was much older than me. She decided to teach me socialist ideas. I was from a tribal, land-owning, aristocratic background, and whenever I came home and began to talk about what she had taught me, my mother became so angry with me!' She laughed. 'Always quarrels in our house, because of that. She made me read Marx and a book about socialism, about social class. I read it when I was 13 or 14 and I became a socialist. We had many servants in the house, men and women; but my mother didn't let them eat with us or even sit with us, even when they came into the room where we were sitting, they should remain standing. When I told them, "Come and sit down," my mother became angry. "Why are we eating such-and-such and they are not eating with us?" I used to say – they ate less good food than us – "They are human beings like us, why are they not eating with us?" – so she became angry. Again and again, always quarrels!

'But then when I went to college, I began to change my ideas. Little by little, I left my socialist ideas completely and I began to be with PUK. Not PUK as such, there was not PUK at that time, it was Talabani and Barzani at that time, but it was the beginnings of the PUK. There were two factions within the KDP, one Barzani and one Talabani. I was with Talabani, because he was young and I was young! And I began to like his ideas very much, and what he said. It was not quite socialism and it was not quite – how do you say it? – capitalism, but something in between.

'I became a member of the PUK in 1982. We were working in the underground struggle, during the Ba'ath era, from '82 to the uprising in '91. I was an underground activist. But you know, at that time, none of the members of the party knew each other. We had numbers only, not to be known. It was very disciplined. We remained like this till '91.

'In the uprising in '91, on the third day, Nazaneen and I went to the Red Security Building to see what had been going on there. This was after the *peshmerga* had taken control of the building. When we went in we saw so many horrible things. We saw the execution room and we saw the isolation cells and we saw the torture tools and we saw many items of women's underwear, here and there in different parts of the prison, in the yard and in the corridors, everywhere. Many people had been in before us, but we saw women's clothes in every part of the building. And we saw blood on the walls. Till now sometimes at night I dream of it. I often have bad dreams.'

Suddenly she sighed deeply and her voice dropped to a whisper. 'He's like a nightmare, he's always sitting on our chest! I don't know when will he go; can you tell us?' She turned to me with a look of desperation.

'You know,' she went on after a moment, 'he is not the only one who has tortured the Kurdish people like this. Every time when a new government came to power in Baghdad, they promised to do something for the Kurds, and then after, when they became strong and stable, they rejected the Kurds. They began to fight us. Again and again and again. Always the same...'

'Do you have any hope of it changing?'

'I don't know. Sometimes I feel I have many great hopes and sometimes I am very hopeless. Sometimes things go so slowly – that makes you hopeless. But sometimes when you hear promises from our leaders, like Talabani for example, you become hopeful. That's the way, so we are just sitting and waiting. And we hope that Saddam will not be able to come back again. If he does come back, I promise I am going to kill myself, that's my idea. I am very much rather killing myself than seeing him again in Sulaymaniyah, around us, taking us over.'

In 1991, when the uprising in Sulaymaniyah was crushed, Sirwa and her sister fled together to the Iranian border near Tawella. They walked for three days and three nights, without food or drink, along with thousands of others who were going the same way. But when they reached the border, neither of them had the heart to go to Iran, a country which they both disliked intensely. They stayed on the border for a few hours and then turned round and walked all the way back home again. That took another two or three days and nights; and still no food and no sleep.

'When we reached Sulaymaniyah we were very afraid. There was nobody, the whole town was empty. Everybody had left! When we came to our street, we saw just two soldiers and all the houses were empty. We came into our house and hid ourselves.'

'Did you have food?'

'No food. Everything in the house had been looted. There was nothing and we were afraid to go out. And we were so tired! We were sick with exhaustion.'

'What did you do?'

'We stayed in the house for a week. We didn't light lamps and we pretended we weren't there, because we were afraid of the soldiers knowing. None of our neighbours was here. It was very strange, Sulaymaniyah was like a ghost city. Then, after a week, the people started to come back. And we went out to the *souq*, which was beginning to start up again, and bought rice. Just rice, that was all we could get, but we had to eat something.

'I was very ill after this. When things got closer to normal, I went to Baghdad to see doctors and they did tests on my stomach, which was giving me trouble. They said, "Nothing wrong with you. Only you need rest." They told me I should take one month of complete rest.'

'And did you?'

She smiled. 'No, of course I did not. But, gradually, I got better.'

chapter twenty

'NO ELECTRICITY, NO GAS, NO PARAFFIN...'

Nazaneen and Sirwa had been friends since they were in their teens. Often when I called on Naza at lunchtime Sirwa would be there already, sitting in an armchair near the open door of the living room, drawing thoughtfully on one of her long, thin cigarettes.

The difference in their two personalities was striking when I saw them together in Naza's house: Sirwa sitting very still, with the strong presence of a woman who was always busy with her own thoughts, occasionally calling out a deep-voiced 'Naza!' with a ripple of amusement in her eyes when she remembered something she wanted to tell her friend; Naza more flamboyant, a larger physical presence, moving around the room, talking, making tea and being called away to the telephone every two minutes.

Sometimes, instead of going back to the hotel to sleep in the afternoons, I would stay at Nazaneen's and try to work on my computer. After lunch she would usually go out to a meeting or the Zhi-nan office and for a brief period the house would be quiet.

One afternoon I was sitting on the floor in the less-used of the two front rooms with my laptop perched on a little wooden table. A lorry was unloading something in the road and a group of young boys were banging dustbin lids and shouting to one another; Naza had gone out, Drakushan was lying down. The wealthy neighbour from Baghdad whose daughter had got married the previous week was on the phone in the kitchen, sleek as usual in a matronly navy blue dress with a little white collar, her short grey hair crisp on her neck and her curious but warm eyes wandering over me as I walked into the kitchen to fetch watermelon and cold water.

I was enjoying the hush and looking forward to an hour writing my journal, but before I had put the watermelon down on the floor Drakushan appeared and followed me into the room with an envelope full of photographs.

Drakushan usually held herself slightly aloof from the constant comings and goings in the household, and gave the impression of being very strong. Her black hair was henna'd in the front and she wore it tied back in a pony tail, revealing fleshy, dark cheeks. She was a striking woman, with playful, intelligent eyes and a heavy, voluptuous body. She carried her weight well and I had often watched her moving around the house very slowly in her dark red dress, like a large cat who is feeling the heat and anyway sees no reason to hurry.

'Look, Teresa, this is sports day at my school,' she began in her husky voice, taking out a bunch of photos of uniformed girls standing in rows in a sports ground and pulling me down onto the sofa beside her. I started to leaf through the photos, but suddenly Drakushan changed the subject and began to tell me how hard life was for her and Nazaneen. I realised with shock that she was on the point of tears.

She turned to me and said, 'No electricity, very hot!' in a dramatic tone, as if it were a new development. The electricity had been off more often than it had been on during the last three days.

'In winter, very cold!' she went on, holding her face near to mine as a sad, desperate look clouded her eyes.

'No electricity, no gas, no paraffin ... nothing!' She looked at me intently.

'Five gallons of paraffin, 140 dinars! And our salary, only 280 dinars!'

'280 a month?'

'A month, yes. We buy paraffin, 140 dinars, and it lasts for half of one week!' She looked even closer to tears and pretended to shiver, hunching up her large frame into a miserable bundle.

'God, don't you get ill?'

'Ill, yes, now I am very ill!'

'Now?' I had thought she might get ill in winter, not that she looked ill now.

Drakushan wrinkled up her face into a frown. 'My back, my baby place' – she gestured at her womb – 'my tummy – all of me, I am very ill now.'

This was startling, but when I thought about it I wasn't really surprised. Conditions in Kurdistan were not conducive to good health and the medical care available was very rudimentary. The lack of exercise and the heat alone were enough to make me feel run down. But somehow I had been under the illusion that the women I was meeting felt well in this environment.

'It wasn't like this before,' Drakushan went on. 'We had money, we went out for visits, to England in '77, to France twice, to Italia, Bulgaria, Romania, Turkia...' She brightened momentarily. 'But now, what can we do?' She was gazing at me with a look that beseeched pity and support.

But before I could say anything the door opened and the wealthy neighbour came in to ask Drakushan to help her with something in her house across the street. She got up slowly, flashed me an intimate little smile and went out, shutting the door to the garden behind her, making it dark and hot in the room. I looked through the photos desultorily, then slid down from the sofa to my place on the floor beside the computer. And now the only sounds were the niece Jwan washing up in the kitchen and the soft voice of Sirwa talking on the telephone.

chapter twenty-one

A DESERT CITY
AND AN IRAQI TANK

Nazaneen was urging me to visit Sumud, a collective town where a lot of *Anfal* widows lived. It was in Germiyan, the southernmost district of Kurdistan.

She warned me that it would be even hotter in Sumud than in Sulaymaniyah. Germiyan means literally 'hot place': unlike the rest of Kurdistan it is mainly flat, being the beginning of the vast desert plain which extends all the way to Baghdad, 2½ hours' drive further south. The front line between the Kurds and the Iraqi government ran just south of the town of Kifri, half an hour beyond Sumud. Omar had relatives in Kifri and said that if we went to Sumud, we should go and visit them.

I was alarmed at the idea of going so close to the front line, but after Omar and Mohammed had said half a dozen times, 'Don't worry, we'll take care of you,' curiosity got the better of me. I didn't intend to stay very long, though; Kifri had a checkpoint through which people entered 'Free Kurdistan' from the government-controlled areas, and was sure to be full of government agents.

Naza didn't have time to accompany us, but Bayan, a young woman who had been translating for me, said she would try to come. We were planning to stay overnight, so she would first have to convince her parents that she would be safe with us and that nothing compromising would happen to her.

We set off at around 7 a.m. on a Monday morning, skimming out of Sulaymaniyah in a hired Landcruiser with Najad, a Zhinan guard, at the wheel. The men sat in the front, Mohammed with his arm around Omar's shoulders, and Bayan and I rode behind with the Kalashnikovs, the bottles of water and the bags.

Bayan was small with dark, shoulder-length hair and lovely skin. She was 27, single and taught English in a secondary school. Her spoken English was not perfect – not surprisingly, since she had never travelled abroad and had been taught by non-native speakers – but when she didn't know how to translate something, she would always struggle to find a way of explaining it. She had been shy and reserved when she first started translating for me, but now we had grown to like each other and were good friends. She was a believer, her brothers were Islamicists and we had had some interesting talks about religion.

There was little traffic on the road as we wound through the low rocky hills for the first hour going south. By 8.30 we were passing the sparkling waters of Dobendikan Lake, which runs east all the way to the Iranian border, and the little town of the same name. South of the town the road began to twist and turn through a strange, flat landscape which Mohammed said was the beginnings of Germiyan. A river ran close to the road on the left, flanked by deep beds of rushes – *Awa Spi*, or White Water. Both Omar and Mohammed had been fighters here and they turned round to explain to me what difficult terrain it was for guerrilla warfare. The country was bare and open, making it easy for planes to fly low and almost impossible for fighters on the ground to hide.

'The *peshmerga* who fought here had it harder than anywhere else in Kurdistan,' Omar remarked. 'Imagine, trying to move around in this terrain when the government have tanks, planes and helicopters.' He tutted disgustedly and shook his head. 'And this is the poorest part of Kurdistan,' he went on, 'the people of Germiyan have nothing … but you won't find better people *anywhere*!'

An hour later we were driving through a desert of sand and scrub, passing the occasional flock of goats tended by a ragged child. We passed the sign to the old town of Kalar and a few minutes later, a quarter of a mile from the road, a vast city of flat-roofed concrete bungalows appeared, partially hidden in a cloud of dust. Najad turned onto a dirt track and headed across the sand.

As we approached I could see that the wide, unpaved streets of Sumud were laid out on a grid. Driving down the first one, we came upon a group of women crowding together at a corner. When we got closer I saw water gushing out of a stand pipe several feet above their heads, and the women jostling to fill tin cans. Some had already finished and were balancing their cans on their heads as they stood talking. They turned and stared at us as we passed. Apart from the group of women, the streets were deserted and extraordinarily desolate: high concrete walls fronted the houses, so that all you saw was the wide channels of churned-up sand rippling like flood water between the rows of houses, and electricity pylons rearing up like masts.

Naza had given me a letter to Amina, the woman in charge of Zhinan in Sumud. Amina, she had said, would take care of us, and we could sleep at the office. The Zhinan building was a two-roomed house in a walled yard of baked mud, with a narrow third room tacked on the side. Although the gate was open the house was deserted when we arrived, but a neighbour sent a child to fetch Amina. She came within a few minutes, read the letter and welcomed us dutifully.

Amina hadn't been expecting us and looked harassed; her thin face was lined and worn-looking, although I was sure she was no older than me and might even be younger. Her blue Western dress seemed out of place in Sumud, suggesting she was educated and had once lived a better life. I had the feeling that we were just one more thing to cope with and understood Amina to be asking Najad in Kurdish why Nazaneen hadn't come with us. He explained that Naza was busy, whereupon Amina shrugged her shoulders resignedly and said she would arrange for some of the Zhinan women to come in and cook us lunch.

Within 10 minutes three women in *dishdashas* and headscarves had arrived and were discussing food with Amina, Omar and Mohammed. One of the three, who was unusually tall, caught my eye. She was wearing a silvery-black headscarf and a long dark blue *dishdasha*, and reminded me of Renaissance paintings of the Virgin Mary. Her dark brown hair hung down at the front in waist-length plaits.

When the women had left for the *souq*, Amina, Bayan and I retreated to the cool of the office, which was furnished with several battered armchairs and a sofa. When I explained why I had come, she mentioned that the tall woman, whose name was Rowsham, had lost both her brother in the *peshmerga* and her husband in the *Anfal*, as well as being arrested four times herself. I said I would like to talk with her, and Amina agreed that when the women got back from the *souq*, Rowsham could sit and talk with me while the others made lunch. While we were waiting, Amina began to tell us about Sumud. I soon realised that she was very shy and wondered if that was why she would have preferred it if Naza had come with us.

'Sumud,' she said softly, 'was built by the Iraqi army in 1987. When it was finished, the government announced that the people from all the villages of Germiyan should abandon their homes and come and live here. Many villagers thought it was a plan to kill them and they didn't come. But later in the year, the villages near the main road to Kifri were destroyed by the government and so their people were forced to come to Sumud. When they arrived, they were given houses. The government waited another year for the people from the more distant villages of Germiyan, far from the main road, to follow the ones whose villages had been destroyed.

'But the people didn't come and so in 1988 those villages became a target of the *Anfal* campaign. Thousands of villagers disappeared and the villages were dynamited and bulldozed into the ground. The women and children who didn't disappear ended up in Sumud, but in worse conditions than those who had come here voluntarily in '87.'

When the women returned from the *souq*, Rowsham came into the office, introduced herself and sat down in an armchair. She was the tallest Kurdish woman I had seen and her lean face with its Roman nose was strikingly intelligent. She sat with her legs crossed in her long blue *dishdasha*, with one bony knee pointing through. I noticed her hands: long and thin, with agile fingers. She wore a simple gold wedding ring.

After we had been talking for some time, a little girl with brown hair streaked with blond came in and climbed onto Rowsham's lap. She was wearing a red cotton dress and although she looked about five or six, she cuddled up to her mother like a toddler. Rowsham sat with her legs apart and let the little girl sit between them, cradling her in her arms. Her elegant hands came together in front of the child and although the focus of her attention scarcely wavered from what she was telling me, she was entirely there for her daughter at the same time.

'I am from Duanzaymam,' Rowsham began, 'a village close to Kifri, about 10 minutes from the main road. I came here after my husband was taken in the *Anfal*. When I was a girl in Duanzaymam we weren't so poor. We didn't have our own land, but my brother was a construction worker in Baghdad and my father worked as a labourer on other people's land and the produce was shared. He grew wheat, okra, tomatoes and barley. We were eight in the family, six sisters and two brothers, and we had our own house.

'I'm 40 years old and I've been arrested four times for helping the *peshmerga*. The first time was in March '79, when I was 26, when they arrested me and my father because my brother was a *peshmerga*. My brother was in hiding at the time and they didn't find him.

'It was lunchtime and we were about to eat when three cars and more than 20 security men came to the house. They took me and my father to the security building in Kifri, held us separately and questioned us. The officer who questioned me accused me of helping the *peshmerga* in many different ways: cooking for them, washing their clothes, and so on. It was true that I had helped my brother and his friends, but I denied it because I thought if I confessed they would kill me without more ado.'

Rowsham gazed at me steadily as she spoke.

'When I failed to confess, they took me to the torture room. The first thing they did was to beat me with a thick cable, till I bled. Then they got some pliers and pinched the flesh on my arms, leaving blue bruises. And then they tied my wrists to the ceiling fan and spun it. After 10 minutes I passed out.

'I was taken to be tortured three times in the first 24 hours. They took my watch away when I arrived at the security building, probably to disorientate me, but I'm sure the torture was more than two hours each time. They would start off by questioning me, but when I didn't confess they would get fed up and send me to the torture room.

'They called me lots of bad names and said that if I didn't confess, all their men would rape me. They said that was "their right". It terrified me when they said this, but what could I do? In fact it turned out to be only a threat and they didn't carry it out. After they had finished torturing me they put me in a small cell with my father. They left me there for the next three days and nights, till they released me.

'We gave them money and once a day they brought us something to eat – usually a sandwich of egg or *kubba*. They brought us water to drink, but no tea.

'Every day they took my father out and tortured him. He was tortured worse than I was.' She pulled a face and her eyes met mine. 'They didn't release him till eight days after they released me ... and he had been so badly tortured that he couldn't sit down.'

Rowsham's daughter was still lying in her arms and was becoming fretful. Rowsham unbuttoned her *dishdasha*, pulled out her breast and offered it to the child, who accepted eagerly. I noticed little gold ear-rings in between the wisps of her red-blond hair.

'What's her name?' I asked.

'Nasreen. She is seven but she still likes to have a suck.'

'Do you have any other children?'

'I had another baby daughter, but she died at 20 days. That's all, I don't have any sons.'

She looked very sad and I wished I hadn't asked.

'I was released after only four days because a relative of ours knew someone in the Ba'ath party and he went to them and said he would guarantee my behaviour from now on. He had to pay them some money, of course. Before I was released the security people said that if I told anyone I had been tortured, they would arrest me and torture me again. Then they let me go and I went back to my village.'

'And did you go on helping the peshmerga?'

Rowsham broke into a huge, knowing smile which lit up the room. 'Of course! My brother used to tell his *peshmerga* friends from other villages where we lived and that his sister was ready to help them in any way she could. I would dress as a man and go out with them at night, leading them by special routes to avoid being caught by the army. I knew the area like the back of my hand. I was still single at that time. I had to keep on helping the *peshmerga*, because we Kurds have been so badly treated.'

Cooking smells were wafting through the open door and Amina called us to come and eat in the other room. Bayan, Amina, Mohammed, Omar, Najad and I sat on thin mattresses round a cloth laid out on the floor for our meal of rice, fried eggs, stewed okra and bread; Rowsham and the two cooks ate theirs outside.

When we had finished Bayan got up quietly and went out. She reappeared a few minutes later with her head wrapped in a towel and whispered to me that she was going to pray in the office. She had wet her hair as part of her ablutions. When she had finished, Rowsham, Bayan and I went back into the office and Rowsham carried on with her story.

'I was arrested again in January 1980. One day the *peshmerga* asked me to take a message to someone who was working for them underground in Baghdad. The message was written on a small sheet of paper, rolled up into a tiny ball, so that if something went wrong I could swallow it. I was stopped at the checkpoint outside Kifri, on the road to Baghdad. I hadn't disguised myself and they recognised me, so I immediately swallowed the ball of paper. They asked me why I was going to Baghdad and I said I was unwell and was on my way to see a doctor. They took me to the security building in Kifri and held me for a week. Luckily I had warned my family about what I was doing and had told them that if I was caught this was what I would say.

'At the security building, they asked me again why I was travelling to Baghdad. Then they told me they wanted me to work with them as an informer. They wanted me to continue my work with the *peshmerga*, but to inform the security about their activities. They offered me a lot of money. They said, "These *peshmerga* are not true Iraqis, they are not good patriots." They also tried to tell me that the *peshmerga* were working as agents of the Americans.

'The man who was questioning me was the same one who had questioned me before. He told me that the *peshmerga* were "liars" and "thieves" and that their work would not endure, "unlike that of those who work for the Iraqi government". Their work, he said, would be "honoured by posterity".

'They didn't torture me this time, or hit me. All they did was to call me bad names and swear at me, and after a week I was released. When I got home, I discovered that my family had bribed the head of the local police to get me out. He was an Arab and he had influence with the security people. My family had given him some sheep and he had gone to the security people and told them he could guarantee my good behaviour in future.

'A week after I was released, the *peshmerga* leader came to me and asked what I had done with the message, and I told him the story. Then I agreed to try again to go to Baghdad. They wrote the message out again and screwed it up into a tiny ball. I set off for Baghdad via a different route this time and delivered the message successfully! And I returned home safely without being arrested.'

Rowsham's eyes gleamed and her silver headscarf glittered as she smiled at me. Nasreen was sleeping now in her arms.

'The next time I was arrested was at the end of that year, in December 1980. This time I wasn't interrogated or tortured. I was taken to prison in Ba'qouba, an hour's drive from Baghdad. They held me for 15 months, until March 1982, without any family visits and without taking me to court to be sentenced.

'There were about 50 women in the prison. Most of us were Kurds, but about five were Arab. It was a special prison for the relatives of *peshmerga*. My dad was held too, in the men's wing. He was 60 when we were arrested and he went blind in there. All 50 women were held in one room, in very crowded conditions. They fed us, but the food was very bad and often we couldn't eat it. They used to give us half a roll and soup for breakfast. Usually the food was several days old when they gave it to us. They used to give us lunch at five in the afternoon, when we'd had nothing since breakfast. Dinner was at 1 a.m., by which time most of us were asleep. Then they would change the mealtimes suddenly, to confuse us.

'The toilet was next to the room we were in, and the smell was terrible. I think the conditions in that place were specially designed as a kind of psychological torture. The worst thing was when they let us get very, very hungry and then brought us food which was bad.

'Most of us were in poor health. Our skin turned yellow and sometimes we vomited due to the smell from the toilet. We got head lice. The only way to wash was using the water pipe in the toilet. In the winter it was very cold, so we were glad to be crowded together, but in summer the heat was terrible! There were no fans and all we had to drink was the water from the pipe in the toilet.

'There was one young girl who was taken out of the cell for questioning every month, and when they brought her back her teeth were broken and she seemed to be in another world. She wouldn't speak, she would just sit and stare into space. She was about 16 or 17, a school girl. The other prisoners and I thought, from the state of her, that she had been raped. We used to try to comfort her by saying that if she had been raped, it wasn't her fault. But she would never say what had happened.

'They released me, and my father, in March 1982. The reason they released us was that they had killed my *peshmerga* brother. He was killed in combat in a village and they flew the body to Chemchemal.' She paused, and her face clouded over. 'The government people tied his body to their car and drove around the town, dragging him behind to make an example of him.'

'When they had finished they buried him by shovelling earth over his body. We waited three weeks and then we went at night, took the body and buried him in a village. You see, when someone was martyred, the government usually tried to prevent the family from holding the traditional three-day wake. After my brother was killed and my father and I returned to Duanzaymam, the security people watched us for three months to make sure we didn't hold a wake.

'Everybody in Duanzaymam knew I had been in prison for 15 months. When I went home my friends and close relatives treated me well, but people who didn't know me so well avoided me, because they assumed I would have been raped in prison. People knew I had been arrested several times although, in fact, I hadn't been raped.

'In 1986 I married my cousin. He wasn't at all worried by my having been in prison and he said he trusted me completely. People said that I was marrying my cousin so that no one outside the family would find out what had happened to me. It was upsetting, of course, when they said these things, but not everyone was like that.

There were other people who were very good to me. My husband was from Qani Kadr village, in the area of Touz Khurmatu, and I went to live with him there. The day we married, he said to me that if I had been raped, he wanted to take on this "scar" too, so that he could share the burden of it with me.

'Look, my daughter has a photo of her dad in this locket round her neck and a photo of my brother who was martyred on the other side.'

Rowsham lifted the locket chain gently over her daughter's head and passed it to me. Both of the tiny photos showed men with dark hair, pale skin and moustaches. The brother had a look of anxiety in his eyes.

Rowsham sighed deeply and went on, 'In April '88 my husband was taken in the *Anfal*. Nasreen was only 11 months old then and I was pregnant. After he was taken I stayed in Kifri for six months, in hiding. Then when the general amnesty was announced, I was free to go and I came here to Sumud with my daughter.

'When we first came, I took in sewing to make money, but for the last two years my right shoulder has been so bad that I can't sew. It has never been right since my first arrest, when they hung me from the fan. If I use my right arm a lot, at night I am in so much pain that I can't sleep.

'Now I live in the house of my other brother and I am supported by organisations that give money to the victims of the *Anfal*.'

It was well into the afternoon by the time Rowsham finished telling her story. Amina had arranged for me to meet some other women, so, although Bayan and I were feeling weary, we walked through the hot sandy streets past another gushing standpipe to a house shared by three sisters. A crowd of children followed us and hung over the wall of the yard as we sat on the porch and talked with the women.

We returned to the Zhinan building at dusk and spent the evening sitting out in the yard, resting and talking. Rowshan and her friends reheated the leftovers from lunch and this time they ate with us; we sat on the baked mud floor with our backs resting against the wall of the house next door.

Najad had driven the Landrover into the yard for security and a youth with a Kalashnikov was posted at the gate. Rowsham said I was the first foreigner to visit Sumud for as long as she could remember. I sensed danger, but knew I was not the only one taking a risk: Kurds who guard, drive or tell their stories to foreigners are all seen as targets by Iraqi government agents.

After our meal we sat drinking tea in the warm dark air by the light of a hurricane lamp. Rowsham presented a striking sight in the semi-darkness, sitting cross-legged on the ground with Nasreen asleep in her lap and a Kalashnikov in her hands; the long thin metal barrel of the gun echoed the angularity of her lean, determined body and the crescent-shaped magazine echoed the curves of the sleeping child.

At 11 that night Bayan and I changed into *dishdashas* and climbed the outside staircase to the roof, where the Zhinan women had laid two mattresses side by side for us. Their own beds were only a few feet away, to afford us company and protection. I looked out over the benighted shanty town from the edge of the roof. Perversely, the electricity had come on just now and lights glowed eerily in the deserted streets. We lay down under a bright half-moon and talked in whispers till we fell asleep.

I woke with the sun to find the women already cooking breakfast in the yard and the men washing beside the rusty water tank. I decided to risk a shower, which meant carrying half a bucket of water into a little concrete shed in the yard and throwing it over myself with a plastic cup. I had learned in the last few weeks how little water I really needed to keep clean and that a shower with six cups of water was infinitely preferable to no shower at all.

Bayan prayed in the office and then we sat down to a breakfast of more reheated leftovers and freshly fried eggs.

We exchanged warm good-byes and left at 8 a.m. on the road to Kifri. As Sumud disappeared into its cloud of dust I felt a sense of relief, but at the same time satisfaction that I had experienced what it was like there. I couldn't imagine a bleaker or more soul-less place to live. I felt how terrible it would be to have lived all one's life in a Kurdish village and then be forcibly transferred to a place like Sumud. It had not escaped me that the Arabic word *sumud* literally means 'endurance'.

*   *   *

It was a clear, lovely morning and the road was empty apart from the occasional truck coming the other way. In the sandy scrub by the side of the road we passed herds of goats and sheep tended by little boys. It felt strange to be driving through land which was flat as far as the horizon and I remembered with a shiver of apprehension that, if we kept going south for a couple more hours, we would reach Baghdad.

On the outskirts of Kifri we passed palm trees, tall and thin and graceful, the first I had seen in Iraq. We came upon a cattle market on some flat open ground by the side of the road, and decided to stop and take a look. Pitifully thin cows were standing with flies crawling over their faces, while men haggled in little groups. Several of the men were wearing white *dishdashas* and *keffiyahs* hung over their heads and shoulders. It reminded me of Egypt.

'First time I've seen an Arab in ages,' Mohammed muttered, and I realised slowly what was different: Kurdish men didn't wear *dishdashas*, or *keffiyahs* hung like that. We were on the fringes of Arab Iraq. We got back into the car and drove slowly into the town. It too looked very different from any other I had seen in Kurdistan. The houses were old one-storey stone dwellings built close together, each one with its own walled courtyard. It reminded me of the backstreets of small towns on the Nile delta.

I was nervous now, knowing we were so close to the Iraqi army. It had been foolish to get out of the car at the cattle market, thereby announcing my presence.

Omar thought his cousin would know women I could talk to in Kifri so we drove to his house in a side street near the town centre, where we were given the usual warm welcome. The house had four rooms and was cool and spotlessly clean, with a baked earth courtyard where the women cooked and made bread and did the washing. Inside there was a tall refrigerator and a functioning fan. There were no power cuts in Kifri, it being close to government-controlled territory. The cousin's wife made tea while Omar and he went out and Bayan and I chatted with her mother-in-law, who was rocking their newborn baby in a traditional wooden cradle at the back of the room. The men returned an hour later with three women cloaked in black *abayas* with a clutch of six children between them. They were *Anfal* widows and their self-appointed spokeswoman angrily told me the now-familiar story of how their village had been surrounded by the army, the men taken away, never to be seen again, and the women imprisoned for six months. I wrote it all down and took photos of the women, but the story no longer shocked me, although it confirmed to me how enormously thorough and far-reaching the *Anfal* operations had been.

After the widows had left, I wandered out into the yard, hoping to give Bayan the chance to pray. Lunch was bubbling over an open fire in one corner, fanned by the cousin, who was squatting down beside his wife.

Mohammed was perched at the top of a flight of outdoor steps.

'Teresa, come!' he called down to me softly.

'What's up there?'

'Come and see.'

It was very hot now and I climbed the steps slowly, not wanting to get dizzy. At the top I followed Mohammed across the flat roof of the house, past a washing line to another half flight of steps. This led to a vantage point from which you could see up and down the street.

Mohammed skipped ahead of me, then lent down, took my hand and helped me to the top.

'Look,' he said, pointing south down the street towards the heat-shimmering horizon.

I followed the line of his extended arm and saw the glimmer of something silver. It was about half a mile away, but even from this distance it looked three times as wide as the street.

'What is it?' I asked. I thought I knew, but I wanted him to say.

'A government tank.'

chapter twenty-two

THE POMEGRANATE ORCHARD

I had been in Sulaymaniyah a month and, although I wanted to stay, it was time to move on.

On the morning before I left, I went to say goodbye to Sirwa at her school. We sat on an old rickety sofa in the large, bare staff room and promised to write to each other. I was on the point of tears, but Sirwa told me sternly 'Don't cry, Teresa, ple-ease!' Mohammed, standing at a discreet distance, shot me a look which said more gently 'Try not to, it'll upset her.' In a culture where almost everyone is standing on a mountain of pain and grief, tears are dangerous things, not to be given in to lightly. Sirwa said that she and Naza had been talking about me: 'Why do you come, people like you, and then you go again? Wha-y?' Her voice expressed both affection and reproach.

I felt terrible, knowing that she meant it kindly but unable to forget what she had said to me a few days earlier: that if Saddam reoccupied Kurdistan she was going to kill herself.

At one o'clock I was lying on the couch in Naza's living room with my head resting comfortably on her fat pillow, waiting for her to get back from school. We were to have lunch together for the last time and then say goodbye; I would leave for Shaqlawa in the morning. I could hear Drakushan's soft voice chattering away to Mohammed in the kitchen and it didn't matter that I didn't know what they were saying. The big knife went thud, thud as Drakushan cut up tomatoes and Mohammed's voice rose at intervals, laughing, questioning. Drakushan had told me he was like a brother to her now, having eaten in her house and accompanied us on picnics so many times.

Outside the lunchtime street was quiet. It was 2 October and the new school term had begun. Drifting on the edge of sleep, I heard the outer gate rattle. The door opened with a soft click and Naza walked in.

'*Choni*, Teresa, *chaki*, how are you?' she sang as I slowly sat up. She was wearing a white muslin blouse with a large collar. It looked really pretty on her and I said so, but she stood in front of the mirror and said, 'But I am fat!' with disgust.

She said she would like to be like me and I said, 'No, you are beautiful as you are, I am too thin!' and we both wrinkled up our noses and laughed.

Omar and Fareed had already returned to Arbil, leaving Mohammed and I to travel on public transport. I felt sad as we slipped out of Sulaymaniyah in a taxi in the cool of the early morning. Saying goodbye to Naza, Drakushan and Sirwa had made me realise how fond of them I had become. They were like a new set of older sisters I had acquired all at once and it felt too soon to be leaving them. The uncertainty of the situation in Kurdistan made it worse – no one really knew what the future held and, although things felt calm, it was possible that acute danger was lurking close by. And once I left the city I wouldn't be able to reach them by telephone and could only send letters if I found people travelling to Sulaymaniyah to deliver them.

We stopped in a queue for petrol and I opened the door to get a breath of air. The windscreen of the taxi was badly damaged, with cracks fanning out in a spider's web from what looked like a bullet-hole.

While we waited Mohammed took out his pack of Aspen, gave one to the driver and took one for himself. This was a regular ritual on every long taxi ride; it was unthinkable in Kurdistan to smoke without first offering your cigarettes around.

Our driver was a stocky man with square shoulders and a black moustache. He had nodded at me when I got in but made no attempt to converse. Mohammed and he exchanged remarks from time to time and after the usual polite interval I understood him to ask Mohammed where I was from and what I was doing in Kurdistan. It always felt strange to be discussed in Kurdish, but by now I had got used to it. On mornings like this, when my mind was full of thoughts and feelings, not being expected to talk had its advantages.

We had left Sulaymaniyah by the road which went to Shaqlawa via the east of Dokhan Lake. We were well out of the city now, riding up a flat valley bottom at the foot of a ridge of mountains. Flanks of pink and gold rock rose steeply behind the cultivated fields like the rippling folds of a full skirt, towering into sharp, jagged peaks. The ridge ran almost the whole way to Shaqlawa and for an hour my eyes wandered over the sunlit rock face, delighting at the way the stratum of pink blended seamlessly into the stratum of yellow-gold below. I wished we could stop and spend a couple of days exploring on foot, but nobody walked for pleasure in Kurdistan and the lower slopes were likely to be littered with unexploded land mines.

Shaqlawa was a 'massif', a small leafy mountain town with a pleasant climate which had once been a holiday resort to which Jordanians, Gulf Arabs and wealthy Iraqis had come in search of relief from the summer heat. Now most of the hotels were occupied by Shi'a Arab refugees from the south, who lived as guests of Ahmed Chalabi, the leading Arab figure in the Iraqi National Congress (INC), the umbrella organisation for the Iraqi opposition.

I had arranged to stay at the English Language Resource Centre (ELRC), which was run by an Australian Christian whom I had met on my first visit to Kurdistan. She had appeared out of the night like a guardian angel in a moment of crisis, when we had arrived in Shaqlawa to find that the hotel we were to stay in was closed for maintenance. We were sitting in a roadside restaurant in the main street wondering what on earth to do, when an old silver Mercedes drew up, driven by a middle-aged *peshmerga*. Diane had gaily wound down the window and called out, 'Hi there! You guys need some help?'

Diane and her group, who were mainly Americans, had settled in Shaqlawa after the uprising and were running English courses for local people, with – if their library was anything to go by – a heavy dose of Christianity sprinkled in. Shaqlawa had a sizable Christian community, although I learned later that one of the local priests had forbidden his congregation from going to the Centre.

The ELRC was in a large white-washed building constructed on three sides of a square with a neat green lawn in the centre. It had something of the look of a Spanish colonial dwelling and the atmosphere of a friendly mission. A Kurdish family lived in an apartment at the back of the building and their teenage sons worked as caretaker-guards.

When we got out of the taxi at the gate of the ELRC I caught the smouldering scent of autumn in the clear air. The guards told us that Diane was away for the day, but they knew I was coming and showed me to a guest room at the back of the building, facing the family's vegetable patch. After leaving our bags we walked down the steep hill into the town, enjoying the rustling of leaves from the hundreds of trees, and ate lunch at the same restaurant where I had first met Diane. It was large and airy with a glass front onto the deserted main street and the tables were empty apart from a handful of *peshmerga* eating noisily in one corner. We ate a heavy plateful of beans and rice and sauntered back to the Centre. Shaqlawa was much cooler than Sulaymaniyah, but still it was an effort to walk uphill in the afternoon sun.

Inside the guestroom it was delightfully cool and the decor was fresh and calm. The walls were white-washed and there were white-and-turquoise spotted cotton covers on the beds, with matching curtains. Two single beds were arranged along the walls like sofas, scattered with turquoise cushions, and a pair of bunk beds stood in the corner.

I opened a little cupboard and found everything you could hope for in an English holiday cottage. There were little plastic jars labelled 'TEA', 'SUGAR', 'MILK POWDER', 'DETERGENT' in neat handwriting. There were tins of processed cheese and raspberry jam. There were red plastic picnic plates and cups, and even two jars of peanut butter. I had an odd feeling as I opened the containers one by one that this was a foretaste of the hygiene-obsessed, meticulously labelled world I would be returning to in under three weeks' time. It gave me a sinking feeling, whispering that my adventures were drawing to a close, but I pushed the feeling away and tried the gas ring. It was going to be a treat to have my own stove and kettle and be able to drink tea independently of the outside world.

It was hot and I wanted to sleep. Mohammed was lounging in the doorway with his back to me, blowing smoke rings into the garden. He was to sleep at night in one of the language labs, but it was locked during the day.

'You can sleep here if you want,' I said, gesturing at the bed nearest the door. 'We'll leave the door open.' I knew I had to be careful about what people thought, but it seemed ridiculous, when there were four beds, that he could not use one of them.

'OK.'

I climbed onto the top bunk as he finished his cigarette, threw it into the vegetable patch and removed his trainers.

I woke at 5.30 to the waning light and the beautiful mountains shadowy and lovely. The day was fading into night so fast that I could hardly see the objects in the room. I could just make out the bulk of my suitcase in the middle of the floor like a sleeping animal, the sharp plane of the open door and a carrier bag at the foot of the bunks. Mohammed was awake and we lay for a while murmuring conversation, until thirst dragged me up to make tea. When it grew completely dark I lit the oil lamp and we sat at the little table in the window.

On the far side of the vegetable patch there was a corrugated iron door in the fence with 'STOP' daubed on it in white paint. I had glanced at it with curiosity when we arrived, wondering where it led. The next morning as I was washing some clothes at the outside tap an old woman appeared and began tending the vegetables. Mohammed was squatting in the sun playing with the cat and the old woman pointed to me and said, 'Why don't you take her into the orchard to eat some fruit?'

The corrugated iron door swung open easily and we stepped into a new and marvellously private world. The orchard sloped down the hillside towards the town, but although you could hear cars you couldn't see the road and you could scarcely see any buildings. It was the first time in Kurdistan that I saw the possibility of being out of doors yet unobserved: the perfect place to sit, write my journal and recuperate from the hectic month in Sulaymaniyah.

The trees were laden with pomegranates – bulging, leathery orange fruits that pulled the branches towards earth like the udders of an unmilked cow – and there were apple trees bearing large, yellow, unripe apples. Mohammed went to get his cigarettes, leaving his gun cocked at my side with instructions to fire should a snake come up close. But snakes were unlikely, we agreed, as the soil was damp and it was cold – by Kurdish ideas of warm and cold. For me the weather was perfect, fresh and sunny, and the morning light shone dappled on the leafy ground. I spread out a blanket and opened my journal. Behind me, further down the slope, a large white chicken with a red headdress was pecking and rustling under the trees.

Mohammed came back, knelt down beside me and crouched over the earth to open a pomegranate. The orange skin was tough and he had to use the muscles of his hands to break the fruit into segments, opening out each one, folding it back on itself and sucking out the crimson seeds as the juice dripped like blood onto the carpet of clover.

I spent two whole days sitting in the orchard, drinking in the privacy and peace, stepping back into the outside world only briefly for meals. Intermittently I wrote my journal, but much of the time I watched the chickens strutting about, listened to the creaking of branches and chatted with Mohammed.

On the second afternoon we left the orchard to eat lunch in one of the restaurants on the main street. We ordered rice, stewed okra and salad, but they brought too much and one untouched plate remained on the table. It was a beautifully arranged salad of diced cucumber, tomato and lettuce, ringed with slices of a giant purple radish.

Mohammed was telling me about his experiences as a *peshmerga*.

'When I started I was very young, 18 or maybe 19. To begin with they don't let you do very much. Just you go with them and when they are doing operations you stay some distance away and you wait for them and you watch.'

'What kind of operations? I don't know anything about guerilla warfare – what sort of things do they do?'

Mohammed hesitated for a moment.

'Look, here is Touz,' he lifted his gun from under the tablecloth and laid it on the table, 'and here is the main road,' his file of bullets parallel to the gun, 'and here all this area is mountain.' He drew the plate of salad to within 6 inches of the bullets.

'Germiyan?'

'Germiyan. There is a village, far, far from the road, and in the village there are *peshmerga*.' He placed the salt cellar close to the salad.

'OK, so here is Touz,' he lifted up the gun and replaced it, 'and here is the main road,' touching the bullets, 'and all this is mountain,' lifting up the salad and putting it down again carefully in the same place, 'and here,' he picked up some slices of the giant radish and began to lay them out on the table at right angles to the file of bullets, wending between the bullets and the gun, the main road and Touz, 'and there is water, Awa Spi, remember?'

I did remember, it was a poetic name.

'A lot of water?'

Mohammed thought for a moment.

'A lot in winter and a little in summer. So, here is Touz and the *peshmerga* are in the mountains, far from the government. But by night the *peshmerga* are in control of Touz, it's only by day that the government are in control. So the *peshmerga* do their operations by night, on the main road, outside Touz. There's a checkpoint controlled by the *peshmerga*.'

'How do they control it?'

'Just like any checkpoint: they stop the cars, they ask for ID. If it's just a Kurd and the ID is in order, they let them go. If it's Military Intelligence personnel, they take them in.'

'How do they know someone is Military Intelligence?'

I had a mental picture of an Arab male in a black leather jacket at the wheel of a Landcruiser, being asked for his ID in the dead of night.

'They know from the ID.'

'They carry ID which says they are Military Intelligence? Surely not!'

'They carry two IDs. One is normal, the other one says Military Intelligence. If the driver is Arab and he shows the normal ID, they ask for the other one.'

'And if he doesn't produce it?'

Mohammed smiled. 'They search him.'

He patted himself under his arms with both hands and down his body.

'And if he's armed?'

'They take the weapon off him. The *peshmerga* at the checkpoint are all armed. They take what they want.'

'And if they find he *is* Military Intelligence?'

'They take him, they question him, they beat him.'

Momentarily I was taken aback at the idea of Kurdish *peshmerga* actually having the upper hand over Iraqi security personnel. But when I thought about it, it made sense: if the *peshmerga* hadn't sometimes had the upper hand, they would not have been able to maintain a war against central government for the last 30 years.

Next Mohammed described the operations the *peshmerga* carried out inside Touz, although he hadn't participated in many of these.

'Why didn't you?'

'I was afraid.'

A rare admission and I liked it.

'I was very young and my family were in Touz. And they had had so much hassle from the government, first because my brother who was killed had been a *peshmerga* and then because of me.

'By day the government controlled Touz and by night we did. If there were police, they were in their building and not on the streets. They were very afraid of the *peshmerga* and they knew we controlled the city by night. The government were very afraid of us.

'A small group would go into Touz on foot, walking from the mountains, entering the city after dark. They wore *keffiyahs* wrapped round their faces with only their eyes showing. There were people working with the *peshmerga* inside Touz, underground activists. They would be waiting for them.'

'So what would they do in Touz? Give me an example.'

Mohammed lit a cigarette and looked at me while he thought.

'OK, here's an example. It's not a real operation, just an example of the sort of thing they used to do. Imagine a Ba'athist officer, let's call him "Wathban". Married with a child. He comes home in the dark to his nice house, by car and with a gun in his hand, but without guards, and he finds himself surrounded by four *peshmerga* who are hiding in the garden or just outside in the shadows. And as he opens the door already there are two guys inside who have frightened his wife and who immediately disarm him and tell him they are taking him away. Wathban pleads with them, "Don't kill me, don't take me, please, please, my wife, my child!" but they take him and they march him through the night to their base far away in the mountains.'

'How many hours' march?'

'Four, five, six – it depends.' Mohammed drew on his cigarette. 'When they reach the base they take him into one of their buildings and lock him in the outhouse, and then they interrogate him.'

'Do they hit him?'

'If he doesn't talk, sure they do.'

'What with?'

'With pieces of wood – but he talks, because he's terrified; and they take his ID off him and keep it, because later it may be useful; and then they send an old man to Touz, to the government, to say, "We've got Wathban and whom are you willing to exchange him for of our *peshmerga* prisoners?" And eventually a deal is agreed, and the *peshmerga* get their money or their prisoners, and in the middle of another night they release Wathban and send him off to walk back alone the four- or five-hour walk into Touz...'

'Why don't they kill him?' I was fascinated and wanted to understand it all, however horrible.

'Sometimes they do. If Wathban had been a big guy in the security police, for example, they would have killed him rather than doing a deal.'

'Whom else might they take when they go on operations in Touz?'

'Sometimes they take men who are *jash*, and then they don't kill them, because after all they are Kurds, but they hold the families to ransom for large sums of money. The families get the money off the government, because the government are behind the *jash*, and have it brought to the *peshmerga* in the mountains, and in the same way as with Wathban, the *jash* get released.'

The last story Mohammed told me was about how the *peshmerga* carry out raids on military posts. He had participated in one or two of these raids, but not many, because he was too young and inexperienced. He took the plate of salad ringed with the circular slices of radish, and said, 'Let's say there is a *nuqta*, a military post. All around it is a barbed wire fence, and then landmines and then more barbed wire. See? In the centre are eight or so government soldiers, camping out in tents. There's a guard outside on one side of the circle, and on the far side is a path without mines, which they use as their way in, with another guard.'

'Whereabouts is this *nuqta*?'

'Near to Touz.'

'So the group of *peshmerga* – four or eight of them – creep up on the post and wait till the soldiers are asleep, and then they approach by the path, and kill the guard – either by shooting him or, better, with a knife, because it makes no sound – and then they can get really close to the soldiers and they either kill them or disarm them and take them prisoner.'

He looked at me to see if I had understood. 'And then they capture all the weapons and ammunition which is in the *nuqta*. In one operation which I was involved in we captured all the soldiers alive and marched them off through the night into the mountains. And when we got within earshot of the village, far, far from Touz, we fired into the air with a special rhythm to let the villagers know that the operation had been successful.'

chapter twenty-three

THE CHEMICALS
AT SHEIKH WISAN

Late one afternoon when I had been in Shaqlawa a few days, I went to the hospital to meet a woman called Vian. Diane had told me she was dying of injuries to her lungs sustained in the chemical attack in 1987 on the village of Sheikh Wisan in the Balisan valley. I was accompanied by Marywan, who ran the local Committee for Martyrs, and Sherzad, an ex-*peshmerga* who had offered to act as my translator.

When we arrived, Vian was sitting in the shade on the stoop of the hospital doorway with her sister Sozan, who was acting as her nurse. Sozan helped Vian to her feet, took her arm and led us slowly down a long corridor to a small consulting room. Vian was dressed in a long black dress and a black headscarf which trailed down her back, held in place by a headband. Her skin was sallow and there were big shadows under her eyes, making her look much older than her 25 years. Sozan looked younger, although she too appeared tired and lethargic and her cheeks were scarred with pock-marks.

Vian and I sat down next to each other on a pair of black plastic chairs fixed to the floor. She was clearly uncomfortable and would have been better off lying down, but there was nowhere to do so.

'My family are from Sheikh Wisan,' she began in a weary voice. 'I was married at the time of the chemical attack, I was 19 then and had two little daughters aged one and two. I was seven months pregnant with my third child, but he was born prematurely following the chemicals and he died.' She paused for breath.

'Can you remember the day of the attack?'

'Slowly, slowly because I can't talk too much.' Vian was hugging her right knee and looking from Sherzad to me as she spoke, with a cool, distant expression in her eyes.

'It was nearly dark. I was sitting on the balcony of my home, sewing. The men were returning from the mountain to the village when we heard the noise. At first I thought it was a tractor. When I realised it was a plane I said to my husband, "It's your fault if the planes come to destroy us! You wanted us to come back to the village early today." Most days we didn't return to the village till it was dark, because the airforce were always bombing us. I used to keep the children with me on the mountainside during the day – do you think I would leave them behind? – but on that day we had come back to the village early because someone had come with a trailer full of chickens and my husband wanted me to buy one and cook it for supper.

'The planes shot at us and dropped their bombs and it went dark with black smoke. I left the children on the balcony with my husband and jumped down to the ground, a drop of more than 10 feet.

'Someone told me that my cousin Hashem's house had been hit directly by a bomb. I went there and found he was injured with shrapnel in his back and left buttock. As I arrived the skin on the back of my right hand began to burn and peel. I sat down on the ground and took Hashem's head on my lap. He had been heavily contaminated with the mustard gas, and the skin of my leg and hand began to peel while I was sitting there.'

As Vian was speaking the door opened and two little girls, perhaps eight years old, came in. One sat with Sozan and the other came and stood beside Vian. Both had long straight hair which gleamed a rich dark brown in the light, tied back in identical pony tails. They were wearing knee-length dresses, stained in many places. But what I noticed most about these children was their sharp, intelligent faces. The one who sat next to her mother listened intently to every word she said. I felt uneasy, but I supposed she knew the story already.

'While I was sitting with Hashem, my husband sent a message that the girls were crying and he couldn't comfort them and would I come back. I didn't go straight away, but he sent a second message and then I went. When I got home, one of our relatives was there, saying, "Let's go to the city." But my husband was against the idea. He said, "I'm not going back to the city, if I go the government will be sure to arrest me."

'I had started to vomit before I reached the house. Now my husband tried to take care of me but I couldn't even lie down. He tried to get me to eat but I was vomiting a lot. Then he said, "Let's leave the village," and he picked up the girls and we set off. It was dark everywhere, with the thick black smoke from the bombs. As we reached the edge of the village my husband began to vomit too and there was blood in it. Our eyes were affected by the gas, but we could still see. But before we reached the edge of the village we both collapsed, unable to walk any further. We lay where we fell with the children, on the ground. I told my husband that I could feel my feet touching the body of a strange man, but he said, "It doesn't matter, this is not the time to worry about shame."

'We lay on the ground all night, till sunrise. The children vomited, but were not as ill as we were. In the morning a message was brought from the head of the *jash*, that he was coming to take care of us and that he would not be handing us over to the government. He would take us to a special place and people from nearby villages would be sending tractors and trailers to collect us.

'I said to my husband, "What shall we do?" He said, "You and the girls go with the *jash* and then maybe you can go on to Arbil to stay with your parents. I will stay here, because I'm afraid of what the government will do to me if I go." He insisted he would not come down the valley with us. He said, "If the government are dropping chemicals on us, they won't stop short of killing us or burying us alive. It would be madness for me to go down to the city." He was an underground activist and had reason to fear the government, but I never saw him again.

'I had blisters full of water on my burnt skin, and one on my belly which was very big and painful. It was so painful that I nearly passed out. As I lay on the ground I heard someone saying they thought I was dead and someone else saying, "No, she's not dead." They lifted me onto the trailer with my daughters.

"The tractor pulling the trailer drove off, taking us away. On the journey my skin was burning and very painful and it was peeling, but by the time we arrived I could no longer feel anything. I heard someone saying, "She's the daughter of so-and-so.' A man came and lifted me out of the tractor. He tore off my clothes and dressed me in a new *dishdasha*, then put us into another vehicle. Everyone else in that vehicle died, except me and my daughters. I was blind by now, but I could hear the sounds of the people dying all around me.

'I don't know what happened to me during the next two weeks. At some point I lost the baby I was carrying, but I don't know when or how it happened. All I know is that when my sight began to return, I was no longer pregnant. I found myself in a prison cell with just two small windows high up. My children were with me and there were two mothers of *peshmerga* also in the cell. We were in the Red Security Building in Sulaymaniyah.'

I went back to see Vian again a few days later, by which time she had left the hospital and was staying at her father-in-law's house in a suburb of Shaqlawa. She was lying on a mattress on the verandah. Sozan was with her and Vian's two little girls. She sat up momentarily as we started talking, but soon lay down again. Fatima, my translator, sat beside her and Vian talked lying on her side and looking up at us. Every 10 or 15 minutes I asked Fatima to ask Vian if she was tired and wanted to stop, but each time the answer was, 'No, I want to talk.'

'After we had been in Sulaymaniyah about five weeks, a Kurdish nurse came to me. Her name was Fenig. I offered her my gold earrings and a ring if she would take a message to my family. She started to cry and refused to take the jewellery. I asked her to phone my father in the cigarette factory where he worked in Arbil.

'Shortly afterwards my father came to Sulaymaniyah, but they wouldn't let him see me. They only allowed him to see my daughters. When I asked the girls who the visitor was, they said it was their grandfather and that he was crying. Fenig said he had wanted to take us home, but the security people said he could not because we were to be treated like *peshmerga*.

'After my father came to the security building and asked for me, the authorities said they would deprive me of food for six days and torture me with electricity to make me tell them how I had sent the message to him. Fenig had to take me to the torture room, but I wasn't tortured. Afterwards Fenig brought me sweet biscuits and crumbled them up and fed them to me. Back in the cell I was sharing with the two mothers of *peshmerga*, she secretly brought me ointment for my skin. My whole torso was burned from my chest to my hips. She was allowed to peel off the burnt skin but was forbidden to give me any real medical treatment.

'Meanwhile, as I found out later, my father had gone to the head of the *jash* in Betwatar near Balisan and asked him for help. He took him some gifts and said he must help him to get his daughter back. The *jash* head sent his son, Anwar Beg, to the security building in Sulaymaniyah. When he arrived he pretended to be my uncle and the authorities called me in. I was very frightened, because I didn't know him and I thought perhaps I had been called in to be given electric shocks.

'Before they called me in, the authorities gave me a clean *dish-dasha* because the one I was wearing was covered in blood. My skin was very dry and had begun to bleed a lot. I said to Anwar Beg, "I will die if you don't save me!" The authorities were very angry, and asked me again who had sent the message to my father, and reminded me that my detention was meant to be secret. They threatened to beat me and to tear the flesh from my body unless I told them how the message had reached my father. I was terrified, but I said I didn't know. I couldn't tell them that the nurse, Fenig, had sent the message.

'Anwar Beg told me that he would prepare a document and send it to the First Army Battalion and that after three days I would be released. That night, after Anwar Beg had left, Fenig came and told me that there were three men from my valley who were still alive, two from Balisan and one from Sheikh Wisan, and did I want to see them? The room where the men were being held was next to our room. Fenig said that when the guards had left, I could see them. I thought it might make me feel better, so I agreed.

'When I was in the cell I had a cage over my body, which the nurse had brought me, because my burns made it unbearable to wear clothes. She had been forbidden from washing me, so my skin was still saturated with the chemicals. My hair, which in those days I wore in long plaits down my back, was caked with chemicals and very dry. That night when the men came to visit me, all I had over me was a dirty *dishdasha*, but the shame was gone – everything was finished, I felt I was dying – so I showed them the burns on my body.

'One of the men, Hoshit, was from Sheikh Wisan. I told him I was dying. He said, "No, Vian, you are not dying, you are in good shape. I am very tired, maybe I am dying." His lips were very dark.

'Hoshit said, "I am worried about my children, I don't know where they are and haven't had any news of them." Poor Hoshit: the skin on his lips and inside his mouth was damaged and peeling; and his testicles were badly injured.

'The two men from Balisan were in better shape than Hoshit. Their lungs had been affected, like mine. The next morning I asked Fenig to give me a *dishdasha* and take me to see Hoshit, because I wanted to talk to him again. Fenig said he had been taken to a different room and I began to cry. Every day for three days I asked to see him and every time when she said I couldn't, I cried. Eventually Fenig admitted to me that he was dead. He had died after he had come to see me, that same night. When I heard this I became afraid; I thought it was the end. I told Fenig that I too was going to die there, but I didn't want to die in the Security Building...

'After that the two men from Balisan came and left me a message saying that if Anwar Beg's son came, I was to inform him that they too were prisoners here, because nobody outside knew about them. One day my mother came to the Security Building and was allowed to see me. I put the message from the Balisan men in my shoe before I walked over to meet her and I managed to give it to her. She passed the message to the families of the two men and they tried to get Anwar Beg to help them.

'Three days after my mother's visit, without any warning, we were all released – me and my daughters and the two men from Balisan. When we came out of the building into the sunlight, we were blinded and our eyes became very painful. We wanted to rent a car to take us back to our families, but as we were standing in the street, a boy who had a shop called us in and gave all of us new clothes. He gave my daughters traditional Kurdish outfits. Then he brought a car and paid for it himself and took us all to Ranya. One of the Balisan men's relatives was living in Ranya, so we went to him. I was very ill when we arrived. They cut my hair and washed my body in warm water. All my skin peeled off and it was so painful that I went numb. I was having great difficulty breathing. The water hurt my belly and thighs a lot.

'The family in Ranya helped me so much. There were lots of boys in that family and they cried when they saw the condition I was in. They took me to the hospital in Ranya, although it was forbidden for me to go there. The hospital treated me secretly, giving me injections which helped my breathing. The family gave me liver to eat. They said, "We will do anything for you, just tell us what you want." They desperately wanted to help me. I thanked them, but I wanted to go to my father's house in Arbil. So they rented a car and took me to him.'

I could see that Vian was getting tired. She lay back on her pillow and closed her eyes for a few moments. Then she turned to Fatima again and went on.

'Many members of my family had died in the chemical attack. In my uncle's household, in Sheikh Wisan, there were 18 people. All of them died except for him. Another uncle had two wives and seven children, and they all died together in Sheikh Wisan. My father and mother were in Arbil at the time of the chemical attack, so they were all right. My cousin and one of my brothers and my uncle had all survived as well, because they were *peshmerga* and not in the area at the time. My two sisters, Sarzan and Sozan, survived, but all the rest of my family were dead. After the attack, my father took in the children of other people who had died. My father now has seven orphans whom he cares for in Arbil.

'For the last six years since the attack I have been living between Arbil and Shaqlawa. Sometimes I stay in Arbil with my parents, which they like because they can take care of me, sometimes I come here to my father-in-law's. I prefer it here.'

The two girls were sitting with their mother, one crouched against the wall listening and watching, and the other at the foot of the bed.

'What are their names?' I asked.

'Runak and Rayzan. Runak is in the third class of primary school and is top of her class. Rayzan is in the same class, because they are so close in age.'

We had reached the end of Vian's story. For me it was one of the most disturbing I had heard; I would not be able to get it out of my mind for months to come.

'Is there anything else you want me to write about you?' I asked her.

Vian looked at me.

'All I want is to be better. Can you help me to get medical treatment in the West?'

The next day I called on Marywan in the office of the Committee for Martyrs to find out more about what had happened at Sheikh Wisan.

Marywan was a lovely man, with a pointed, sensitive face, soft golden skin and gentle eyes. His grey *sharwal* hung on him loosely, as he was quite thin; it was invariably spotless and pressed with creases down the outside of the arms. When I appeared in the doorway of his office he jumped to his feet, welcomed me warmly and sent out for tea.

Marywan told me that there had been about 100 families living in Sheikh Wisan at the time of the attack, which meant about 600–700 people. Four hundred and eighty-five were affected by the chemicals, and 153 died. He pointed to a chart on the wall, a handwritten list of the names of the martyrs, arranged by family. In some families, almost no one had survived. The name *Kimia* – 'Chemical' – appeared here and there, beside the dates of birth of several babies born in the days following the attack.

Marywan told me that the attack on Sheikh Wisan on 17 April 1987 was Ali Hassan al-Majid's first act after he was given the brief to find a solution to the 'Kurdish question' once and for all. From 1980 to 1987, the Balisan valley and its 42 villages had been under peshmerga control and a 'no-go' area for the government. One of the PUK's four *malbands* or headquarters was situated in the valley and Sheikh Wisan had a *peshmerga* base and many *peshmerga*, renowned for their bravery.

On 14–16 April 1987, PUK *peshmerga* undertook a major operation in the Jafati valley, which runs southeast from Dokhan Lake towards Sulaymaniyah, in the course of which they captured over

100 government military posts. Most of the *peshmerga* from Balisan were involved in this operation. On the following day, 17 April 1987, government troops bombed and captured the Balisan valley in an act of reprisal.

Sheikh Wisan is less than two hours' drive from Shaqlawa and I decided I would like to go there. Marywan suggested I should ask Sherzad, the *peshmerga* who had translated during my first meeting with Vian, to take me. He had been based there for five years and had been involved in helping the survivors of the chemical attack in the days after it occurred.

Sherzad picked us up at eight the next morning, in a dark red car rented for the day complete with a plump, smiling driver. We stopped for Marywan in the town and he climbed in the back beside Mohammed and me. Sherzad was a small stocky man in his forties who had retired from being a *peshmerga* and worked now as a translator. At first glance he appeared strong but his complexion was sallow and he moved about very slowly. He had himself been badly affected by the chemicals and had lost much of his former strength. Some time after the attack he and a *peshmerga* friend had undergone fertility tests in a hospital in Iran and had found their sperm counts to be very low; the friend had been impotent for two years after the attack.

We drove through the quiet early morning, down the road towards Diyana. Balisan is not far from Shaqlawa across the mountains, but by road one has to go the long way round, following the valleys. Shortly before reaching the town of Khalifan we turned off to the right and entered the Balisan valley at its top. The valley floor was wide and lush, planted with rice and fruit trees, with a small river running close to the road; behind, the hills rose up broad and chunky like the Yorkshire hills. The lower meadows were pale yellow, covered with dry stubble and lightly scattered with dark green young trees: it was obvious that there had been a scourge and the trees were struggling to re-establish themselves. In winter, Sherzad said, the hillsides would be covered in snow.

As we drove along, Sherzad pointed out caves he had hidden in when he was a *peshmerga*. After the chemical bombing, he told me,

2,000 Iraqi soldiers had been brought in to comb the valley. Sherzad had been one of a group of only 14 *peshmerga* who remained in the area, helping the injured villagers and trying to avoid detection.

After half an hour the driver turned onto a track of stone and earth and the car began to bounce and groan. After Balisan village the track climbed steadily and suddenly Sherzad announced that we were arriving in Sheikh Wisan.

The village was situated at a point where two mountains met forming a right angle. In 1987 the planes had dropped the chemical bombs on the slopes above Sheikh Wisan and the gas, which was heavy, had drifted down the valley towards some of the other villages. Later in the day we saw the crumpled remains of one of the bombs in a tobacco patch in Balisan. Its thin metal shell was painted pale green.

The two mountains rose up steeply behind the village. The lower slopes were covered in dry yellow grass studded with almond trees and I made out bright flashes of colour as women moved among the trees. Lower down near the houses, a donkey was ambling along slowly, pulling a cart. As we got out of the car a crowd of men and children came to meet us: Marywan and Sherzad were old friends of the villagers.

The present-day village was a scattering of houses separated by rough ground. There were piles of stones and mounds of earth with weeds, scrub and animal droppings, heaps of concrete blocks – the remains of walls which had collapsed in the bombing – and, here and there, craters where bombs had landed. Sherzad told me that prior to 1987 the houses had stood close together and it had been a big village. Now, although quite a few families had returned, at best it was a sprawling hamlet.

The houses were built of mud and thatch, with roofs made from a base of wooden poles laid horizontally, with mud and straw packed down tightly in between. When it rained, Marywan said, the people got up on the roofs with a big smooth stone and rolled the turf to get the moisture out; that way the houses stayed dry all winter.

On a roof near where we were standing a little girl was unrolling a cloth containing fresh tobacco leaves. On the other corner of the same roof, red slices of tomato were glinting in the sun, drying for the winter.

I liked the atmosphere in the village, although it was clearly a place of poverty whose people had been severely beaten and were struggling to drag themselves back up. Everybody was thin and most were dressed in rags.

We spent the morning wandering from house to house calling on people and chatting to them. At noon Marywan led us to the home of a friend of his who lived on the edge of the village. We were ushered in and served rice and stewed okra with the men of the family, sitting on the earth floor of a bare, newly built room. Afterwards, at my insistence, the driver drove back to the tarmac road alone, leaving us to walk a mile cross-country to Kanibarda to visit Marywan's parents.

The low slopes of the mountains were peaceful and lovely in the warmth of the afternoon. Halfway down the path we stepped over the trail of a snake which had recently crossed it in two places, leaving a zig-zag furrow in the sandy dirt, like the print of a bicycle tyre.

We found Marywan's parents sitting under an awning outside their house, looking out over a broad sweep of valley. His mother welcomed us and made tea on a wood fire, kindling it in a matter of seconds just beside where we were sitting. Behind her a border of yellow and pink flowers turned their faces to the sun.

Marywan's father sat rolling home-grown tobacco into fat cigarettes and smoking through a hand-carved wooden filter. A black-and-white *keffiyah* was wrapped around his head in a turban and he regarded me coolly from his position half sitting, half lying on the ground. Sherzad chatted with him while Mohammed and I watched four blond little girls playing nearby, the children of the neighbour.

From Kanibarda we walked back along the path and rejoined the dirt track which led to the road. But before we reached Balisan, a man called out to us from his vegetable garden and invited us to sit under another awning while the three women of the house brought pomegranates and fresh walnuts in shells, and a pick-axe head to break them open. There was a flower garden here too, with golden chrysanthemums shaking their heads in the breeze.

Back in Balisan, Sherzad showed us the site of the house he had lived in when he was based in the valley and the two bomb shelters he had built with his own hands in underground caves dug into the rock. The house had been flattened by a bomb and grass was growing over the site.

There was to be a wedding party that night for Marywan's neighbour's son, and Mohammed and I were invited. It was nearly 10 p.m. by the time we had changed and eaten supper with Sherzad's family.

Sherzad put on a new russet *sharwal* with a freshly-pressed cummerbund which he wound round his waist several times before tying it in an elaborate knot. Diane was with us, glamorous in a fine set of traditional Kurdish clothes in turquoise and pink. I had put on the best dress I had with me, but it couldn't compete with the glitz and shimmer of a traditional Kurdish party outfit.

The nights were cold in Shaqlawa now and we walked quickly up the hill to the neighbour's home to find the wedding party in full swing in a large open space at the back of the house. The electricity was off but lamps had been rigged up in a tree beside a generator, the roar of which was muted by the fiercely energetic tunes being played by three ancient musicians. A ring of at least 60 dancers was slowly rotating under the trees, with the trio of two pipers and an *oud* player circling on the inside. The musicians would prance a few bow-legged paces, then stop in front of a particular dancer, and the elder piper would blow so hard that his cheeks filled out like red balloons and I wondered that he didn't have a heart attack.

About three quarters of the dancers were men, with a few spangled women sprinkled among them, mostly at one end of the circle. I watched and thought there was something timid about the way they danced, as if they were unsure of whether they really ought to be in the circle. The remaining women and children crowded the garden between the dancers and the house.

'Let's dance!' cried Sherzad, and Diane, Mohammed and I followed him through the crowd. He seized Diane's hand, who in turn grabbed mine and I Mohammed's. People would often join or leave the dance without waiting for a break in the music, so that the shape of the circle was forever changing. The footwork here was different from in Sulaymaniyah, but it didn't take me long to get it and the shoulder-shaking was the same, although I half wondered if it was seemly for a foreign woman to shake her shoulders as vigorously as the men. There was something wildly sexual and abandoned about the way the men would suddenly start to lift and drop their shoulders and swing their hips as they pranced back and forth, on the cue of a speeding-up of the music.

chapter twenty-four

LEAVING KURDISTAN

After two weeks in Shaqlawa I returned to Arbil for my final three days. On the last evening, Mohammed and I visited his cousin Rashid. He was a schoolteacher in his late thirties and lived with his shy, plump young wife and their four children in a residential district not far from the centre of the city. Their four-room house was cool and spacious, and they had a little concrete garden in the front with a walnut tree and a space for their ancient rusting white car. The car had seen better days for in 1991 they had fled in it to Iran in the great exodus at the end of the Gulf War.

Rashid taught English and spoke it well and he and I spent the evening talking avidly about Kurdish politics. He was cynical about the ability of the Kurdish political parties to sort out the mess the region was in and told me that the Kurdish struggle had for many years been dogged by poor leadership. He traced the current situation back to the 1920s when, he said, Sheikh Mahmud Barzinji had been offered Kurdish autonomy in exchange for supporting the British, but had chosen instead to fight them.

Shooting reverberated round the city that night as we lay on mattresses under the stars beside the open front door. A light breeze was rustling the leaves of the walnut tree and I had a sense of the neighbourhood lying awake, listening and waiting. I was wakeful anyway because my heart was aching: I had realised in the last few days that, although I was tired and ready for a break, leaving Kurdistan was going to be painful.

In the course of this second trip I had become powerfully attached to the place. There were so many things I had found difficult at the beginning which now I could cope with. I could sleep on a wafer-thin mattress on concrete in the open air with a rough blanket and no sheet; I could use any toilet, however filthy; drink *piyalas* of tea with an inch of sugar in the bottom; live for days on end on a diet of rice and okra; and I had finally got used to the heat, which was subsiding now and giving way to the crisp, sunny warmth of early autumn.

I hadn't got used to the extreme pain in the stories people told me everywhere I went; but somewhere in my system I was gradually integrating it with the many things Kurdish which I felt were wonderful: the natural beauty of the place, the tremendous human warmth I encountered daily and my sense that people were slowly picking themselves up and trying to move on. I had been deeply moved by many of the people I had met, and had learned something through spending time with them which I had never come close to experiencing anywhere else.

About 1 a.m. I got up and tiptoed inside to the toilet, past the six sleeping bodies of Rashid and his family stretched out in a row on the living room floor. Mum lay at the far end, nearest the centre of the house, and Dad by the open door.

Mohammed was stirring as I came back outside.

'*Choni?*' he murmured.

'*Yani,*' I replied. '*Tu choni?*'

'*Bashem.*'

I lay down on my side on my mattress, three feet away. He had the blanket pulled up over his head, but as I lay there watching he pushed it away and opened one eye.

'Frightened?' he asked, meaning by the shooting.

'No.'

I wasn't, and that was another thing: I had got used to living with danger, up to a point anyway.

'I don't want to leave,' I whispered, and a tear rolled down my cheek.

He began to stretch as his other eye slowly opened. 'Stay then, Teresa! Stay here. Don't go back to England!' His dark sleepy eyes were full of tenderness and as my second tear fell and then my third, he stretched out an arm and took my hand across the concrete.

*　　*　　*

In the morning we took a 'special' taxi to D'hok, retracing the journey I had made seven weeks earlier. We stopped for tea halfway at the same roadside café we had visited then, and I reflected on the strangeness of life and the speed with which it rushes by. I had been so nervous then, wondering how I would survive and half-doubting the wisdom of my being in Kurdistan at all. Now all I felt was love for the place and a deep reluctance to leave.

In D'hok I spent the last hour before dusk in the *souq*, shopping for presents to take home and things that would remind me of Kurdistan. I bought half a dozen black wool women's headscarves edged with gold tassels and spangled with sequins, and two packets of cardamom seeds.

The next morning we left early, changing taxis in Zakho for the 10-minute ride to the border. Mohammed sat beside me in the back of the taxi, urging me not to cry when we said goodbye. 'I'll cry too, if you do!' he warned, and I believed him. We had been together constantly for the last six weeks and he had become like a brother to me.

The car drew up at the Kurdish administration building in the dazzling sunlight and we stepped out into a crowd of men: truck-drivers, would-be refugees leaving to seek asylum in the West, money-changers, taxi-drivers, hawkers. I was the only foreigner and I saw only two other women among perhaps 100. For a second I hesitated; then I took a deep breath, steeled myself and walked into the dusty building, leaving Mohammed with my bags.

When I came out 20 minutes later Mohammed was arranging for me to share a taxi to Silopi, just inside Turkey, with a young Kurdish couple who were emigrating.

'Go with them,' he told me, 'you'll be with another woman and it's better that way.'

I was too upset to argue. The seething, bristling crowd was like a harbinger of the world I was about to re-enter, a world full of people struggling to survive the cold indifference of a neo-Western country. Soon I too would be free-wheeling into what, compared to Iraqi Kurdistan, felt like an alien land; and I would be alone.

'OK?' Mohammed asked, reminding me with his eyes of my promise not to cry.

'OK.'

He was loading my bags into the taxi with the resignation of an old man and as he faced me to say goodbye I could tell that he wanted this moment of my leaving to be over as quickly as possible.

I swallowed hard, hugged him and kissed him on both cheeks, feeling the eyes of the amazed crowd piercing through my back. Public demonstrations of affection between men and women are considered shameful in the Middle East, except between brothers and sisters or mothers and sons.

'Thank you for being a brilliant guard,' I murmured. 'I couldn't have managed without you!'

On the far side of the bridge the crowd at the Turkish post was smaller. As I stood numbly waiting with my papers, my eye lighted on Jack, a young American Christian aid worker I had met in Shaqlawa. He was climbing out of a shiny pick-up truck with his passport in his hand.

'Hi!' he called out. 'Where ya goin'?'

'Dyarbakir.'

'Wanna ride?'

I had first seen Jack at the wedding in Shaqlawa, dressed in a honey-coloured *sharwal*, a lone blond head dancing very competently in the long line of Kurdish men. Mohammed had muttered, 'How come he knows the steps, when I don't?' I was astonished to see Jack here.

'Have you got room?'

'Sure, I got room. It'll save you a few bucks, anyways. Give me your bags and I'll meet you in the post office in Silopi at 11.'

I reached Silopi early and wandered unsteadily down the main street. It was the first time I had gone anywhere on my own in seven weeks and I had a strange feeling of being like a child learning to walk for the first time, trying out her legs, not sure if they would hold up.

I wanted to buy bread and someone sent me round the corner to a bakery. Then, searching for cheese, I entered a shop with large square tins of olives on the floor. I tried using the Arabic word but the man didn't understand; by pointing and tasting we reached a large tin with huge cubes of salty white cheese floating in water. I bought half a cube for the equivalent of more than two dollars, a sum which across the border would have fed a whole family for two weeks.

Two hours down the long, straight, beautiful road, Jack stopped for refreshment on the outskirts of Mardin. We sat at a little wooden table on a pavement amongst men playing dice, at the foot of a steep sandy hillside covered with painted shacks. The town was tense, the men looked poor and the cloudy air hovered thick and still and white.

'Think I prefer Shaqlawa,' Jack grinned across the table. He had been explaining to me that he was taking a year out doing 'missionary work' before starting college.

The Turkish tea tasted bitter. It was the same clear golden colour, but had a factory-processed taste which sent a cold unyielding message into my stomach. They served it in *piyalas* on tiny saucers like in Iraqi Kurdistan, but the *piyala* was larger and fluted on a twist. The sweet, mellow taste of tea brewed with cardamom was not there. And the glass was not filled to the top – which in Iraqi Kurdistan is a sign of bad luck. Mohammed had once sent back a glass of tea I'd been brought because it was not quite full. The Turkish tea in these more affluent, extravagant glasses said, 'You are no longer in Iraqi Kurdistan. You have left the land of magic and light; you are still in the East but approaching Europe and to prepare you we are throwing something abrasive at your tastebuds... Here we still have sunlight and we still have rocks and rivers, but there are many cars and smooth road surfaces and our tea tastes bitter because it comes out of a box packed in a factory, not from a hessian sack propped open on an earth floor.'

Diyarbakir the city mirrored the boxes the tea was packed in. For the last 12 miles the road ran through a pinkish-brown rocky canyon, very lovely, small-scale and intimate. Then we came over a rise and before us, in the middle of the plain, a city of tall blocks rose up in numbed indifference. Dyarbakir was said to have grown in the last eight years from 350,000 to well over one million inhabitants, due largely to the Turkish government forcibly transferring Turkish Kurds out of their villages into the city. There had been a frantic construction campaign, with cheap flats being flung up to create new suburbs. Later I learned that there was no work for the displaced villagers and that they were obliged to spend the little money they had earned selling up their goats and chickens on buying one of the flats, the walls of which then became the horizon of their new world. It was not difficult to imagine their misery.

The evening flight from Dyarbakir to Istanbul was full, so I took a room in the Karavanserai, a famous old Ottoman hotel used by travellers to and from the East from the time when Dyarbakir was an important staging post on the caravan routes. It was a graceful stone building constructed around a courtyard. A series of arches fronted both storeys, forming a portico on the ground floor and a gallery above.

After I had put down my bags it was a relief to sit at a table in the courtyard and take in the fact that the day's travelling was over. I looked around at the shapely trees and shrubs, and the green creeper trailing down the grey stone walls. The sun was warm on the top of my head, but it was a mild, sweet, late October sun. Half a dozen people were sitting at white tables with pale blue and pink table cloths, drinking coffee and beer but making almost no sound. In the centre of the courtyard chunks of water melon were displayed around the central column of a stone fountain like slabs of flesh; a jet of water spurted softly from the top. It was strange to find myself in such a comfortable environment. The Karavanserai was in the heart of Dyarbakir at the foot of the Byzantine city walls and, although the people in the street outside looked poor, the hotel guests clearly had money.

I spent the next day resting and wandering the streets near the hotel. I found a pool in a second courtyard and went for a long swim, ignoring the protests of a waiter that the water was too cold. Later, beside the city walls, I found a long straight street with small square shops selling headscarves and rugs, and a fruit market in the middle of the road. Men in Druze-style trousers hobbled bow-legged up and down, and boys sold bananas and grapes from wooden barrows. I passed down the street perhaps six times, but although people stared it didn't bother me. I had learned how to deal with curious male eyes by now.

In the afternoon I went and sat on the far side of the courtyard in the shade, and opened my journal. I was thinking endless thoughts about the differences between rich and poor, East and West – not exactly thoughts, more feelings and questions. I had seen and heard and felt so much in the last few weeks, and there had been little time to sit down and digest, much less to articulate my responses.

On the roads and in the villages, in Qushtapa, the Red Security Building, Sumud and Sheikh Wisan I had come into closer contact with real poverty and appalling suffering than ever before, and yet my sense was of having had an incredibly vibrant experience. I don't mean to gloss over the level of sheer trauma suffered by the Iraqi Kurds in recent years: no one can deny that Kurdistan is a ravaged land whose battered, wounded people walk side by side with countless ghosts. There are many parallels with the Nazi Holocaust and these were never far from my mind. The collective pain is colossal and will take many decades to heal; perhaps the longer since many of the young are leaving to seek asylum in the West. But despite or perhaps because of the depth of the Kurds' pain, I felt that my journey had taken me to the heart of human existence.

Everywhere I went I was exposed to the raw elements of life: pain, separation, despair; recovery, reunion, love and hope. And I found in ordinary people, from young children to the very old, a vitality that one rarely finds in Western countries. Somehow that had made me feel much more alive myself. I had got close to people much more quickly than I do at home: Mohammed, Sirwa, Nazaneen and Drakushan had become very dear friends in the space of a few weeks. I felt a bond, too, with many of the women who had told me their stories; they would remain in my heart for a long time to come.

It was dusk now and lights were burning in each archway on the first and second storeys of the hotel. Lamps had been lit, too, on low stands among the flowerbeds and people were moving around and talking in low voices.

I felt overawed by the thought that in the evening I would be travelling to Istanbul and that when I woke on Sunday morning London would be only a few hours away. The dark courtyard was lovely but I felt suffocated, wishing I dared to turn around and go straight back to Zakho.

It felt horribly cold when I left the hotel at 5.30 and took a cab to the airport through the city of boxey sky-scrapers, ugly and sharp-edged in the darkness. Outside the airport doors I had a row with the driver about how much I was going to pay. Inside I found a hall full of sad, silent people and nobody I knew or could be sure was an Iraqi Kurd, although I searched their faces for clues.

Istanbul smelled and looked as squalid as only a Western city could. As the taxi drove me round Laleli in search of a cheap hotel, the Saturday night streets seemed to be crowded with half-dressed young people getting drunk, getting high, getting old fast by living badly.

I took a tiny L-shaped room in the Hotel Visa, in the grottiest conditions yet but for the highest price. After the splendour and security of the Karavanserai, it was a shock. The room was scarcely larger than the bed and the smell was more unpleasant than in any Kurdish hotel. I fell into an uneasy sleep, but woke at two to what sounded like a key rattling in the lock and the door sliding inwards across the carpet. I lay frozen in fear for a few seconds, then reached for Mohammed's gun. But it wasn't there and my hand hit the bed-side light which fell to the floor with a thud. I held my breath for a long minute, then got up and tiptoed to the door: it was shut.

Tired and miserable when I rose at six I had another row, this time with the manager about breakfast not being available when they had said and the manager not having any change when I tried to pay him. I was in angry-Western-woman mode by now, cold and assertive. But I got my breakfast and my change. It was stale rolls with processed cheese in silver foil and plastic sachets of jam and butter. The tea, even more bitter than in Mardin, was tepid.

As I was leaving the manager asked me if I'd be back in Istanbul the next time Manchester played Turkey, and I sullenly told him,

'I didn't come for the football, I've come from Iraq, Kurdistan.' His face lit up and he exclaimed, 'I am Kurdish people! My city, Mardin!' I flushed with shame, apologised and shook his hand.

In the departure lounge at Atatürk airport there was a hold up, but I didn't mind. Having got through the security queue to enter the building, the queue to check-in, the queue for passport control and the queue for checking hand baggage at the gate, I was happy to sit down.

It was time to lift myself up and smile at life. I tried to picture Mohammed going about everyday things in Arbil, with the sun shining as it was beginning to here in Istanbul, turning the colourless dawn into a fine, mild, October morning. Soon I will be flying home, I told myself, to see my friends and the green fields around Bristol and the red and yellow trees. And then I can write it all down.

EPILOGUE

At the time of my second visit to Kurdistan, in September-October 1993, although the Kurdish administration was struggling to make headway in the face of the dual burdens of UN sanctions and Saddam Hussein's economic blockade, a spirit of hope pervaded the land. The sense of excitement and pride which Kurds had felt at the time of the elections in May 1992 was still present in people's hearts and, for many, the fact that they were no longer ruled by Saddam more than made up for economic hardship. I heard occasional comments about the ineffectiveness of the Kurdish administration, but most people seemed to accept that their activities were restricted by lack of material resources. Food and medicines were in short supply, however, and a minority had begun to grumble to the effect that they had been 'better off' under Saddam.

Less than eight weeks after I left Kurdistan, the situation there deteriorated seriously. In the third week of December, fighting broke out between the forces of the PUK and those of the Islamic Movement in Kurdistan (IMIK). The clashes began in the Kifri region, but soon spread to towns and cities in the governorates of Sulaymaniyah and Arbil and continued for about two weeks. By the end of December the IMIK were forced to retreat to their bases near the Iranian border. Both sides had sustained heavy casualties: Amnesty International reported that the total number of combatants and civilians killed may have amounted to 500. Both sides had taken prisoners and in the aftermath of the fighting each accused the other of torture and the wanton killing of prisoners who had surrendered. Amnesty subsequently interviewed IMIK detainees in PUK detention, ex-detainees on both sides and hospital staff who had dealt with the injured and dead; it found their allegations convincing.

On 1 May 1994, widespread military clashes began again, this time involving the PUK, KDP and IMIK. Fighting was intense throughout the month, followed by sporadic clashes in June and July and further fighting in August until a ceasefire was eventually agreed and observed.

The May 1994 fighting began with a conflict over the ownership of a small piece of land in Qala Diza, in the Sulaymaniyah Governorate. This sparked local fighting between forces of the KDP and PUK, but it was not long before KDP personnel in D'hok took over the PUK office there, PUK personnel in Sulaymaniyah similarly interfered with the KDP office and fighting spread throughout the region. This was the beginning of the division of the Kurdish-administered enclave into zones of political and military control, the northwest falling under the KDP and the southeast under the PUK, with the IMIK intermittently controlling parts of the Iranian border region. This process led to the establishment of a blockade by the KDP whereby they prevented food supplies brought into Kurdistan from Turkey from reaching the PUK-controlled areas.

Inevitably, in view of its geographical location and political importance, Arbil was the most heavily contested area. Both KDP and PUK tried to gain control of the parliament building, but the PUK were the more successful of the two and for much of the summer it was under their control. Parliamentary sessions ceased altogether.

In June 1994, 300 women marched from Sulaymaniyah to Arbil to protest against the fighting and the disastrous effect it was having on the lives of ordinary people, many of whom had been killed or injured or had lost their livelihoods. The women, who were from across the political spectrum, marched for five days and nights; when they arrived in Arbil they camped out in the parliament building. Nazaneen was among them.

The May–June fighting was widely reported in the Western press. It seriously shook the trust of many Western sympathisers in the leadership of the PUK and KDP, the two parties who were supposedly trying to establish democracy in the region. Aid agencies began to question the advisability of continuing to run projects in a region where law and order were breaking down; those who were critical of the use of resources by the Western Gulf War allies to maintain Operation Provide Comfort pointed to the evident inability of the Kurdish parties to put partisan interests aside.

Independent Kurdish intellectuals living in Western cities spoke out against the folly of the PUK and KDP leadership, but had little power to influence events. Saddam Hussein, it must be assumed, sat in Baghdad rubbing his hands together in glee.

The Iraqi National Congress (INC) saw the inter-Kurdish fighting as an opportunity to show that they had something constructive to offer. For a period in the summer of 1994, INC militias played a major role in keeping apart the *peshmerga* of the PUK and the KDP and ensuring that the city of Arbil did not fall under the exclusive control of either party.

Meanwhile both combatants and civilians were dying in the course of the fighting. Amnesty International put the figure at between 600 and 2,000 dead. The use of heavy weaponry inside the big cities undoubtedly contributed to the large number of casualties and again there were reports of appalling human rights abuses committed on all sides. On 1 June 1994, Amnesty called on leaders of the political parties involved in the conflict to 'stop deliberately killing and mutilating prisoners in their custody, and abducting, killing and torturing civilians based on their political ties'.[1]

Although a ceasefire was agreed at the end of August 1994, it was clear by now that an unstoppable power struggle was underway between the KDP and PUK for the outright control of the Kurdish enclave. In short, this was civil war. The tribal rivalries which had dominated Kurdish politics and society for centuries and which prevented the emergence of a cohesive nationalist movement in the years leading up to the First World War were once again coming to the fore. As in the past, these rivalries were undermining the Kurds' chances of dealing

---

[1] Amnesty International report *Human Rights Abuses in Iraqi Kurdistan since 1991*, 28 February 1995.

effectively with their non-Kurdish enemies. Masoud Barzani admitted publicly that the attempt at establishing democracy had failed and at one point suggested to a Western journalist that the best solution would be to bring in the UN to run the enclave. Jalal Talabani was much more evasive in his comments to the press and had spent much of the early part of the fighting in Damascus, alleging that it would not be safe for him to return to Kurdistan because he would be obliged to travel through KDP-controlled territory.

The impact of the situation on ordinary Kurds was incalculable. Not only did many families lose a son or a father, but many had to flee as fighting around their homes made daily life impossible. Inflation, already out of control since the Gulf War, now made the price of many foods quite out of reach of even the middle classes. Unemployment grew and eventually Kurdish government employees ceased to receive their salaries.

As political tensions increased, freedom of speech was curtailed so that by now most of the smaller parties which had flourished in the first months after the uprising had been forced to merge with one or other of the two main parties. To be a KDP supporter living in the area controlled by the PUK was highly dangerous, and vice versa.

A further round of serious fighting began in December 1994. This time the PUK accused the KDP, who control the border with Turkey, of embezzling tax money levied on lorries entering the enclave at Khabur. In the course of this phase of the conflict the PUK seized control of Arbil and thus came into existence a deadlock whereby the KDP refused to hand over the tax money until the PUK vacated the city, but the PUK would not do so until the money was received.

The inter-Kurdish conflict was not the only military pressure. In March 1995 the Turkish army launched a massive incursion over the border into the KDP part of the enclave, allegedly in pursuit of PKK fighters. This was one of many such incursions between 1992 and 1996. In addition, Saddam's troops continued to pound and harass areas of the enclave within shelling range. In this climate it is not surprising that many families, having lost all hope of a peaceful, secure existence, began to sell their possessions and leave Kurdistan to seek refuge in Western countries.

In the spring and early summer of 1995, Iran called representatives of the KDP and PUK to Teheran for discussions. During the same period, Baghdad was making overtures and rumours were rife as to which of the two parties was most likely to reach a deal with Saddam. By midsummer the US government, uneasy at the prospect that Iran might step in to fill the power vacuum that now existed in northern Iraq, sent envoys to persuade the PUK and KDP to engage in US-brokered peace talks. These took place in August 1995 in the Republic of Ireland and resulted in a provisional agreement between senior personnel of the two politbureaux. At the next stage of negotiations, however, when attempts were made to flesh out the details of the agreement and bring together Barzani and Talabani, deadlock resumed over the twin issues of occupied Arbil and the tax money.

From late 1995 until summer 1996 the situation was one of stalemate. There had been no serious fighting in Iraqi Kurdistan since the summer of 1995, but the propaganda war between the factions continued.

From 2 July to 16 July 1996, Iran closed its border with Iraqi Kurdistan in an attempt to thwart the cross-border activities of an Iranian Kurdish opposition group, the KDP-I, which was then encamped outside Koysanjaq. The PUK claimed to have lost 50 million Iraqi dinars (US$ 50,000) as a result, its main source of income being taxes levied on illicit traders moving between Iran, Iraq and Turkey. On 28 July, PUK forces guided the Iranian government's Islamic Guards into Iraqi Kurdistan to launch an attack on the KDP-I bases.

The PUK's collusion with Teheran was widely condemned by Kurds both in Iraq and abroad, and led to a serious deterioration in the PUK's popular support. Meanwhile the KDP, which was celebrating the fiftieth anniversary of its foundation in July 1946, seized every opportunity to criticise the PUK.

Early in August, fresh fighting broke out between the PUK and KDP at Kasnazan, near Arbil. US-brokered talks were held in London in an attempt to settle the differences between the two parties and agree a ceasefire, but to no avail. Behind the scenes, it would appear, the KDP had for some time been negotiating with Baghdad, and on 31 August 450 Iraqi government tanks escorted KDP forces into Arbil and the Republican Guards raised the national flag on the Kurdish parliament building, alongside the KDP's yellow flag.

By 4 September the Iraqi troops withdrew to positions southeast of the city, leaving behind large numbers of *mukhaberaat* – government secret police. The people of Arbil described seeing men dressed in *sharwal* who did not speak Kurdish accompanying the *peshmerga* of the KDP as they patrolled the city. Then, using information given to them by the KDP, the secret police began making house-to-house searches which resulted in the arrest of over 2,000 people from the ranks of the Iraqi opposition, the Turkoman community and the PUK. Offices of political organisations were ransacked and records and information seized. Ninety-six Iraqi government deserters, who had been living in a camp outside Arbil for several years, were among those executed. The Kurdish parliament building became a secret police headquarters.

Despite Iraq's claim to have withdrawn its troops from the area, divisions were observed by Western journalists to be digging themselves into positions on the road between Arbil and Sulaymaniyah. First the town of Koysanjaq, and then, on 9 September, the city of Sulaymaniyah, fell to the KDP. Very little resistance was offered by the PUK, many of whose fighters had already fled to the Iranian border, as had a group of 50,000–100,000 refugees.

The Western response to Iraq's incursion into the Safe Haven was confused and ineffective. Cruise missile attacks by the US on Iraq's air defences in the south appeared to have more to do with electioneering by President Clinton than any serious desire to defend the Kurds. Many Arab and Western countries objected to the strikes and it seems that the US, though embarrassed by Saddam's audacity, may have been relieved to find an excuse to abandon the increasingly problematic Kurdish enclave. The lack of a coherent US policy towards Iraq was exposed.

*   *   *

The future for the Iraqi Kurds is not yet clear, but it has rarely looked bleaker. Masoud Barzani's protestations that his alliance with Baghdad is over have little credibility, although on 20 September he attended talks with US representatives in Ankara and asked for renewed US protection. In any event the Iraqi government is now in possession of detailed intelligence relating to both the Iraqi opposition and a significant portion of the Kurdish nationalist movement. This means that ordinary Kurds with anti-Saddam or PUK sympathies must return to living in fear for their lives, as they did prior to 1991, and Kurdistan can no longer be used as a base from which the Iraqi opposition attempts to overthrow Saddam Hussein. The Safe Haven has collapsed, many of the aid agencies have been obliged to leave and it is difficult to see how the KDP will be able to resist domination by Baghdad, even should it attempt to do so.

While the Iraqi Kurdish political leaders have much to answer for in the demise of the Safe Haven and the five-year experiment in self-rule, the West must also take some blame. Having hurriedly created the Safe Haven in 1991 in response to public concern at the Kurds' predicament, Western governments failed to ensure its viability by providing adequate economic and strategic support. Political instability was to some extent an inevitable consequence of the Kurdish parliament's inability to deliver the basic necessities of life, in the face of unremitting UN sanctions. Operation Provide Comfort did nothing to protect the Kurds from military harassment by Turkey and Iran, and the temporary nature of the operation made it difficult for aid agencies to plan their support. Even with excellent leadership, these were hardly the conditions in which a fledgling democracy could thrive.

As things have turned out, Kurds must ask themselves why their leaders were unwilling to commit themselves to parliamentary government and power-sharing; why so much Kurdish blood has been shed at the hand of Kurds; and why the desire of each party to gain the upper hand over the other was allowed to outweigh the importance of keeping the common enemy at bay.

Many of the people I became friends with during my time in Kurdistan have managed to leave in the last two years and are now living in Europe as asylum-seekers; others are at this moment making their way through Iran and Turkey. My heart goes out to them, as it does to the relatives and friends they have left behind.